THE EVERYTHING
Business Plan
Book

Dear Reader,

Have a business idea that you'd *love* to start? Don't know *where* to start?

You've found the right starting point: this book. In it, you'll learn how to plan your business for success. It includes practical information and advice on everything from analyzing and testing your idea to finding customers and overcoming competition to getting free help. It includes everything you need to know!

I'm a business strategist. I've owned numerous retail and services businesses over the past four decades. I now coach others on how to start and run successful businesses. My writing partner on this project is Steve Windhaus, a professional business-plan writer. Together, we have developed a comprehensive map for you to follow in developing your own business idea into a successful business plan. It includes numerous real-world business plans that you can learn from and use.

In addition, the CD with this book includes more than sixty complete business plans that you can borrow from, along with the sample business plans used in illustrating this book.

So get ready to take the first real step toward your new business: your winning business plan!

To your success,

Dan Ramsey

Welcome to the EVERYTHING Series!

These handy, accessible books give you all you need to tackle a difficult project, gain a new hobby, comprehend a fascinating topic, prepare for an exam, or even brush up on something you learned back in school but have since forgotten.

You can choose to read an *Everything*® book from cover to cover or just pick out the information you want from our four useful boxes: e-questions, e-facts, e-alerts, and e-ssentials.

We give you everything you need to know on the subject, but throw in a lot of fun stuff along the way, too.

We now have more than 400 *Everything*® books in print, spanning such wide-ranging categories as weddings, pregnancy, cooking, music instruction, foreign language, crafts, pets, New Age, and so much more. When you're done reading them all, you can finally say you know *Everything*®!

QUESTION?
Answers to
common questions

FACTS
Important snippets
of information

ALERTS!
Urgent
warnings

ESSENTIALS
Quick
handy tips

PUBLISHER Karen Cooper

DIRECTOR OF ACQUISITIONS AND INNOVATION Paula Munier

MANAGING EDITOR, EVERYTHING SERIES Lisa Laing

COPY CHIEF Casey Ebert

ACQUISITIONS EDITOR Lisa Laing

SENIOR DEVELOPMENT EDITOR Brett Palana-Shanahan

EDITORIAL ASSISTANT Hillary Thompson

Visit the entire Everything® series at *www.everything.com*

THE
EVERYTHING®
BUSINESS PLAN
BOOK

All you need to succeed in a new
or growing business

Dan Ramsey and Stephen Windhaus

Avon, Massachusetts

To the success of our readers in finding and enjoying their new business.

An Everything® Series Book.
Everything® and everything.com® are registered trademarks of F+W Media, Inc.

Published by Adams Media, a division of F+W Media, Inc.
57 Littlefield Street, Avon, MA 02322 U.S.A.
www.adamsmedia.com

ISBN 10: 1-59869-822-2
ISBN 13: 978-1-59869-822-0

Printed in the United States of America.

J   I   H   G   F   E

Library of Congress Cataloging-in-Publication Data
is available from the publisher.

This publication is designed to provide accurate and authoritative information with regard to the subject matter covered. It is sold with the understanding that the publisher is not engaged in rendering legal, accounting, or other professional advice. If legal advice or other expert assistance is required, the services of a competent professional person should be sought.

—From a *Declaration of Principles* jointly adopted by a Committee of the American Bar Association and a Committee of Publishers and Associations

Many of the designations used by manufacturers and sellers to distinguish their products are claimed as trademarks. Where those designations appear in this book and Adams Media was aware of a trademark claim, the designations have been printed with initial capital letters.

This book is available at quantity discounts for bulk purchases.
For information, please call 1-800-289-0963.

Contents

Acknowledgments

This book is the product of a long and successful career in business design, management, and education. Thanks especially go to Steve Windhaus, a dynamic resource of knowledge and skill. His business-plan examples, modified from real client plans, are effective teaching tools. Thanks also go to Tim Berry, president and founder of Palo Alto Software and developer of Business Plan Pro. Thanks also go to editors Lisa Laing and Brett Palana-Shanahan, and agent Bob Diforio, who parented this project.

Top Ten Questions
Your Business Plan *Must* Answer

1. What business am I in?

2. What are my business objectives?

3. How will I manage this business?

4. What products and/or services am I selling?

5. To whom will I sell?

6. How will I sell them?

7. How will I price to ensure long-term profits?

8. Who are my competitors and how can I outsmart them?

9. Who are my primary suppliers and how will I make them work hard for me?

10. What financial records do I need to keep and why?

Introduction

▶ STARTING A BUSINESS of any size can be overwhelming: finding products, developing services, searching for customers, promoting the brand, analyzing risks, estimating costs, securing start-up equipment, finding a location, and getting the money together to make it happen. Every year, thousands of great business ideas languish because entrepreneurs don't have a solid business plan.

Once a business has begun, the problems get larger. Opportunities arise, competitors loom, markets change, costs increase. Profitable businesses can become unprofitable overnight without an influx of new capital. Owners need to find and educate investors on risks and rewards. They need a business plan.

A business plan is a formal statement of business goals and how they will be attained. The plan guides owners, investors, managers, and major suppliers in understanding what the business is about and how it will make a profit. Business plans can be simple three-page documents or can fill a large binder. All have the same purpose and components. All are written to plan for success.

The Everything® Business Plan Book with CD is developed logically. It begins with the basics and advice on getting valuable help in writing your business plan. The Executive Summary (Chapter 3) is the most important component of your business plan. Many plan readers won't go any further; sell them here or lose them. The next eleven chapters walk you through each practical component of winning business plans—including product or service description, market analysis, customer definition, competitive analysis, and marketing strategy. It also includes an important chapter on pricing and profitability. Then come the financial documents: income statement, cash flow forecast, and the balance sheet. With examples from actual business plans, you'll soon learn how to make your plan more effective.

This book also includes four invaluable appendices. There's a full example business plan for a product business and a service business (editable copies are on the CD). There's also a comprehensive business glossary as well as a list of more than 500 business plans available separately.

Sidebars offer additional information that you put to work right now as you plan or expand your small business. The sidebars include E-Facts (facts and statistics), E-Alerts (cautions), E-ssentials (tips), and E-Questions (questions and answers), written to clarify and guide you in writing your business plan. This book also includes numerous examples to help you see how successful business plans are written.

CHAPTER 1

Business Plan Basics

You're considering starting a business. Congratulations! It's a major step in developing a financial investment that can change your life. But where do you start? Buying inventory? Gathering customers? Hiring employees? Meeting with an accountant and attorney? None of the above. Instead, you start by developing a business plan. This first chapter explains winning business plans and how they are used to chart your course toward success. It starts you out on the right foot on your business journey.

Business Plans 101

Imagine starting out on a journey without a map. You want to visit Timbuktu, but you're not sure exactly where it is. Across the sea somewhere. You have many questions:

- Which sea?
- Which continent?
- Where on the continent?
- What will you need to get there?
- How long will it take?
- How will you know when you've arrived?
- What will you do there?
- What languages do they speak?

So you look Timbuktu up online and learn that it's in the West African nation of Mali. You call a travel agent for flights and accommodations. A guide book suggests what to visit when you're there. A language book helps you learn Koyra Chiini. You've developed a travel plan.

A business plan is similar. It helps you analyze and decide:

- What business you will be in
- How you will set it up and run it
- What it will cost
- How much profit it will make
- Who will buy from you
- Who you need to hire

In addition, your business plan may answer operational questions that will guide you in day-to-day decisions about finding resources, paying debt, and growing your business. Your business plan will be the most important step in realizing your desire to own and profit from a successful business.

Business Plans Defined

A business plan is a goal document. It is a written plan for accomplishing specific business objectives. Other than a common purpose and structure, business plans have few things in common. They can range from three-page summaries to hundreds of pages of goals, plans, and supporting data. In that way, they are again like travel plans. An itinerary for a trip to the next town is much simpler than one to Timbuktu.

As your concept for a business evolves, so will your business plan. In fact, you can use a business plan as a thinking document that helps you ask and answer essential questions toward your goal of a successful business. It will guide you in documenting your business strategies.

Types of Businesses

One of the primary tasks of your business plan will be to help you analyze and define what type of business you will be in. As you answer, you may adjust how and maybe even where you will operate your business, but the type probably will not change.

First, you will decide whether your business will sell to consumers (the general public) or to other businesses. Selling to consumers, such as retail stores and restaurants, is called business-to-consumers and abbreviated B2C. If your clients are other businesses, you will operate a business-to-business (B2B) venture. There's also business-to-government (B2G) selling, but it's similar to B2B.

Second, you can categorize you business as offering products, services, or both. A retail store sells products, a consultant offers a service, a restaurant sells a combination of products and services.

Third, your business will be categorized by what level in the marketing process it functions in. For example, a toy store is retail, a company that sells toys to toy stores is a wholesaler, and a business that makes toys is a manufacturer. Some businesses import or distribute toys, offering them to wholesalers or directly to retailers.

Fourth, your business can be categorized by its size. Depending on the industry, a small business is one with less than 100 employees, a medium-size business has up to 500 employees, and a large business has more. In the European Union, businesses are often smaller and these category numbers are halved: 50, 250, etc.

As your business begins or grows, you will consider it within these four categories and, chances are, the category won't change over the life of the business. A service business typically stays a service business; a wholesaler remains a wholesaler; B2B usually doesn't sell to consumers, though sometimes a wholesaler will open a separate retail division. For now, consider what categories your venture falls into and the answer will help you make writing a business plan easier.

QUESTION?

What does a typical business plan look like?
Short or long, simple or complex, business plans come in all types. The CD that accompanies this book offers sixty-eight sample business plans in PDF format as well as examples from this book in Microsoft Word .doc format, written by coauthor Stephen Windhaus. Additional sample business plans are available online at *www.sba.gov.*

Plan Components

Even though there are numerous types of businesses and various lengths of plans, the structure is similar. That's because business plans are developed to answer the same questions, no matter what the size and structure:

- How is it going to make a profit?
- How is it going to pay back the investment of money and time?

Later in this chapter, you'll learn what the common components of business plans are and find out how they answer these two questions. However, be aware that there is no one-size-fits-all business-plan structure. Every business will have a unique plan, tailored to the specifics of the opportunity and of the readers. In addition, plans will be different depending on whether they are intended to plan the start-up or the growth of a business.

Start-Up Plans

Start-up business plans can be intimidating. In many cases, they are written by people who have never written a business plan before. What should be included? What should be left out? How much detail is enough? These are a few of the many questions that come to mind when considering a start-up business plan. They require answers.

Remember the two primary questions that *every* business plan must answer: How is it going to make a profit? and How is it going to pay back the investment of money and time? Those are the questions that your start-up plan must answer. Anything else is supporting information.

FACT

Many new businesses get lost in the details because they forget to clearly answer a primary question: What business am I in? The answer can be expanded as your business grows, but it should not dramatically change. If you start a coffee shop but it evolves into a day-care center, you really didn't know what business you were in. That's why developing a well-researched business plan is so important.

Perspective

The principal difference between a start-up and growth business plan is that a start-up is written before the business opens and a growth plan is compiled after. The difference is perspective—where the business is when you write it. Because the business is in a different status, so are the answers to your two primary questions.

The start-up plan must address questions like:

- What do I need to start the business?
- How much will it cost?
- Where should the business be located and why?
- Who will my customers be?

Answers are projected into the future: If I do this, the results will be that. It's educated guessing. Of course, for success, the guesses must be realistic and defensible. You must rely on what others have learned about starting up similar businesses. You must follow their successes and learn from their mistakes. You shouldn't attempt to design a new business model until you've developed the knowledge and experience needed to gamble lots of time and money on the outcome.

Knowledge and Experience

Your prospective in developing a new business will be based on your current knowledge and experience as well as anything that you can learn before you open for business or take it to the next level. That's why it is imperative that you prepare yourself before you prepare your business. If you've never worked in a restaurant, don't try to start one. If you don't know much about widgets, don't attempt to sell or repair them. Much of what you will be offering your customers is based on your knowledge and experience. An importer must know product resources and international trade laws. A retailer must understand profitable marketing. An auto repair shop must know how to efficiently diagnose and repair cars.

Business is the trading of knowledge for money. A consultant sells her business knowledge for money. A customer trades his money for someone's knowledge of how to make a tasty latte. A doctor trades medical knowledge for money. To succeed in business, find an area in which you can be an expert and sell your expertise to those who benefit from it— and will pay you money for the benefits.

The more you know about what you sell or offer, the greater opportunities you will have to profit from that knowledge and experience. That's Business 101. Keep that in mind as you write your business plan from the perspective of a start-up venture.

Structure

Your start-up business plan will also be dictated by the business structure you use. For example, an individual setting up a business will have a simple business plan compared to a corporation that sets up the same business. The primary reason is that an individual's business plan may only have a few readers, while the corporation's plan may be read by dozens. Each reader will have a different perspective on the business and be looking for specific information that others may not require. But they all want to know where the profit is coming from and how the debt will be paid.

Another factor in designing your start-up business plan is what model you are using. That is, will your business be independent or will it be a franchise? A franchise is a business that is modeled after another business, often using its name and modified business plan. Franchises aren't free. A franchise for a successful restaurant chain, for example, can cost a million dollars or more. In addition, being a franchisee may require that you follow strict rules in how you set up and operate your business. On the plus side, the franchisor will help you develop your business plan.

QUESTION?

How can I make sure that my business doesn't break any laws?
Many small businesses only need to pay their taxes on time. Others deal with import and export laws, employment laws, fair-trade laws, and other legal factors. As you develop your business plan, discuss your business with an attorney who can tell you how to operate legally and safely.

An independent business is self-governing within the law. As long as the business keeps adequate income and expense records to pay accurate taxes and follows business laws and employment regulations, that business may operate with great latitude. No official will come in to your business and say, "Hey, you can't sell blue widgets—only red ones!" The majority of small start-up businesses are independent. Thousands of them open up for business every day.

Growth Plans

The other use of a business plan is to help an existing business grow. Your wholesale business has been in operation for a few years and now needs to expand to be competitive. Your restaurant is considering adding more seats or more employees and needs to borrow some cash. Your retail store is so successful that you are considering franchising it. These are growth opportunities.

Build Your Business

Once your business is up and running, you will be making decisions that impact the growth of your venture. Most of these decisions will be small and self-funded. You have sufficient profits and capital to add a new line; but what if you need more money than you have? You discover an opportunity to double your business by moving into a new shopping mall. Then you probably need to write a new growth business plan, updating your existing plan and describing the opportunity and costs.

FACT

Business plans can become out of date. Decide right now to update your business plan at least once a year. Not only will it help you stay focused on what your overall plan is, you will be prepared when you need it in a hurry. For example, someone may walk in and ask to buy your business for a good price—if you can document your success. Your refreshed business plan can help you stay on track and adaptable.

Build a Second Business

In growing marketplaces, you may discover an opportunity to set up a clone of your successful business. It may be in a similar shopping center in a nearby town or community. Or it may be a related business, operated independently by the same owners.

Your growth business plan will use the success of your first business to design the second one. If financing is required, the growth plan will show investors how you plan to profit and pay back your loans. If you are hiring a manager for the second location, a business plan can help you attract qualified candidates.

Build a Purchased Business

As your first business succeeds, you may get the opportunity to buy out one of your competitors. Or you may opt to venture into business by buying an existing business where a plan is already in operation. What you will write in each case is a growth plan. You will show yourself and others how you plan to expand and operate an existing business.

Be cautious of any business opportunities that sound too good to be true. You can lose thousands of dollars in get-rich-quick business ideas that sound good but don't follow the basic tenets of business as outlined in this book.

Sell Your Business

If you someday decide to sell your business, you don't really need a business plan; you need a results document. Guess what? An up-to-date business plan can serve as your Offering Memorandum, a document that tells about your business. By changing the perspective of the document and its readership, you will have a paper that will guide prospective buyers in understanding the value of your business.

Growth business plans are different from start-up plans because of perspective, but the components are essentially the same and both answer the same business questions. In addition, they have similar components.

Plan Components

All books are different. However, nearly all have a title page, table of contents, introduction, chapters, maybe an appendix or two, and an index. Those are the common components in all books.

Business plans also have common components. As diverse as their content is, they include groupings of information that make it easier for readers to get answers to their primary questions. For more insight into business-plan structure, following are some common formats.

SBA Structure

The Small Business Administration (*www.sba.gov*) is a vital resource in helping people start and grow small businesses. They offer information, classes, advice, and assistance finding funding. They suggest that although there is no single formula for developing a business plan, some elements are common to all business plans. The elements include:

- **Introduction:** cover sheet, statement of purpose, table of contents
- **Business information:** description, marketing, competition, operating procedures, personnel, business insurance
- **Financial data:** loan applications, capital equipment and supply list, balance sheet, breakeven analysis, pro-forma income projections, three-year summary, assumptions, pro-forma cash flow
- **Supporting documents:** resumes and tax returns of principal owners and managers, copy of proposed lease or purchase agreement, licenses and other legal documents, letters of intent from suppliers

There's a lot of information in the SBA business-plan structure, all of it vital to those who need to understand how the business will make a profit and pay off the investment.

FACT

The SBA and other business organizations also offer SBIs, small business incubators. These opportunities offer a business location, shared with other entrepreneurs, and on-call consultants who can answer your questions as you incubate your business opportunity. Contact the SBA and local business bankers for more information.

Everything Structure

Most business plans include all of these components in varying order and complexity. This book follows a proven structure that is similar, but more user friendly. It offers an introduction, business information, financial data, and supporting documents in the following order:

- Executive Summary (Chapter 3)
- Present Situation and Objectives (Chapter 4)
- Management (Chapter 5)

- Product/Service Description (Chapter 6)
- Market Analysis (Chapter 7)
- Customers (Chapter 8)
- Competition (Chapter 9)
- Analyzing Risks (Chapter 10)
- Marketing Strategy (Chapter 11)
- Pricing and Profitability (Chapter 12)
- Advertising and Promotion (Chapter 13)
- Sales and Distribution (Chapter 14)
- Suppliers and Resources (Chapter 15)
- Income Statement (Chapter 16)
- Cash-Flow Forecast (Chapter 17)
- Balance Sheet (Chapter 18)
- Break-Even and Ratio Analysis (Chapter 19)
- Present Your Business Plan (Chapter 20)

The structure of this book offers necessary information in a logical development order. Your investors, lenders, or others may prefer to see your business plan components in a slightly different presentation order. That's okay. Write it for your audience. Some readers care less about the financials than they do about how the business will be marketed.

ALERT!

There is no one preferred presentation order for small-business plans. The SBA suggests one; this book offers another. Business-plan software programs have their own structure, as do business-plan writers. In addition, these structures are modified based on the focus and complexity of the business and of the readers. As long as the plan answers the two basic questions, the structure is less important than the content.

Plan Audiences

Who will read your business plan? Hopefully, people with open minds and open wallets. Before you begin developing your business plan, you must identify the audience so you can be sure to answer the primary questions from their perspective.

The audiences differ from plan to plan. Smaller businesses self-financed and operated by a couple don't need the details required by a team of investors in a new technology company. However, these audiences can be categorized into owners, lenders, and suppliers. Each wants to know that the business will be profitable and pay off the investment, but each also has a primary focus within the plan. Determine who your audience is, what each component wants to know, and make sure that your business plan offers trustworthy answers.

Owners

The owners of a business, be they individuals or a corporation, want to know about profitability and payback, just like all plan readers. However, owners are often responsible for the daily management of the business and need to know more details than lenders and suppliers. What do they want to know?

- Who specifically are the business' customers?
- How can those customers be effectively reached?
- How will employees be selected, trained, and managed?
- What products/services will be sold and what are their sources?
- Who are the competition and how should they be trumped?
- What are the day-to-day operations of the business?

The "owners" include the individual investors who manage the business either directly or indirectly. In many small businesses, a manager is hired to operate the daily business, overseen by the owners. In other businesses, it is the owner(s) who manages daily operations. The owners can be an individual, a partnership, or a corporation (Chapter 5). Before you begin writing your business plan, analyze ownership and describe what each participant needs to know about the business from the plan.

Lenders and Investors

Most businesses, even small businesses, require outside capital to start up and grow; few businesses are fully self-funded. Attracting a lender or other financial investor is different than telling an owner or manager what is needed for daily operations. Lenders want to know:

- How much capital (money and other assets) do the business owners have to invest?
- How much capital is required to start up or grow this business?
- How much capital do the owners need from lenders?
- What return do the owners offer for the lender's investment?
- Is the business sufficiently profitable to pay back lenders and investors?

In addition to the owner/manager questions, a business plan must answer those of lenders and investors. Lenders are those who loan the business (or individual owners) money and expect a specific rate of return, a percentage of interest. Lenders are typically commercial banks and other traditional sources of business capital.

ESSENTIAL

Know your audience before you begin writing. Identify individual readers, their needs and abilities, and keep them in mind as you develop your business plan. Know what questions they need your business plan to answer. Help them see your vision.

Investors invest money in the business and accept some of the risk of its operation. The investor may get a very high rate of return or may lose the entire investment. Investors accept more potential risk (Chapter 10) and more potential reward. So their questions also cover management: How do I know that my investment won't be lost?

There are various types of investors. Venture capital is private equity capital (not banks), usually pooled from diverse investors looking for a greater profit from loaning their funds than they could get at the bank. They realize that the risks are higher and do whatever they can to reduce those risks. Venture capitalists (VCs) that will consider higher-risk ventures are called angel investors or angels, and typically require partial ownership or management of the business. You'll learn more about these capital sources in this book and through online resources. For now, be aware that investors need more financial details than other readers of your business plan may require.

ALERT!

Venture capitalists are sometimes referred to as vulture capitalists, a term developed during the 1990s when needy businesses met greedy investors who took over successful companies in which they had invested. The dot-com bubble burst in the late 1990s, driving many of them out of business. Hire a proven business advisor if you are considering venture capital investments.

Suppliers

In some new or growing businesses, additional capital comes from suppliers. For example, if you're starting a new restaurant, a restaurant equipment supplier may sell you needed equipment—and even fixtures—on credit. The supplier, in a sense, is investing in the success of your business. That supplier will probably require a peek at your business plan, or at least portions of it that answer relevant questions. Chapter 15 covers working with suppliers and other business resources.

- What supplies or equipment does your business need?
- Will you have debt to other major suppliers?
- How profitable will your business be and when?
- Who holds title to the supplies or equipment furnished?
- How will you pay off the supplies or equipment furnished?
- What access does the supplier have to the business' financial records?

There will be other questions, depending on what the supplier is investing, how much, and whether the supplies are used in the business or resold to customers. As you develop your business plan, you will be identifying suppliers who may be asked to participate in your business. Some will only require a credit application. Others will need to see your business plan. Make sure that the plan you write addresses their specific needs.

FACT

What does your credit look like? You can find out for free! The Fair Credit Reporting Act managed by the Federal Trade Commission allows all customers to obtain a free copy of their credit report once a year. More information is available at *www.annualcreditreport.com*. Be careful, as this is the *only* site authorized to offer free credit reports. In addition, the credit-reporting services will attempt to sell you additional services.

Starting Your Plan

That's a summary of how small-business plans are designed and developed. The remainder of this book will focus on the specifics and guide you in writing a successful plan. But you don't have to wait. You can begin right now, gathering and organizing your plan so it comes together smoothly and isn't held up by missing components.

What to Gather

As you can see from the above outline of business-plan components, most of what you'll need to gather are facts or data. You'll need data about products or services, profitability, the marketplace, costs, suppliers and other resources, and management tools. Begin gathering this information right now. You probably have a handle on your business idea or you wouldn't be considering it. If you're planning a retail store, you probably know much about what it will sell and to whom. You may even know where it should be located. Start gathering that information, but don't lock yourself into a decision just yet. Keep your mind open. You may have the perfect store location identified, but you really won't know if it is perfect until you do some comparative research. So gather information on a few different locations. If nothing else, later you will be able to analyze why your business will be more successful in one location than another.

QUESTION?

Do I have to have a building for my business?
For most businesses, yes. However, you only need a well-located and showy location if your customers need it. Many modern businesses begin by sharing a location with another company or set up an office in an office suite with a common reception area and receptionist. Others set up virtual companies with all business done over the Internet. You have options.

How to Organize

Data will be useless if you can't find it. Fortunately, there are numerous methods of organizing information for your business plan. The simplest is to purchase a file box and file folders, placing information in the appropriate category: management, customers, competition, financials, etc.

Alternately, you can begin collecting electronic files on a computer. You may use a word processor for writing the plan, a spreadsheet for the financials, and maybe a presentation program for giving presentations to prospective investors. These are covered in Chapter 2.

Because developing a business plan can be complex as well as adaptable, many entrepreneurs opt to organize their plans using one of the primary business-planning tools. Palo Alto Software (*www.paloalto.com*) is one of the most popular resources; there are others. Each is developed to help you organize your thoughts and your facts toward an efficient and productive business plan.

CHAPTER 2

Getting Help

Writing a business plan is a big job. Fortunately, you don't have to do it alone. There are hundreds of valuable resources that you can call upon to ensure that your plan is successful. Finding them isn't always easy, but, with diligence, you can gather the information needed to profitably focus your business. This chapter introduces many of these resources and shows how you can put them to work.

Planning Process

Business plans don't just fall into place. You will need to gather the various components, analyze them, and include appropriate information that the plan readers need to make an informed decision. Where do you start? How do you proceed? When will you be done?

Initial Planning

You start with a preliminary outline, following the one suggested in Chapter 1 or one from another resource: a lender's preferred formation, a prior business plan, or a chosen software program. You modify the outline as required to better fit your business' design: retail or wholesale, product or service, start-up or growth, etc. You then begin gathering the needed data from reliable sources as outlined in this chapter. You will be done when your business plan answers the primary questions for your audience:

- How is it going to make a profit?
- How is it going to pay back the investment of money and time?

Your plan also may need to answer a question posed by managers: How will the business operate on a daily basis? Or it must answer questions asked by suppliers, franchisors, or others. Initial planning requires that you know what questions your business plan needs to answer before you start writing it.

Gathering

By defining the questions, you will begin to identify the resources. If the answer depends on gathering sales statistics in your chosen industry, contact industry resources and get them. If you need to better understand the local marketplace for your enterprise, use a market-research company or do your own market research to answer the question.

Often, asking a single question will bring additional questions to mind. You're analyzing customers for your service business: Who are they? Why do they buy? What do they need? As you ask, you discover that prospective customers come from a variety of buying groups. So the question is expanded to: Who are these groups and are their needs and buying habits different from your core customers? Depending on the importance of these secondary buying groups and your market-research budget, you may or may not decide to gather detailed information on them. If in doubt, return to the primary questions that your business plan is intended to answer.

FACT

An excellent and free source of market data is the U.S. Census Bureau (*www.census.gov*). It includes current and historic data on people and households, business, industry, and geography. It should be the first place you look for population numbers. In addition, you can analyze the makeup of that population by a variety of criteria including age, race, economics, and other factors that impact business.

Review

Once gathered, the information is compiled into your business plan following your chosen outline. In fact, the data you use may dictate changes in the outline. You may discover reliable resources that point to a previously undiscovered secondary market. From that discovery, you may decide to refocus your business to reach it.

Many families already have successful business people among them. If yours does, ask for suggestions and tips on developing your business concept. Not only might you get some practical advice, you may also earn a referral to a potential investor or advisor.

Develop a preliminary business plan that includes all of the elements, but isn't yet ready for distribution. The prelim should answer all of the planning questions; it just needs someone else to read and comment on it. Once gathered, you should get an external review. Ask a lender or a business-plan consultant to review your preliminary business plan, looking for missing elements. Then incorporate those elements into your business plan before distribution.

Distribution

Your business plan is a valuable document. It may cost you a few hundred or a few thousand dollars in time and services to develop. It is produced to make you many times more. If well written, your business plan could be used by anyone to start their own business. If read by a competitor, your plan could help them and hurt your business. You certainly don't want to pass your plan around without getting a promise of confidentiality.

A confidentiality agreement should be signed before others are allowed to read your business plan. Business people know this and will have no issues with signing it. A standard confidentiality agreement is part of each of the sample business plans on the CD included with this book.

In addition, keep a record of all persons who receive a copy of your business plan and when. Use this list to follow up with each to determine their interest. If they are no longer interested, ask them to return the plan to you and to destroy any copies. Chapter 20 offers more suggestions on presenting your business plan for success.

Planning Tools

Developing business plans is a major step in starting or growing a business. For every business that is started, many plans will be written. Some will be revised; others will not find funding.

Many software programs are available in trial versions. They are typically limited by the number of days of use, the number of entries, or the features available. Use a search engine to find demos of specific products or visit *www.download.com* and similar sites.

Fortunately, there are numerous tools, and that can help you focus on the details rather than the structure. This book is one of them. In addition, there are numerous computer programs specifically designed to help you plan, gather, review, and distribute your business plan. Following are some of the primary tools.

Business Plan Pro

Business Plan Pro (*www.bplans.com*) is a Windows-based program that helps compile business plans in a logical system. It's developed by Palo Alto Software (*www.paloalto.com*) of Eugene, Oregon. BPP is the most popular of the business-planning programs and is recommended by many professional planners as well as the Small Business Administration.

There are currently two versions of BPP: Standard and Premier. Premier has all the components of the Standard version as well as business valuation analysis, cash-flow planning tools, planning tools, and other features. In addition, Premier imports spreadsheet data directly from Microsoft Excel. Both versions include more than 500 sample business plans for a variety of small businesses.

BPP is relatively easy to use. Once the business is broadly defined in the initial setup, the program presents a number of tasks. You complete each task, following instructions with examples, and your input is added to the business plan at the appropriate location. The resulting business plan can be printed directly, exported to MS Word or in rich-text format (RTF), exported as HTML web pages, or as Microsoft PowerPoint presentation files.

In addition, BPP offers a variety of resources and associate services. For the relatively low cost—less than $200—it is a proven and time-saving tool for developing business plans.

BizPlanBuilder

Another business-planning program that has been in the marketplace for more than a decade, BizPlanBuilder is published by JIAN (*www.jian .com*) of Chico, California. Similar to BPP in structure and results, BizPlan-Builder focuses on flexibility. Numerous templates walk you through every step from cover to appendix with numerous examples.

BizPlanBuilder sells for less than $150. It is also available within a suite of business start-up software programs from JIAN: Agreement Builder, Stock Options Builder, and a business training book. The suite package price is less than $200. BizPlanBuilder is a popular program for people with no prior business-planning experience.

Other Business-Planning Programs

Though Business Plan Pro and BizPlanBuilder share most of the market, there are other programs available. Plan Write (*www.brs-inc.com*) offers three editions: for loans, for business, and the Expert edition with expanded features. Smart Business Plan (*www.smartonline.com*) offers numerous formatting options.

Other Software

Thousands of successful business plans have been developed the old-fashioned way, with word processing and spreadsheet programs. You can use your favorite word processor to develop the text, a spreadsheet program for the calculations, and integrate the two resources. You don't need to buy a business plan development program; in fact, you don't even need a computer and software. You can develop your business plan with a typewriter or even in longhand and have someone format it. However, there are many advantages to using software, including being able to easily modify and reprint documents. Considering the stakes involved, purchasing and learning a proven business-plan development program is a sound investment.

QUESTION?

Where can I find some trial versions of business software?
You can often find them on the publisher's website. In addition, you can check freeware and shareware resources such as *www.download.com*, operated by CNet. Use the site's category and search features to find and download trial versions.

Small Business Administration

Wouldn't it be great if small business had a friend in the federal government? Well, it does. The mandate of the Small Business Administration (*www.sba.gov*) is to "aid, counsel, assist, and protect the interest of small business concerns." The feds recognize that small business is an integral part of the nation's economy. And they know that small business isn't small.

The SBA has been in operation for more than fifty years and currently offers a variety of assistance for small businesses and people interested in starting a business. The SBA offers technical advice, training and counseling, financial assistance, help getting government contracts, disaster assistance, and help for special interests such as women and veterans.

QUESTION?

How big is the SBA?
The Small Business Administration has been shrinking over the past decade. However, 2008 budget increases brought its budget for core programs to $569 million, less than $2 per U.S. citizen. In a recent year, the SBA backed $12.3 billion in business loans, $1 billion in disaster loans, and coordinated more than $40 billion in government contracts with small businesses. The other services provided by the SBA make it a valuable asset to small business.

Technical Assistance

The SBA offers training and counseling for start-up and established small businesses, including entrepreneurial development that focuses on helping people find business opportunities. Training, classes, and mentoring is offered at no or reduced cost. If you need additional training on the accounting or marketing side of your business venture, contact the SBA for guidance and instruction.

The SBA has Small Business Development Centers (SBDCs) in most metropolitan areas. SBDCs offer one-stop assistance to current and prospective small business owners, ranging from classes to consultation. The SBA website offers additional information and locations of SBDCs.

SCORE (*www.score.org*) is an association of business advisors sponsored by the SBA. In many cases, the SCORE advisors are retired business owners who offer assistance to those who are starting or growing a small business. Depending on local availability, you may be assigned a SCORE mentor who will answer specific questions and offer experienced advice on the daily operation of your business. The counseling can be face to face or online. There are more than 10,000 volunteers in the SCORE program.

Financial Assistance

Need some money for your new business? The SBA can be a go-between for entrepreneurs and lenders, helping both find a working relationship. The SBA certifies some lenders as "preferred" and helps borrowers prepare the needed paperwork to meet lending requirements.

There are various loan programs available through the SBA. Visit *www. sba.gov* for the latest opportunities and requirements. Millions of small businesses got their start with SBA loans.

Contracting Assistance

Will your business sell products or services to the government? The SBA has a contracting assistance program that can help find governmental buyers and teach you how to meet the bidding requirements. The contracting assistance program assists all small businesses sell to government entities, but it focuses on helping small disadvantaged businesses as well as technology firms.

FACT

The SBA can help you find and apply for subcontracts with the federal government. Visit *www.sba.gov/services/contractingopportunities* for specific information and resources.

In addition, the SBA offers surety guarantees that help small businesses meet the bonding requirements of some government sales.

Disaster Assistance

Small businesses suffer from disasters, too. Hurricanes, tornados, earthquakes, and other natural disasters can put a small business out of business in a day. The SBA disaster-assistance program helps small businesses prepare for common disasters as well as recover from ones that occur.

In addition to advice, the SBA disaster-assistance program offers short-term loans and financial aid to help businesses recover from damage and the loss of business. In fact, the SBA disaster-assistance loans are available to homeowners and renters as well as to businesses.

Special Interests

The SBA encourages businesses established by groups such as women, veterans of the armed forces, Native Americans, and young entrepreneurs. Specialized programs are developed for these and other groups. The assistance comes in the form of needs-based training and loan assistance.

The Small Business Administration is a dynamic resource for people wanting to start or grow a business. In addition, many state governments have their own small business programs or ones that function in conjunction with SBDCs.

Business Associations

No matter what business you start, chances are good that there is already at least one association representing it. Such associations offer a meeting place for competitors, a source of data and advice, and a voice in legislation. A few of the thousands of business associations serving small business include:

- American Small Business Alliance (*www.asbanet.org*)
- American Small Business Association (*www.asbaonline.org*)
- National Business Association (*www.nationalbusiness.org*)
- National Federation of Independent Business (*www.nfib.com*)
- National Small Business Association (*www.nsba.biz*)
- Small Business Association of America (*www.sbaa.org*)
- U.S. Chamber of Commerce (*www.uschamber.com*)

In addition, most states have at least one association that focuses on a specific business group. Use an online search engine to find ones in your state or region.

There are also associations for specific types of businesses. For example:

- American Wholesale Booksellers Association (*www.awba.com*)
- International Housewares Association (*www.housewares.org*)
- International Wholesale Furniture Association (*www.iwfa.net*)
- National Association of Wholesaler-Distributors (*www.naw.org*)
- National Retail Federation (*www.nrf.com*)
- North American Retail Hardware Association (*www.nrha.org*)
- Retail Merchants Association (*www.retailmerchants.com*)

The list of specialized small business associations is extensive. An online search for your specialty will yield many. In addition, public libraries have directories of associations. You will also find them advertised or promoted in magazines published for your trade. Alternately, your business suppliers can tell you what the primary associations are for your type of business.

ALERT!

Be wary of business associations that promise unrealistic services, such as a directory of resources that can "save you thousands of dollars." Any business directory can do that with effort. Instead, select a trade association that your competitors are members of. Also, look for associations that can advise you on special tax problems or offer group rates on health insurance. Verify the claims before joining, as some associations earn referral fees and don't thoroughly check out the offered services.

Professional Business Planners

Developing a successful business plan doesn't require that you do all the work. In fact, it can be productive to hire out at least part of the project to professionals who have experience in this area. They can be market-research services, accountants, small business advisors, or professional business planners. You can hire an expert to advise you before starting and review your final efforts. You can hire an accountant to gather and analyze the financial data. You can hire a plan writer to polish your business plan. You have many choices.

Hiring a professional business planner is a partnership. You don't simply write a short concept and write a check; you participate in the development of your business plan. How much you participate depends on what you want and what you're paying for. You can hire coaching or mentoring and or review services for start-up and growth business plans.

Start-Up Plans

Professional business planners offer a variety of services, including:

- Developing a logical outline
- Conducting market research
- Developing sales projections
- Estimating start-up costs
- Calculating operating costs
- Producing financial projections

You can hire a business planner to perform any or all of these services for you in the development of your unique business plan.

Growth Plans

Your business planning needs are different if you have an established business that wants to grow. Your small business may need to expand or downsize or you may want to acquire another business. You'll need a business plan to focus your efforts and document your needs. This book can guide you.

However, you may decide to hire a professional business planner or advisor to help you in producing an effective growth plan. Some of the services available include:

- Analyzing your current marketplace to look for opportunities
- Evaluating products and services for methods of reducing costs
- Re-evaluating your competition
- Reviewing all expenses to determine opportunities to make them more efficient
- Considering the advantages and disadvantages of specific financing options

Each of these services requires your participation to make them valuable, but you will be relying on a business planner or analyst to ensure that the plan is accurate and viable. Your investment can be multiplied many times by an experienced professional.

Coaching

You may not need any of these services. You can do most of them yourself and only need some direction from an experienced business planner. Most professional planners offer coaching or mentoring services, typically on an hourly basis. You have a question, they offer you an answer and point you in the direction of additional information. A pro planner can save you many hours of effort with a short consultation.

If you choose to hire a planner to coach you, make sure that the planner has experience with the type of business you are developing. Some specialize in retail start-ups. Others focus on expanding an existing franchise operation.

ESSENTIAL

If you hire a professional business planner, do your homework before the first interview. Ask for references. Talk with other clients. Then set up a meeting with a sample question, such as "How did you help another distributor find additional markets?" Listen to how the planner responds as well as what is said. Do you get succinct answers or does he ramble? Do the answers have sufficient value to you?

Review Services

If you're comfortable with writing your own business plan, consider hiring a professional planner to review the final document for possible problems. The input can be invaluable, polishing your words and your focus to meet the requirements of each reader.

A business-plan review may reveal that you need more data. Or it will give you the confidence to present your plan with only a few changes. If your advisor recommends a major revision and you agree, the costs of revision will probably be lower than if you had hired the planner to write the entire document. As important, you will have participated in drafting your plan and understand its strengths and weaknesses better.

Financial Data

Business is driven by money. How much will it cost? How much will it sell? How much profit will be left? These are measurable elements to your business plan and necessary to understanding how your venture is going to make a profit and pay back investments.

QUESTION?

How reputable must the financial data be?
Your business—and your investors—are going to depend heavily on the financial data that you present in your business plan. You, and they, will be gambling in a sense. Smart gamblers know to play the odds and leave emotion out of the equation. If the odds are against a specific bet, they don't make it. You cannot make up the financial data that you use. It must be specific, reliable, and verifiable. You're betting a lot on the outcome.

Finance is the management of money and other assets. Data is pieces of information. So financial data is information about money. You'll need lots of it as you develop your business plan, and your business. Where can you get financial data? There are many sources, depending on what financial data you need. Typical start-up costs? Sales forecasts? Equipment costs?

Profitability? Finding and using those resources is a big part of the work you will do in developing your business plan.

Hoover's

Dun & Bradstreet (*www.dnb.com*) is known for gathering reputable credit information on U.S. businesses. One division, Hoover's (*www.hoovers.com*), specializes in developing and selling industry-specific financial data. For example, you can purchase a financial report on publicly traded companies, private companies, and subsidiaries. You can buy financial data about your competitors, suppliers, and businesses you're trying to emulate. A report on Acme Widget Co. includes name and location(s), annual sales, total number of employees, and other basic data. Further reports can offer specific financial information including competition.

Industry information is useful when you're trying to determine the size of the marketplace. For example, you can buy an industry report on catering services. The report will include:

- Industry overview
- Competitive landscape
- Products, operations, and technology
- Quarterly industry updates
- Trends and opportunities
- Financial information
- Industry forecasts
- Related financial data

When entering into any business, especially one in which you aren't fully familiar, financial reports are vital to your understanding of the challenges and opportunities. Even if you only compete on the local level, gather industry and national competitive financial data so you will know how your small business stacks up. Your investors will want to know.

Integra Information

D&B gathers financial information on the majority of businesses, but not all of them. Some are too small to be seen on their radar. If you are starting a small independent business, sometimes called a mom and pop, you want financial data that is more relevant to your business size. Integra Information (*www.integrainfo.com*) is one of many services that collect and sell this data.

A benchmark is a standard for evaluation. Benchmark information is used to determine the value of a specific property by comparison to similar properties. Benchmark information is used in both valuing and evaluating business opportunities. Integra Information and similar services sell benchmark data on businesses. The data can be from one of nine revenue ranges, such as catering businesses with annual sales between $250,000 and $499,000. If your business is projected to be in this range, financial data and benchmarks can be invaluable in developing your business plan.

Industry data reports typically include information about various financial-statement ratios. (What percentage of income is usually spent on labor?) In addition, these reports include industry forecasts. The reports from Integra Information are available in thirteen revenue ranges from below $250,000 to above $500,000,000.

ALERT!

Are you buying an existing small business? Use industry data reports to analyze opportunities as well as determine whether the business is healthy and positioned to grow. If not, reports can indicate the cause of current problems (high expenses, low stock turnover, insufficient capital, etc.). With this knowledge, you can defend a purchase-price reduction as well as plan a path to higher profitability.

Accountants

Depending on the business you're planning, you may want to hire an accountant early in the process to consult with you regarding the financial side. A professional accountant (PA) or certified professional accountant (CPA) can offer guidelines, benchmarks, ratios, and financial advice that can give you a competitive edge and save you money.

Ratios are a critical component of business. Chapter 19 will explain ratios in greater detail. For now, a *ratio* is a comparative number. If there are thirty students in a class with one teacher, the ratio is 30:1 or thirty-to-one. The second number is always the smallest of the two.

ESSENTIAL

Want to see some business ratios right now? BankRate.com (*www. bankrate.com*) offers small business ratio calculators online. Included are liquidity (ability to pay off short-term debts), debt-to-asset ratios, return-on-asset ratios, and a gross profit margin calculator. Become familiar with these terms, as you will be using them in your business plan and in your business operations.

Ratios are important in business because they can help guide your decisions. If employee costs in your industry are typically 4:1—$4 in sales for every $1 of employee costs—you will know to estimate about $100,000 a year in employee costs for $400,000 in annual sales.

Financial ratios are important to lenders who may not know your business but understand that, to be profitable, your business must meet specific ratios. There are many of them, as will be presented in Chapter 19. Meantime, financial data and industry reports will help you establish ratios for your business.

CHAPTER 3

Executive Summary

Your business plan will be a thorough document, complete with details on how you will start or grow your business. But not everyone wants all the details. Some readers will focus on your market analysis, or financial statements, or product profitability. Other than that, they just want an overview. In addition, you want to build a solid foundation under your business plan. This chapter shows you how to develop a dual-function executive summary that guides both you and your reader through your business document.

Purposes of the Executive Summary

It's said that executive summaries are written for lazy readers. It's not true. An executive summary is written for smart readers who want to know where they are going. Instead of plodding through a long business plan looking for recognizable signposts, the reader can first examine the executive summary as a road map. From it, the reader can decide which paths to take to get to a specific destination or decision.

The executive summary has a second purpose. It is an opportunity for you, the plan writer, to establish and verify the signposts along the chosen path. It's the point where you start as well as where you end.

In fact, the executive summary will be the first component of the plan that you begin and the last component that you finalize. Once you're done with all other components, you'll return to it and make needed changes to ensure consistency and accuracy. Or better, you will use it as you develop your business plan, pulling it out and revising it as needed. When you reach your ultimate destination, a complete and thorough business plan, your executive summary will be ready to serve as its map.

Contents

What are the typical components of a business plan? The answer depends on the specifics of the plan. However, as most business plans include the same types of information, some generalizations can be made. For example, most business-plan executive summaries include:

- Concept
- Background
- Mission statement
- Marketing
- Keys to success
- Capital requirements

The order of these components will be dictated by the type of business. Fortunately, it is easy to reorder components of your business plan and your executive summary as it grows.

Drafts

A business plan is a dynamic document that grows in leaps and spurts. You may be able to build one section in a day, while another takes a week or more. In most plans, you will also modify one section as you write another. Financial data may require that you change your marketing goals or adjust your start-up plans.

Many business plans are developed in three drafts: initial, complete, and reviewed. The initial draft is written as you focus on data, even though some data is missing. In fact, you may not even realize all the data you need until you begin writing the initial or first draft. Once the initial draft is done, you will thoroughly evaluate it for completeness. You will make sure that the facts are accurate and the development is logical. Finally, you will ask a knowledgeable friend, business associate, or consultant to read and critique your business plan. You will make needed changes to the reviewed plan before submitting your business plan to powers that be.

QUESTION?

Once done, to whom should I first submit my business plan?
Submit your plan first to someone who can offer the best advice on its effectiveness. If possible, don't submit it to the reader who has the most power. You don't want to get rejected due to an unrecognized error on page 14. Submit it first to a lender or financier with limited authority. Consider this submission a dress rehearsal. Learn from it and make appropriate changes before the primary decision-makers see it.

Revisions

Your plan's executive summary should be kept nearby as you write other components of the plan. You can update the summary as needed. As important, the summary will help you to focus and summarize other components. If, in writing your plan, you get lost in the details, refer to the executive summary's latest draft as your road map.

To ensure that you don't lose your valuable efforts, make backups or copies of your business plan and executive summary. If using a computer to develop your plan, make sure you save your files every five minutes or so. In addition, copy the files to another drive or media every few hours. The common rule is: Back up what you cannot afford to lose.

Concept

A concept is an idea. You think that your neighborhood could use a good widget store and an idea is conceived: Why don't you start a widget store? From then on, your concept can grow until the question is answered. The possible answers to the question are:

- There is already a good widget store nearby.
- You don't have enough money to start and run a good widget store.
- There isn't enough profit in selling widgets to pay the costs of a store.
- You'd rather sell wholesale widgets.
- Actually, there are no good reasons not to.

Your business concept will eventually become part of your plan's executive summary. For now, it is the core of your business idea. It is a summary of your question rephrased: Is a widget store in this neighborhood a viable business opportunity for me? To accurately answer that question, another list of questions must be answered:

- What is the local market for widgets?
- Is that market being satisfied?
- Are widgets profitable?
- How can they be made more profitable?
- Is this a business I am qualified to operate?
- Do I have the capital to start and operate this business?
- Do I want to start and run a widget store?
- How will owning a widget store change my life?

These questions will lead to others, each requiring an answer before a decision can be made. Your business plan is a document written to convince yourself and possibly others that such a business concept is viable. If it isn't, the business plan won't get finished.

Here's an example of a business concept from Appendix B:

> *Acme Time Management Consultants, Inc. (ATMC), incorporated under the laws of the State of New York, is a start-up company seeking to establish itself in the professional organizing service industry.*

FACT

You can download sample executive summaries from actual business plans at various websites on the Internet. AllBusiness.com offers many executive summaries for free, though there is a fee for downloading full sample business plans. In addition, many business schools have sample business plans and executive summaries available at no cost.

Background

What makes you believe that you can successfully operate your business concept? What is your background? Do you have relevant training or experience? Do you have related experience? Why do you believe that this is a good opportunity?

As you begin developing your business plan, these questions are increasingly important. You must convince investors that your experience and the market conditions can be profitably merged.

Opportunity Background

Once the business concept is defined (see previous section), you can begin describing the opportunity. An opportunity is a favorable juncture of circumstances. It's being at the right place at the right time. All successful businesses are based on clear opportunities.

The first step in taking advantage of a business opportunity is to determine what opportunities you are looking for. Do you prefer an opportunity to start a new restaurant or would you prefer to import musical instruments or manufacture games? As a practical exercise, list the areas of business opportunities that you are most interested in.

Once you've selected an area of opportunities, begin your research on what specific opportunities are available to you right now or in the near future. If you're reading this book, you probably already have a business opportunity in mind. However, you can make it and the chance for success greater if you make sure that it is the best opportunity for current conditions.

Among the many critical questions that your business-plan development will answer is: Do I want to do this? As the plan progresses, you may determine that the concept won't work, isn't right for you, or will be too expensive or time consuming. If so, your efforts aren't wasted; you've learned an important fact.

Why is this business concept such a good opportunity? Your business plan will attempt to document and convince others of the answer. List the reasons that this business will survive and thrive. The reasons will be expounded in your business plan and abridged in your executive summary.

Following is an example of an opportunity background from Appendix B:

> *People always read and hear how to increase their productivity, take control of time, and create an organized environment in the office and home. However, studies have proven that people learn to change their behavior more effectively when they have hands-on experience to physically adapt to a new strategy.*
>
> *A professional organizer is someone who provides information, products, and or services to help people get organized. This professional should have a good understanding of the tasks to perform, a thorough knowledge of organizing products and services, and, of course, excellent organizational skills.*

Professional organizers assist with many tasks of organization in business, corporate, and home environments. The services we will provide include:

- *Time and paper management*
- *Clutter control*
- *Behavior modification*
- *Space planning*
- *Filing*
- *Training and coaching*
- *Wardrobe and closet systems*
- *Event planning*
- *Financial and records management*
- *Computer usage/software/systems*
- *Public speaking and seminars*

Your Background

Why are you the best person to take advantage of this opportunity? Are you knowledgeable? Do you have relevant training? Do you clearly recognize the concept and background of this opportunity? Are you willing to make the investment and sacrifices needed to bring this concept to fruition?

ALERT!

Experienced business people will tell you: Make sure that the business you select fits your interests and nature. That is, don't try to open a business if it won't be enjoyable. You may soon discover that you're making money, but it isn't fun. To see how a business concept fits you, get a job working for a similar business. If, after six months, you're still in love with the business concept, consider starting your own.

Your business plan will document both your business and personal background. Begin right now by summarizing both in the first draft of your executive summary. Think of the business opportunity as a job for which you are applying. Why are you the most qualified candidate? If your business plan is for an existing business that needs to grow, what is your background and that of your business that makes you the best candidate for growth? For an example of a personal background see Appendix B.

Mission Statement

A mission is a purpose. A mission statement is a written declaration of a purpose. In your business plan, it briefly explains the function of your business. It can be a single sentence or a paragraph. It should use concrete rather than abstract words. Your business' mission statement should be unique and not describe any other business. It should be focused on the opportunity and tell readers specifically what your business is about.

A concise mission statement is the most important and most read component of your business plan. It summarizes what your business does, how it does it, and what results it expects. As your business grows, new opportunities will arise. Your business' mission statement will help you focus on the reasons you got into the business and help keep you on track. If a business is unsuccessful, or less than successful, an imprecise mission statement is often the cause.

How do you come up with an effective mission statement? Think of it as an advertising slogan; it succinctly defines the mission or purpose of your business. Following are some popular ad slogans that provide a summary of the company's mission.

- Connecting people. —Nokia
- Live in your world, play in ours. —Sony Playstation
- No battery is stronger longer. —Duracell
- Empowering financial institutions globally. —IFLEX Solutions
- Buy it. Sell it. Love it. —eBay
- Bank of opportunity. —Bank of America
- Like a good neighbor, State Farm is there. —State Farm Insurance
- Do more, feel better, live longer. —GlaxoSmithKline

Ad slogans are the kernels from which mission statements grow. Conversely, many businesses develop their ad slogans from their mission statements, reducing it to the fewest words that project the core mission. As you develop your business plan, your executive summary, and your mission statement, think of what ad slogan you would develop to succinctly tell others what your business is about. This exercise can help you in defining your business concept, background, opportunities, and mission.

Here's an example of a mission statement (from Appendix B):

The mission of ATMC is to help the business professional balance his/her career and family by professionally organizing time, office, and home environments.

Marketing

Your business plan's mission statement will succinctly describe its marketing strategy. This will be expanded in the marketing strategy section (Chapter 11) of your business plan. For now, all you need is a summary.

Marketing involves finding out what a customer wants and supplying it. There are many components of marketing, including market research, analysis, distribution, sales, and customer relations. All operate under the umbrella of marketing and are vital to your business.

Marketing answers a variety of questions for your business, including: What are you selling? Who buys it? Why do they buy? and How can you sell to them? Before you begin your business, you must know the answers to these questions in detail. For now, all you need is a summary of your market.

FACT

Your new or growing business plan requires a succinct summary of what it is you are selling. Make sure you know what it is and have developed a list of related products and services that your customers are interested in.

What Are You Selling?

This first question may seem like a no-brainer: What are you selling? However, many new businesses get lost quickly because they don't know the answer. For example, a retail bookstore may open, then decide that it wants to sell organic teas. The two product lines are unrelated, the business structures are different, and the customers are not always the same. Either sell books or teas, not both.

Who Buys?

One of the most important questions your business plan answers is: Who are your customers? Who will buy your product or service from you? If you are manufacturing jewelry for wholesale distribution, your customers are retailers. If you are starting a pet-sitting service, your clients are pet owners within a specific geographic region.

In many cases, you are your own typical customer. That is, you have identified a need for a specific business because you are a frustrated buyer who cannot find a needed product or service, so you've decided to start a business supplying it. However, you cannot build a successful business by selling to yourself. You must identify and sell to others who have similar needs.

For now, attempt to summarize who it is you will be selling your defined products and or services to. What is your market? In Chapter 11, you will expand on this topic and thoroughly understand your customers.

Why Do They Buy?

Everything is sold based on a need or want. You buy milk at the store not because the price is low, but because you need it. You purchase a new high-definition television because you want it more than you want the money it costs.

To sell your defined products or services to specific customers, you must understand why they buy. Do the majority of your customers buy on need or on want? What factors initiate the need or develop the desire to buy what you sell? How will you satisfy both types of customers? Your business plan must answer these questions. The plan's executive summary will recap customer purchase motivations. For now, simply put yourself in your potential customers' shoes and consider why they may want to buy from you.

All products and services are designed to solve a specific problem. Before you sell any product or service to another, make sure that you fully understand what explicit problems it solves and for whom. Then you will better understand your market and be able to capitalize on it.

How Can You Sell to Them?

In one room you have sellers with products and services. In another room there are buyers who have related needs and wants. Marketing is the hallway between these rooms. It's the path that sellers and buyers take to meet and transact business. Yes, marketing is a little more complicated than that, but it illustrates the function. Without the hallway, buyers and sellers remain separated. Smart sellers say, "Let's use the hallway to find buyers" or "Let's entice buyers through their senses and they will find us."

There is more to marketing than simply setting up a store, printing a catalog, or building a website. Much more. At this early stage of your business plan, summarize your ideas for marketing what you sell to those who have an associated need or want.

Compelling Reasons to Buy

It's lunchtime at the mall. You head toward the food court. Competitors are lined up to sell you their food. There are Americanized ethnic foods, healthy foods, sweet foods, traditional fare, and variations. From which should you order your lunch?

The one that offers you the most compelling reason to buy. Based on market research, each of these food vendors is guessing what you will buy today. In addition, they are appealing to your senses with photos and smells of delicious foods.

Your business also must offer customers a compelling reason to buy from you rather than from your competitor. This is an important element of your business plan; it's your marketing strategy (Chapter 11). For now, you must begin developing a compelling reason that you will abridge in your plan's executive summary. Following are some compelling reasons for your customers to buy from you, depending on your business:

- Location convenient to customers when they decide to buy
- Lower prices than competitors
- Faster delivery than competitors
- Greater selection than competitors
- Friendlier, more knowledgeable sales staff
- Higher quality than available from competitors
- More comfortable shopping experience
- More trusted brand name
- Easier purchase terms
- More enticing sensory messages (visual, smell, taste, touch)

These compelling reasons are responses to your competitors. That is, if you have no competitors as you sell wholesale widgets in Ohio, you don't really need compelling reasons for buyers to choose your company over another. However, if the marketplace is flooded with widget wholesalers, you can respond with lower, faster, greater, higher, easier, friendlier, and other compelling reasons to choose your business. As you identify and define your competitors (Chapter 9), you will select one or more compelling reasons to buy from you. For now, consider these reasons as you write the first draft of your business plan's executive summary.

Capital Requirements

Chances are you don't have enough to fully fund a start-up or growth business. You'll probably need some financial help. Even if you don't, you need to document the costs of your business. That's a primary function of your business plan.

Capital is accumulated goods of value. Commonly, money is referred to as capital. However, there are other capital assets, including real estate, machinery, fixtures, inventory, licenses, and other things of value. Your business will need capital to start, operate, and grow. Your business plan documents capital requirements in detail. Your plan's executive summary suggests the sources of required capital.

Before you begin developing your business, you should have a good idea of where needed capital will come from and where it will be spent. Further research will expound on capital sources and outflows. For now, you just need to summarize capital requirements.

Start-Up Capital

Start-up capital is the money and other assets you need to set up your business until the day you sell your first product or service. You may already have many of the assets. For example, if you are establishing a computer-training business, you already have knowledge, experience, some equipment, and maybe some money in the bank. If you're developing a manufacturing or product-related business, you typically won't have all of the tools, materials, and money to open the business doors. You'll first need to convince others of the sound investment they can make in your business.

ALERT!

Obviously, if your preliminary summary suggests that capital requirements can't be met by increased income, you must begin adjusting your business plan. The concept may not be profitable as defined. The best time to revise the concept is before you waste lots of money and effort on a project that just won't be a good investment. That's why you should begin drafting your executive summary before the plan is begun.

By developing the first draft of your business plan's executive summary, you are defining what business you will be in, to whom you will sell, and how you will be better than the competition. Your core business concept will be defined, albeit in broad terms subject to further research. This definition can also help you estimate start-up costs. With it, you can list required space with costs, employee training and salary costs, inventory or machinery costs, etc. At this point, you don't know specifics, but you can make educated guesses based on your own business experience and additional research. You need realistic numbers.

Where will this start-up capital come from? Your preliminary executive summary will offer suggestions and, eventually, actual sources. Start-up capital often comes from savings, real estate loans, retirement funds, personal (family, friends) investors, and the sale of other assets. A popular resource is SBA-guaranteed loans (See Chapter 2).

Growth Capital

Growth capital is the money needed to expand an existing business. You may be buying out a competitor, extending your sales territory, adding an online presence, or expanding your store. For example, if your business concept is to expand an existing retail store, you probably already know what costs will be required for additional space, fixtures, inventory, and staffing. If you have a manufacturing operation that would profit from expansion with new equipment, the equipment supplier can provide an estimate of capital requirements as well as payment terms.

Working Capital

How will you make sure that income exceeds expenses? And how will you ensure that sufficient income arrives before expenses are due? These are vital questions to the success of your business operation.

Cash flow is the measure of a business' liquidity, making sure that there is sufficient cash to pay bills when due. More small businesses are strangled to death by cash-flow problems than any other cause. To cover the difference, your business will require working or operating capital. You will need money in the bank for the times when cash doesn't flow fast enough. How much money? For now, estimate your working capital requirements as a cash reserve sufficient to operate your business for three months (for retail) to a year (for manufacturing).

CHAPTER 4

Present Situation and Objectives

A business plan is a goal document, written to illustrate your path from Point A to Point B. Point B is the successful start-up or growth of your small business. Point A is where you are right now; it's how you see your opportunity. It is your analysis of the marketplace, your first comprehensive step on your path toward Point B. This chapter will nudge you on that path as you turn your business ideas into reality.

The Market

Writing a business plan is analogous to building a house. First, you need an overall plan. That's your first draft of the executive summary. Then you need a foundation, built on solid ground that outlines and supports your business. That's your section called Present Situation and Objectives. Some business-plan books and software programs call this by other names, but the function is the same—to start and support business construction. It expands your plan with more details that will be further expanded in subsequent sections of your business plan.

The first component of defining the present situation (also called opportunities) is analyzing the marketplace for what you plan to sell. Your executive summary mentions the market; here's where you discuss it in further detail. What you say about the market depends on the purpose of your business plan and your level of research. For example, if you're writing a start-up plan, your analysis will primarily be as a knowledgeable outsider who has done the research and maybe even worked in a similar field, but not operated this type of business. If you're writing a growth plan, you have experience in the market and can build upon it with new research and insights. Prospective is key.

Market Environment

Even if you have experience in the marketplace in which you plan to build your business, you'll need additional research. For example, if you're selling wholesale widgets throughout your state or region, you will probably need data on how many widgets are currently being sold. Exact numbers will come with market analysis (Chapter 7). For now, you need a sense of what the marketplace for your product or service is doing within your sales territory, whatever that is. Following are some typical market-environment statements:

- The market for wholesale widgets in the Pacific Northwest is rapidly growing.
- The state marketplace for tax services is small but expected to grow later this year due to legislative changes in how businesses are taxed.

- The local market for ethnic restaurants is saturated, but there is a shortage of vegetarian restaurants.
- The market for trade association websites is poised to grow by 25 percent in the coming year according to a recent *Wall Street Journal* article.

A concise definition of the market environment for what you expect to sell can begin expanding your business plan and help you focus on opportunities.

QUESTION?

How can I tell what local opportunities are available for my business model?
Get informed. Read all local publications, especially those with business information. Join the local chamber of commerce and begin developing relationships with members. Ask the chamber manager what local business data is available to you. If there is a nearby college or university, find out if any studies have been done by the business department on the local marketplace. Study similar markets in other areas to determine what opportunities have been developed that could be applied to your market.

Market Opportunities

An opportunity is a favorable juncture of circumstances. A new technology can offer you an opportunity to develop a proven business concept in a new way. For example, print-on-demand services have made the publishing of single-copy books relatively easy and inexpensive, opening up a new market for publishers, authors, and booksellers. Classic books that were too expensive to republish in quantity are now back in print.

Your business concept and market environment can be combined to help you select from among numerous opportunities. If you plan to offer employment services, market opportunities may include:

- Helping newly trained auto mechanics find jobs
- Helping employees caught in a local layoff find new jobs

- Packaging employment services with resume writing for sales executives
- Finding employment online for nurses within a specialty that you are familiar with

Again, a marketing opportunity is a favorable juncture of business opportunities. Consider the many combinations of what you already know and what customers need. At that juncture, opportunities abound.

ALERT!

One of the best ways of learning about local market demographics is to talk with local media salespeople, such as radio and television stations, newspapers, and shopper ad-sales executives. Their business depends on identifying and programming to the local markets. They can help you understand who buys what, why, and how to reach them.

The Product or Service

What is it that you will be selling? Is it a product, a service, or a combination? Is it wholesale, retail, or will you manufacture or import it? Many of these questions you've already answered as you developed your business plan's executive summary. These get expanded and made more specific as you define the present situation that your business opportunity lives within.

Remember that your business plan is a living document. You can and should make changes to it whenever you identify new requirements or opportunities for your business venture. Even after you've delivered your business plan to investors, you should continue updating it to reflect current conditions. It will guide you into the future.

Status

What do you know about the current business circumstances for the product(s) and or service(s) you're planning to sell? What do you know and what can you discover?

A manufacturer may respond: At present, our concept for automatic widgets is in the design stage and will be ready for testing within three months after the business plan is funded. A wholesaler may say: We have signed an exclusive agreement with the world's largest widget manufacturer to import and sell their products to retailers within our state. A service business developer responds: We have tested the marketplace and determined that there is an opportunity for us to sell our proven services to major clients we have identified.

Your response will expand on what you've already said in the executive summary. Later, your analysis of the present situation for your product or service will be expanded further in your business plan's Product/Service Description (Chapter 6). You are developing your business plan in interactive stages.

Life Cycle

Products and services have life cycles—stages of form and function that a thing goes through during its lifetime. People have a life cycle: toddler, child, teen, young adult, mature adult, senior adult. Products and services have a similar life cycle that can be short or long and can even be reversed. For example, the life cycle for a specific product may range from new to mature in six months, then be revitalized and reach a second stage of maturity before expiration.

Whatever you sell will have a life cycle. What is it? If it is based on technology, the life cycle will be shorter and require frequent renewals. If it is a mature service, such as tax consulting, the life cycle is at maturity and will be so until there is a dramatic change in how taxes are calculated and reported.

Why is understanding your product's or service's life cycle so important? Because you don't want to begin selling something that others are discontinuing for lack of profitability, unless you know something they don't. Your business concept may return a nearly expired product life cycle back to maturity or even a growth stage.

FACT

The seven stages of business life are the idea (seed) stage, start-up stage, growth stage, mature stage, expansion stage, decline stage, and exit stage. Most businesses fluctuate among the stages at various points of their life, moving from growth to decline and back to expansion depending on management and market factors. Some businesses will jump right into the mature stage based on the experience and funding of the owners. Others will not get past the idea stage.

Timing

Humorist Will Rogers said, "The best way to make money is to figure out where people are going, get there first, and buy up all of the land." Timing is everything, especially in business. If you knew what stocks would go up tomorrow or when your lucky numbers would be selected in the lottery, you could become rich. Many fortunes have been made and lost by the timing of events.

ALERT!

Markets are dynamic, not static. Make sure that your business plan and your subsequent business venture continually monitor and adjust to changing factors in your marketplace. Be especially aware of changes that impact your customers. If they lose jobs, find more shopping options, or are worried about the economy, your business may be impacted.

Timing is the ability to select the moment to do something for optimum effect. Your business venture requires intelligent timing. Open your small retail store when there is great local need and you will thrive. Open it a month after a major competitor opens with a wider selection and lower prices and your business will probably expire. As you plan your business' present situation, consider its timing. Later, you will analyze the marketplace and do additional research in timing. For now, do some preliminary research on whether your business timing in the present situation is optimum.

Pricing and Profitability

No matter what the business, its primary function is to make a profit for the investor(s). Without that profit, its blood flow, the business will not survive very long. It can have the noblest of ideals and be sanctioned by customers and suppliers, but it will only survive if it is profitable.

Your business plan must answer explicit questions about pricing for profitability (Chapter 12). Before you get that far in your plan, you must answer some basic questions that will help you better define what your business will do to thrive.

Pricing

A price is the amount of money agreed upon for the exchange of a product or service. The tube of toothpaste has a $1.95 price on it. If a customer who needs it agrees with the price, it is purchased. If not, there is no purchase, no exchange of money. Many transactions are more complex than that for toothpaste, but the process is relatively the same. If there is a perceived need and the customer believes the price asked is equal to or lower than the value, an exchange may occur.

What is your business' concept of pricing? Will you aim for the lowest prices in the marketplace for comparable products or services? Will you focus instead on superlative service and not be as concerned about where your pricing falls as long as it is profitable? Is your business model to deliver quickly? Summarize your venture's pricing philosophy now and expand on it as your business plan develops.

Profitability

Profit is income less expenses. It's what's left over after you've paid the bills. Because you have some options in how you price your product or service, you also have choices in profitability. Certainly, you want the highest profits that your business can consistently earn. The problem is that if your profits—based on your prices—are high, they will develop market opportunities for competitors.

Want to know how profitable your competitors are? Many will tell you—if you are one of their investors. If you can, purchase stock in your competitor's business. If the business is a franchise, become a candidate for the franchise and learn what level of profitability is required to maintain the franchise opportunity. Alternately, ask a business consultant who can do the research for you and offer a fairly accurate estimate of the competitor's profitability.

As you develop your business plan, you will study competitors to determine what their profitability is and will decide how your business can be at least as profitable in the long run. You may decide to offer some products or services at prices lower than the competition—called loss leaders—to draw customers who may also buy more profitable products or services. You may learn that a competitor works on an average profit of 12 percent. You may then decide that you can beat the competition with a profitability of 10 percent. In addition, you will offer some loss leaders at no profit and others at 20 percent profitability. You don't have to get into the specifics just yet, but you should develop a profitability goal for your business early on. Otherwise, when you finally do come to the question of profits, you may find that the business model you developed won't support sufficient profits.

Resources

What resources are available to you as you start or grow your business? Who can you count on for sage advice? Where will your money come from? Who can help your business succeed?

A resource is a secondary source. It's someone or something that can assist you in an endeavor. This book is a resource in writing your business plan. It additionally opens the door to many other sources that you can use in starting or growing your business. What types of resources does your business need? Knowledge, financial, and assistive resources.

Knowledge Resources

Business is about profiting from knowledge. A lender profits from in-depth knowledge of financial markets and how to make profitable loans. A restaurant profits from knowing how to attract customers with food and service that is both popular and profitable. Without specialized knowledge on their fields, each will soon be out of business.

Your business venture requires expert knowledge. As you define the present situation and expand your business plan, you must clearly define and document what that knowledge is. If you don't already have it, you must report how you are going to get it. If you're selling your services as a consulting engineer, you need a related degree, accreditation, and proven experience at solving problems for others. If you are manufacturing widgets, you must be able to prove that you can do so profitably. You must identify the sources of this specialized knowledge. Your investors will require it; your customers will depend upon it.

FACT

Bankers are in the business of understanding finance. Use them as your tutor in business finance. In addition to being a resource for money or credit, bankers can answer questions about financial requirements and opportunities you may not have considered. Make friends with your banker.

Financial Resources

Business requires money. Some businesses, called *boot-straps*, can start up with little more than an idea and, very slowly, build profitability. However, even a hot-dog cart business needs money for the cart, the hot dogs and relishes, and business licenses. Where will the money come from? What is its source?

Some of the financial resources for starting or growing a business come from self-funding. The owner has the cash, savings, or equity needed to invest. These are sources. If additional money is required, outside sources must be convinced that the business can and will pay their investment back with interest. Your business plan is written to document the inside and outside sources of needed financing.

Assistive Resources

Chapter 2 offered numerous sources of additional business help, including the Small Business Administration, SCORE, and other resources. As you develop your plan, these assistive resources will be developed and documented. Your investors need to know about them. You need to know about them. As you write about your opportunity's present situation and objectives, find and define the assistive resources that your business needs to start or grow.

You may also list key or secondary employees as business resources. For example, your widget-importing business may rely on hiring an import manager with widget experience.

Once you have considered your business' knowledge, financial, and assistive resources, you can write a summary.

Following is an example of a Resources paragraph for your business plan: "This business will utilize the new owner's twenty-five years of experience in widget marketing to expand the business. Growth will be financed by a $100,000 personal investment plus a secured SBA loan for $400,000. A SCORE mentor with widget experience will advise management during the first year of operation."

Objectives

"If you don't know where you're going, how will you know when you get there?"

Too many new businesses have simple objectives: to make a profit. Yes, but how? One of the primary functions of your business plan is to make you think about and document the business' objectives or goals.

Most businesses have more than one goal. In fact, they often have many complementary goals that must work together to satisfy the overall objective of making a profit. If business-design goals are met but financial goals aren't, the business will not succeed. These goals will be expanded upon as your plan develops. Before you invest more time and money in your business concept, however, you should clearly define them. They describe where your business is going.

Business Goals

Business goals answer the question, "How do you expect to make a profit?" Your response will be something like, "Acme Widgets will profit by offering superior service to wholesalers in the Southern Territory as well as expanding growth opportunities in the Northern Territory." These statements, then, become individual goals. Each will eventually have subgoals.

To offer superior service in the Southern Territory:

- Identify the best wholesale opportunities.
- Interview wholesalers about service needs.
- Establish a proven service manager who will be responsible for the territory.
- Select a transportation vendor that will reduce delivery time at current costs.
- Publicize the improved service structure to existing customers and new prospects.

Of course, your business goals will be different. The above example illustrates that you need to first establish specific goals, then develop actionable subgoals that support them. Each of these components will be expanded upon as your business plan develops.

Financial Goals

Financial goals answer the question, "What profit do you expect to make?" Following the above example, your response may be, "Acme Widgets will increase sales in the Southern Territory by 20 percent and in the Northern Territory by 10 percent during the coming fiscal period." Subgoals will then be developed.

To increase Southern Territory profits by 20 percent:

- Increase on-time deliveries by 25 percent within three months.
- Reduce product returns by one-third within six months.
- Develop markets for high-end widgets within twelve months.
- Promote delivery advantages to new and existing customers.

Each of these subgoals will have numerous steps to their implementation. Those steps may be developed in future components of your business plan or they may be stated as goals with the details worked out later. In addition, your financial goals will identify profitability. How much detail you include depends on how extensive your business plan must be to satisfy your investors.

Return on Investment

Your business plan's present situation and objectives are outlined and developed to answer a vital question: What current conditions offer my business concept opportunities for profit? The answer to this question is important because it helps answer the ultimate business-investment question: How is this business going to reward its investors?

The bottom line to any business is an acceptable ROI. If you can invest the same amount of money in a lower-risk opportunity, do so. If the returns are relatively comparable, go with the one that offers other valuable benefits, such as the satisfaction of operating an independent business. However, keep in mind that, first and foremost, business is an investment opportunity. It must offer a fair return relative to the risk involved.

A key element to business planning is calculating the *return on investment* (ROI). It's the ratio of the money gained or lost on an investment relative to the amount of money invested. For example, a $10,000 investment that earns a profit (or interest) of $1,000 has an ROI of 10 percent (1,000/10,000 = 0.10). This is the number that all of your business investors are looking for. They will then compare it to ROIs for opportunities with comparable risks.

If they can get a 10 percent ROI on a less-risky investment (less chance of loss), they will invest there.

As your business plan grows, make sure that it verifies to all investors that it will provide a ROI that is acceptable for the risk involved. *Risk* is the possibility of loss. If the chance is greater that you will lose your investment in your opportunity than another, it has a higher risk factor. That's okay if the potential rewards, the ROI, are sufficiently greater.

At this early stage of planning your business, make sure that you have considered the factors of risk and rewards. Verify what the risks and rewards are before accepting the business challenge.

Your business plan can include a return-on-investment (ROI) summary like the following:

> *Based on a 10 percent market share for our widgets within one year of start-up, we estimate our return on investment to be 25 percent. The risk factor is moderate, as 70 percent of the initial investment is secured by machinery and other tangible assets.*

Again, your business plan will expound on this ROI summary. However, you should have a realistic understanding of the risks and rewards available in your business opportunity before you and others invest money and effort into developing your concept.

What if the ROI isn't sufficient for the risk? What if you could do as well by investing in a less-risky venture or in putting your investment into a money market fund or certificates of deposit?

In that case, you have some choices. You can search for ways to reduce the risks, you can decide not to make the investment, or you can invest anyway because you believe you can improve the results. Whatever your decision, do the research to accurately analyze the opportunity. Also, use your knowledge and assistive resources to develop and consider options. A modification to your business plan's situation and objectives now can be more profitable and help your opportunity develop a greater chance of success.

CHAPTER 5

Management

Who's the boss? More importantly, how is the boss going to get things done? Management is a critical component of any business and any business plan. Before the door is opened or growth begins, owners and investors must know who is in charge and why that person or team is qualified to do the job. Investors want to be assured that their money is being well managed. This chapter guides you in analyzing and documenting your business structure and management team.

Business Structures

The first businesses had a simple structure: one owner for one business. Then more money was needed and partnerships emerged. Liability became an issue and various corporations were developed. Today, business owners have a variety of structures that can be adopted to the needs and complexities of their venture.

Your small business requires a structure. Which one? The answer depends on many factors as well as state laws. The factors include investment options, liability, and taxation. Your business plan will define the business structure even before it selects a management team. Following is a summary of the most popular configurations. They include sole proprietorship, partnership, limited liability company, S corporation, and C corporation.

ALERT!

The easiest time to set up the most appropriate business structure is in the planning stage. Once the business is established, it is more difficult to change it. Review your various options and seek professional advice from a business attorney and or accountant. An hour or two of consulting can save you time and taxation.

Sole Proprietorship

A proprietor is a business structure with a single owner. The exception is that some states allow a category called sole proprietor, comprised of a married couple. The sole proprietor does business in his/her/their name and pays personal rather than corporate income taxes.

A sole proprietor typically operates under a business or trade name, sometimes called doing business as or DBA. For example, Bob Smith operates his retail widget store as Bob's Widgets. Depending on state law, Bob will register his DBA with a government with jurisdiction where his business is based. He could call the business Acme Widgets or by any other name not already registered. Other than registration, Bob has few legal requirements and can set up his business in a few days.

The profits from the business are treated as the owner's personal income, just as if they were wages. Bob will pay federal and state income tax as well as federal self-employment tax. As an employee, Bob previously had Social Security and Medicare taxes deducted from his wages; his employer paid the other half. As a sole proprietor, Bob must pay both sides of these taxes, currently more than 15 percent of his business profits.

The majority of new businesses started each year begin as sole proprietorships. Some eventually take other business structures to attract capital or reduce owner liability. Others retain this structure as they are passed on. At any time, a business can reorganize under a new structure, though it typically occurs when the business wants to move to a new stage in its development.

FACT

Many states have enacted the Uniform Partnership Act, which defines creation, organization, and dissolution of general partnerships within a state. Limited partnerships are governed by the Uniform Limited Partnership Act in most states.

Partnership

Some businesses require additional knowledge or capital to begin or grow. A partnership is a business structure with two or more individuals as owners. Each partner's contribution to the business is defined, and they agree on how the resulting profits will be split. The specific terms are included in a partnership agreement.

For taxes and liability, partners are treated like separate individuals. If the agreement says that partner A gets two-thirds of the profits, that partner will probably be responsible for paying two-thirds of the taxes—whatever the agreement says. It also outlines who has what management responsibilities.

In a limited partnership, one or more partners are limited in their rights or responsibilities. Partners may be limited in what authority they have in the daily operations or in the business liability that they accept. A partner without these limits is called a general partner. Your attorney or accountant can help you establish the most appropriate business structure for your new or growing venture.

Limited Liability Company

A limited liability company (LLC) is a hybrid. In some situations, owners are treated as individuals and in other conditions as investors in a corporation. The structure is defined in an operating agreement. The LLC business can be managed by an owner-manager or a hired manager selected by the investors.

LLCs are established for two reasons: liability and taxation. The structure is set up to define what will happen if the business loses lots of money. Can creditors come after individual owners? Do they have limited liability? As with other complex business structures, consult with professional advisors to determine which is the most appropriate for your venture.

S Corporation

A corporation is a separate legal unit. It is not the owners; it is, within the law, its own entity. The corporation can be owned by individuals or other corporations, called stockholders. The corporation operates within the law under its own by-laws. Ownership shares are transferable. If an owner dies, the shares are sold or transferred and the corporation lives on. The liability of shareholders is limited, typically to their investment.

An S corporation (S-corp) is a modified corporate structure based on Subchapter S in Chapter 1 of the Internal Revenue Code (IRC). S-corps are different in that the profits made by the corporation are passed on to the shareholders, who must pay taxes on them as individuals. The S-corp does not pay taxes on income; it passes the obligation on.

Corporate law covers everything from small businesses to multinational companies. Make sure you get appropriate legal advice when defining and establishing a business corporation. Setting up a corporation can be expensive, especially if it doesn't reflect your desired business structure and taxation plans.

To become an S-corp, the business must be a domestic corporation or a limited liability company with fewer than 100 shareholders. There must only be one class of stock, and the corporation's profits and losses must be passed on to shareholders proportionately. Setting up an S-corp requires professional assistance, but it isn't as difficult as establishing a full corporation. S-corps are especially popular structures for family businesses and partnerships that want to grow beyond two or three partners. Seek counsel.

C Corporation

A C corporation (C-corp) is a full corporate structure based on Subchapter C in Chapter 1 of the IRC. Unlike S-corps, the C-corp must pay income taxes. The profits or dividends passed on to shareholders are then taxed as income. So-called double taxation is the primary reason why many smaller businesses prefer other business-structure forms.

FACT

A share of stock represents a share of ownership in a corporation, a share in the equity or value of that corporation. A shareholder or stockholder is an individual or business entity (including another corporation) that owns at least one equity share. In most corporations, a shareholder can participate in corporate elections. If publicly traded, the shares can be bought and sold to others through a stock exchange.

The primary advantages to C-corps are that shareholders have limited liability and they are more flexible in ownership. It can have more stockholders than an S-corp and have numerous classes or levels of stock. The New York Stock Exchange (NYSE) and other stock exchanges primarily trade in C-corp stocks. These are termed publicly traded stocks; anyone can buy them and invest in these corporations.

Other options include incorporating in a state other than the one where your business operations are. For example, you can incorporate in Delaware or Nevada. The advantage to a Delaware corporation is the state's laws that benefit business. More than half of all corporations publicly traded on the NYSE are incorporated in Delaware. Nevada incorporations offer similar benefits to privately held corporations. Establishing a C-corp is complex and requires professional advice. As you develop your business plan, understand the opportunities and limitations of each structure.

Management Team

What management skills does your business require to succeed? It's an important question that should be answered and developed in your business plan. Is your business a manufacturer that requires specialized knowledge? Is it a retail business that needs a management team with extensive retail experience? Is it a service business requiring management that thoroughly understands the problems that your service will solve?

ALERT!

Be careful sharing your business plan with management candidates. Even though they sign a confidentiality agreement, they may share what they learn about your business with your competitors. Make sure that you develop and test relationship trust before sharing your valuable business plan with them.

No matter the structure or size of your business, your management team will have the same functions. You will want a person or group to manage the business aspects (administration, finances, taxes, hiring and firing), another for operations (making or selling the product or service), and employees or independent contractors who do the work. In a sole proprietorship, these functions may be managed by a single person or a couple. In a corporation, there may be numerous layers with a business-manager team for each product line or territory. Your business plan must define these management or operational functions and identify the people or teams, at least in general terms. You will be developing job descriptions for your management teams; later, you will identify specific key personnel.

Business Manager

No matter what your business does to make a profit, it needs a manager—a supervisor or director of people toward a specific result. A business manager is responsible for the success of the business. That person or team manages the income, expenses, taxes, and other financial aspects of the venture. In large corporations, these are the chief executive officer

(CEO) and chief financial officer (CFO). Proprietorships often have a single manger who is responsible for the financial side as well as operations.

Before you share your business plan with a potential employee, lender, or supplier, make sure you get a signed confidentiality agreement (Chapter 20.)

Appendix A is a full business plan for a product-based business. Appendix B is a plan for a service business. Refer to these plans for specific examples of successful components. Both are developed by coauthor Stephen Windhaus (*www.windhaus.com*).

It's important to your business' success that you clearly define the responsibilities of your business manager. Use your business plan to develop this summary. It not only helps investors understand the implementation of your vision, it will also help you understand what management skills are required to succeed.

Operations Manager

An operations manager is responsible for the day-to-day processes that will make your business succeed. For example, a retail store manager is hired to supervise the selection of inventory and the activities of employees toward selling products. A plant manager supervises the materials, equipment, and employees needed to make the products you sell.

Many corporations have chief operations officers (COOs) to oversee business activities. If large, offices or plants will have their own operations managers who report to the COO. Smaller businesses may have a store manger. One-person businesses will combine this function with the others; the person who runs the place also keeps the books and pays the taxes.

Think of your own business opportunity and write a job description for your operations manager. Make it as thorough as you can. You may not share every detail with your investors, but it can serve to guide you in defining a successful business. The description will also help you implement your business plan once it is approved and funded.

Support Staff

Some businesses employ or contract with hundreds or thousands of people to provide their products and services to customers. This group is the workers who implement your vision: buying, selling, making, helping. A retail store will have a few clerks, some with specialized product training. A service business may have a receptionist, an input clerk, a bookkeeper, and others who have narrowly defined jobs that contribute to the whole. Again, the smallest businesses may be operated by an individual who does these jobs, too.

Your business plan should include a description of the primary job functions required to make your venture successful. In addition, the job descriptions can include a concise list of requirements, such as: must type sixty words per minute or requires a general radiotelephone license. As with other business-plan elements, include the level of detail required for your readers to make a decision. Additional detail may not help them, but it can assist you as you execute your successful plan.

Key Personnel

Successful businesses need more than comprehensive job descriptions—they need qualified people. You are a key component to your business. You will bring specialized knowledge and skills that can help the business start and grow. You are an asset to your business.

Others may be key to your business operations. A partner, friend, spouse, or known expert may also be an asset for your business. For example, you're starting an auto repair shop and your partner is a locally known ASE-certified mechanic. Your import business will partner with a successful international exporter. Your beauty shop has commitments from three popular local beauticians who will have chairs. Your investors want to know about these key personnel.

You

Most small businesses are built around an individual or a partner who contributes specialized knowledge. In most cases, the person has proven experience that the business will depend upon as it starts or grows. It's probably you. Your business plan must explain this to investors.

Following is an example from the business plan for Widgee World Retailers' Key Corporate Management section (Appendix A):

> *John Doe—John is President and founder. His background includes:*
>
> - *Graduate of Central High School—1996*
> - *Ownership, management, and operational experience (9 years) in the retail industry*
> - *Senior Sales Manager for a telecommunications firm; quarterly regional sales awards*
> - *Store Manager for three years at ABA Retail*
> - *Developed growth strategy and retail concept, which include an experienced management team to implement expansion*
> - *Active volunteer in local charitable organizations*

Your business plan should include a concise resume for its key personnel, starting with your own. Quantify your experience and emphasize results you've earned in the past.

Partners

Many small businesses are developed as partnerships, either with formal partnership agreements or as sole proprietorships (husband and wife). If your partners bring assets to the business, make sure they are summarized in your business plan. For example:

- Partner Frank Sales has twenty-five years of experience in marketing widgets in New England.
- Co-owner Arthur Wrytus will provide accounting services part time through his CPA business.

- Partners Ike and Mike Candy will provide a new truck and work as delivery drivers.

Your partners are valuable assets to your business. Make sure their contributions are documented in your business plan.

Employees

Employees will come and go as your business starts up and grows. However, some businesses depend on specific employees for the product or service that is sold. For example, a furniture repair service may hire a specific upholsterer who has extensive experience that will benefit the business. If so, get a long-term commitment from that employee and include him as a resource in your business plan.

FACT

Not sure that you want to mess with hiring employees? Most states allow coemployment, where another company checks, hires, pays, and fires employees as well as pays payroll taxes. Your job is reduced to managing them. Coemployment services typically charge 20–25 percent of the employee's salary for this service. Ask your banker or accountant about this option.

Other Resources

Your business will depend on other specific resources for its success. If they are known, document them in your business plan.

Here's the Operations section for the business plan of Acme Time Management Consultants (Appendix B):

- *Ms. Jane Black, of Black & Associates, will provide bookkeeping and accounting services.*
- *Mr. John White, a computer consultant and programmer, will provide webmaster services for the websites.*

In addition, if you will be using a specific staffing or employment service, note it in your business plan. Investors will want to know how you expect to hire and train qualified personnel to operate your business.

Compensation and Benefits

As part of your financial section of the business plan, you will estimate the costs of salaries and labor. Before that, you will summarize the costs of compensation and benefits in your management or operations section. For example, in describing yourself, your partner, or a key employee, you may note that they "will be paid $50,000 a year in salary and benefits" or they will receive "a salary of $25,000 a year plus a bonus of 10 percent of profits calculated and paid every six months."

In addition, you can estimate costs for other key personnel, even if you haven't selected and hired the people yet. The management section of your business plan can summarize these costs to help investors and other business-plan readers understand operations.

Responsibilities

Who's in charge here? As a business begins or stalls, areas of responsibility are often clouded. Who hires and fires? Who has the authority to purchase inventory? Who is supposed to take out the trash? The management section of your business plan is a good place to begin defining responsibilities so they are clear to owners, investors, and those who hire and train.

What Needs to Be Done?

To determine responsibilities, review your business plan's executive summary (Chapter 3) and objectives (Chapter 4). Then list the components of your business' processes. For example, if you are building a retail store, the processes include:

- Get customers into the store.
- Help customers buy appropriate products.
- Replace sold inventory.

- Manage income, expenses, profits, and taxes.
- Make the daily decisions needed to keep the store running smoothly.

Each of these processes must be defined and managed. As the business-plan author, it is your responsibility to consider each of these processes and document what needs to be done. You will rely on your own knowledge and experience as well as that from other resources (partners, consultants, books, etc.). If your investors need to know the details, include them in the plan. If not, summarize them so that they guide the business.

Who Is the Best Candidate?

It may be quickly obvious who is supposed to get customers in your store or purchase raw materials for your manufacturing operation. Even so, summarize it in the Management component of your business plan. If unsure of the delegation, note that in the first draft and answer the question before you complete the business plan.

Determining the best candidate for a business process will require that you discuss options with owners, partners, key personnel, and consultants. Get their input. Is your partner comfortable with taking responsibility for a key process or should you? Or should you consider a different partner? Your business plan is a thinking document that requires you to explain your design to investors. In doing so, you will learn about the opportunity, its processes and requirements, and decide on the best path for your business start-up or growth.

Writing Job Descriptions

The management component of your business plan should include job descriptions for key positions. These descriptions will be expanded as the business is established or rebuilt. For now, they help investors understand what your plans are for delegating responsibilities.

Following, from Appendix A, is a typical job description for a Store Manager:

Responsible for the management of operations, which includes:

- *Managing staff and creating a positive work environment*
- *Opening and closing of store*
- *Responsible for cash on hand and safe procedures*
- *Responsible for store maintenance*
- *Responsible for creating positive company exposure and PR*
- *Weekly store inventory and payroll*
- *Insure store and merchandise layouts are consistent with optimum traffic flow*

Not sure how to write a job description for your industry? Find a trade association that serves your type of business and ask what human resource assistance they offer. Many will have hiring guidelines, including common job descriptions that you can use as models for your own.

Job descriptions should be developed for all primary employees, including managing owners and partners. Group positions, such as assemblers or clerks, can be defined more broadly.

Future Management Requirements

Your business plan is a dynamic document that should be updated at least annually to reflect refinements and new directions. It should also talk about the future as you see it. For example, your start-up plan will define the present situation and operations for the first year. It also may summarize in what direction you plan to grow your business during years two and three and beyond. For these, you should also summarize future management requirements.

For example, your import business may be designed to introduce products from West Africa during its first year of operation. That function will require a manager with trade experience in that region. If future growth will depend on imports from East or South Africa, your business plan should note this and summarize what management changes will be needed. You may look for an export partner in that region or you may decide to make your own contacts there and expand your management knowledge. If it will give your business a long-term goal, include it in your business plan.

Your business plan can also summarize what you and any partners expect to do as the business grows. You may want to split the business into two operations in three years to serve additional regional or customer markets. Will you need to hire another manager or will you simply develop the partnership toward that goal? Alternately, you may decide that, once your business is established, you will hire a financial officer to handle the record-keeping while you focus more on sales, manufacturing, or another interest. Again, include your plans in the management section of your business plan.

Your business' management description is vital to the success of your business plan. Investors want to know who is running the business, why they are qualified, and what their responsibilities will be. Depending on your business plan's structure, this description may be in the operations segment or a separate management section. In any case, it is critical that you define who and how your business will be managed for success.

CHAPTER 6

Product/Service Description

What is your business selling? It may not be what you think it is. This chapter guides you in analyzing and defining exactly what your business is or will be selling. It will help you focus on the real function of your business, then steer you toward the most appropriate marketplace (Chapter 7). You'll learn how your product or service can be developed for long-term profits, and you'll understand better what your business is all about.

What You Sell

What is it that you're selling? Widgets? Investment services? Beauty products? Home repair services? Imported gadgets? Ethnic foods?

None of the above. Nor any other product or service!

What your business offers its customers is . . . solutions. For example, if your new venture sells auto parts, it is actually in the business of helping customers solve automotive problems that require parts. The problem may be that a car needs clean oil to ensure long life for the engine. The solution is for you to provide the appropriate oil and filter for the customer's vehicle at competitive prices.

Yes, your business does offer oil and filters and hundreds of other parts, but what the customer wants is a solution. If your business is auto repair, it is your job to analyze the problem for the customer and come up with an appropriate solution before buying parts. Customers for auto part and auto repair are, obviously, auto owners, but they have different problems that require solutions. One type of customer understands what the problem is in specific terms: parts. The other requires that you provide diagnostic services to define the problem and make the appropriate repair. Offering parts is a product business. Offering repair services is a service business.

If you think of your business as a problem-solving venture, you will be more in tune with what customers want. It will help you understand how best to offer products and or services to your customers.

Products

A product is something that is produced or made. Each was designed with a primary function that solves a problem faced by a specific group of potential buyers.

A commodity is product produced in quantity and readily available. For example, hand soap is a commodity that you can buy at numerous locations in any town or shopping center: drug store, grocery store, discount store, etc. Because it is standardized—a branded bar of soap is the same wherever it is purchased—and widely available, pricing can be competitive. If you shop around, you can buy that bar of soap at various prices. Some sellers don't make much profit on the sale of that bar of soap, instead profiting from related sales or quantity sales. Smaller, independent businesses prefer to specialize in offering specialized, noncommodity products with less competition from larger businesses.

Here's an example of a products definition from a typical business plan: "Frank's Furniture offers more than 150 items including, chairs, stools, dressers, book shelves, mirrors, screens, side tables, dining tables, and lounges selected and priced to match the household needs and economic levels of the residents of Smithtown."

FACT

The products that your business offers must be clearly defined in your business plan. Make sure that the definition allows for future expansion to related products that meet the related needs of your customers. Define the product(s) you sell in terms of a customer solution.

Services

A service is work performed for another. Changing the oil and filter on a customer's car is a service, even though products are involved. The services that your business provides to customers must solve specifically defined problems. That's how your customers look at your business. For example, a customer may say, "I know my car is due for an oil change, but I don't want to climb around underneath it trying to figure out where the filter goes—and maybe getting oily in the process."

Following is an example for the services description from a typical business plan: Fuzzy Wuzzy Child Care offers child care services for children ages from three months to six years old. Hours of operation are from 6:00 A.M. to 7:00 P.M., Monday through Friday.

As you develop your business plan, consider what problems your services will solve for potential customers, but state it in terms of the solution. Later, in your market analysis you will expand on these definitions with an analysis of exactly who needs your business services and how to reach them.

Current Products/Services

With a broad definition of the products or services that your business will offer, you can be more specific as to what you will offer in the first year of operation. For example, if you're opening a child-care center you may begin with weekday care for parents who work Monday through Friday. You goal may be to someday offer extended hours, but your current services will be offered weekdays.

Many small businesses are successful by offering both products and services. If the discount store offers only products, consider value-added services that can entice customers to buy from you. Options include technical advice, fast delivery, free delivery, gift wrapping, special orders, satisfaction guarantees, and so on.

Think about the first or next year of your business as you define the current products or services that it plans to offer. Investors will want to know what your short-term plans are. For example, if you're opening an independent bookstore, what types of books will you offer in the first year? Will you focus on a specific genre such as cookbooks, mysteries, or bestsellers? Or will it be a general bookstore? In the first year, will you offer gift certificates, promote reading groups, or offer related products such as bookmarks or reading lights?

Also define what markets you will test during the coming year. For example, if you focus on selling automatic widgets, will you also test the local market for manual widgets? Will you offer gift-wrapping services? Will your automotive oil-change service branch out into simple auto repairs? How can you expand your business by solving additional problems for your defined customer base?

Your business plan can include longer-term product and service goals as well. The purpose of defining these components is to help you focus your business and help investors understand its long-term goals. Before you can sell your customers, you must first sell your investors.

Proprietary Technology

Many businesses are based on unique opportunities that are developed by the owners—a valuable idea that you plan to profit from. Maybe it's a new way of manufacturing widgets or a unique trade name that you can build or you own intellectual property that can be turned into a profitable business.

If your new or existing business will depend on a copyright, patent, or trade secret, your investors will want to know about it. Each of these proprietary products or services has value that you can use to build a brand name. You can profit from your ideas.

Patent

A patent is an exclusive right to something. For example, you can get a patent on your unique method of manufacturing widgets from recycled cell phones. It must be distinctive and not infringe on the patent rights of others.

Patents are documented and issued by the U.S. Patent and Trademark Office (*www.uspto.gov*). Canada has the Canadian Intellectual Property Office (*cipo.gc.ca*). In the European Union it's the European Patent Organization (*www.epo.org*). There are filings and fees involved. If you believe that your concept is unique and patentable, contact an experienced patent attorney for legal advice. Once you've been issued a patent or it is pending, include a summary of it in your business plan.

ALERT!

Your proprietary knowledge is valuable; don't give it away. If your business plan includes proprietary information, make sure that whoever reads your business plan first signs a confidentiality or nondisclosure agreement written by a business attorney. Also, investigate your plan's readers and be comfortable with their honesty before passing along your secrets. Alternately, word your business plan to describe the proprietary element without giving it away.

Trademark

A trademark is a unique word or symbol that has exclusive rights assigned to a person or business. For example, Fix-It Club® is a trademark registered to a business (*www.fixitclub.com*) by the U.S. Patent and Trademark Office.

Trademarks can be developed by proving first-use in the marketplace or through registration. If you start a business called Widgee Widgets, you may be able to trademark the term and use the superscript TM (™) with it. Registering the trademark with the USPTO is a longer and more expensive process, but offers additional legal rights if there is a dispute. If you have a word or symbol that you believe is worthy of a trademark, contact an experienced trademark or intellectual-rights attorney for further advice. Once secured, include specifics of the trademark in your business plan.

You can research trademarks and patents at libraries in many major cities. The Patent and Trade Depository Library Program (PTDLP) maintains searchable data at more than 100 public libraries across the United States. For specific locations, visit *www.uspto.gov*.

Copyright

A copyright is the exclusive right to publish, sell, reproduce, or distribute a communication product such as a book, music, art, or video. A copyright notice and symbol (Copyright ©) are no longer required on publications to protect them under U.S. and International copyright laws. If the originator can prove that he or she is the originator of a communication and has not given up rights to it, then the originator is considered the copyright holder. The most enforceable way to prove rights is to include a copyright notice on the media. Sound recordings use the circle-P symbol ℗.

If your new or business benefits from a copyright, make sure that the facts are included in your business plan. It is an asset that may help attract investors and build profitability.

Trade Secret

Many businesses are built on confidential information, often called trade secrets. Trade secrets can be product formulas, processes, designs, patterns, or compiled information that offers an advantage over competitors.

What can you do with your trade secret? Keep it to yourself! Document it, explaining what it does and, if known, how it does it. Then put the secret away somewhere safe. Don't include the specifics in your business plan. Instead, describe the results in your plan, giving the reader sufficient information to realize the value without your giving the value away. The longer you can keep your trade secret from competitors, the more valuable it will become.

FACT

You can search copyright ownership online. The U.S. Library of Congress manages the United States Copyright Office. The searchable database is at *http://cocatalog.loc.gov.* You can search copyrighted documents by author, title, keyword, or document number.

Features and Benefits

Whatever your business sells is more than a product or a service. It is a solution to a problem that your customers have. The problem may be finding a safe place to care for their children during the workday or eating a healthy and delicious meal where it is convenient to them or reducing the cost of manufacturing equipment by purchasing it from a reputable importer. All consumers are seeking solutions to specific problems. All businesses are established to help consumers solve problems.

How do consumers discover these solutions? Through businesses explaining the features and benefits of their products and services. A feature is a characteristic. Typically, it's a primary or even unique feature. It's a characteristic that buyers are seeking or should be seeking as they make a purchase. More important, a benefit is the reason why they seek the feature. It is what the product or service offers to the buyer. Both of these topics—features and benefits—will be described in greater detail in coming chapters as you develop your business concept and match it to customers. For now, consider the topics as they relate to your business plan's description of products and services offered.

Product Features

The products sold by a business each have features or characteristics. A widget may be made of tempered steel, a computer printer uses low-cost ink cartridges, a car has unique styling. The specific products your business sells will have explicit features. Your business, too, will have characteristics that make it better or unique. Your business plan must not assume that readers will already know what features your products and business have; you must tell them.

Features are included in the product description component of your business plan. For example, Bob's Widget Store will feature the widest selection of name-brand widgets in the Yukon Valley. That's a characteristic of your business and should be prominently noted in your business plan.

Product Benefits

So what? Do your potential customers really care about the primary features of your business? They should. In fact, that's why you even mention the features—to indicate the benefits. Customers of Bob's Widget Store don't need to go anywhere else when looking for name-brand widgets. The primary benefit is ease of shopping.

ESSENTIAL

> Turn on the TV or read a magazine for the ads. You'll see that companies don't sell features; they sell benefits. They don't offer a sleeping pill; they offer and illustrate a restful sleep. Airlines don't fly you anywhere; they give you enjoyable destinations and emotional reunions. Think of the many benefits that your business offers its customers.

Benefits must be described in terms the customer understands. You can find all popular widgets at Bob's—that's the benefit. Your investors want to know what features and benefits your business expects to develop. Your marketing strategy (Chapter 11) will expand on product and business features and benefits.

One important benefit that your business can offer is listening intently to your customers and taking action on what you hear from them. Customers want to know that your business is interested in satisfying their needs and wants. By interviewing customers and using surveys, you can continue to be aware of what customers are thinking and how to keep them coming back to your business.

Service Features

Services aren't tangible, but they still have features. For example, a time-management consultant offers a service that features proven methods and results. The business owners and employees know how to help others manage their time better. That's the service feature.

Businesses typically offer more than one feature. Service businesses, for example, understand what their customers require and offer a variety of services, each with numerous features. A time-management consultant may also offer training classes featuring concise guides that summarize what is learned in the class. This is a secondary service feature. Your investors should know about it.

Service Benefits

Customers want to know: What's in it for me? What's the benefit? Your service business plan should summarize the benefits that customers will receive for primary and secondary services. What do your customers want and how will they benefit from it?

In addition, your business plan should think of investors/readers as customers and answer the same question: What's in it for me? How will the investors benefit from investing in your business opportunity?

Value Added

How will your product or service business stay ahead of the competition? Will you lower costs and prices? Will you have the latest products on the market? Will your business offer superior service to its customers? Curious investors want to know.

Your business plan should tell them. It should explain what value is added to products and services sold by your business. Value is the perceived benefits compared to the price. Value added means additional benefits available from a specific source. For example, many stores within a market sell a particular product, but your store also offers free gift wrapping—a value-added service. In the customer's mind, your products have a greater benefit than the same products available at another store.

QUESTION?

How can I find value-added features and benefits that fit my unique business concept?
Look to other businesses offering what you do. First, start with your competitors. Are there any obvious opportunities that are currently not filled within the local marketplace? Second, look to other marketplaces to discover ways in which similar businesses have developed value-added products and services for their customers.

Make sure that your business plan includes information about value-added products and services that you will offer. It is what differentiates your business from your competitors and makes your opportunity a better investment. Following are some examples.

- **Airport taxi service:** complimentary snacks during drive
- **Auto parts store:** longer weekend hours, free delivery
- **Book store:** expedited special orders, rare book searches
- **Fitness center:** free weight-loss classes
- **Paint store:** professional decorator on staff for free consultations
- **Travel agency:** airport delivery and pick-up services

How can your business opportunity offer greater features and benefits to customers than your competition? How is your business unique and the value of what it sells greater than that available in the local market? These are vital questions that you must answer to be successful. In addition, your investors will want to know that you understand your customers well enough to give them added value.

CHAPTER 7

Market Analysis

Your business plan is progressing well. You've developed an overview, considered present situations and future objectives, established your management goals, and defined your business' products or services. The next step—a vital one—is to analyze the market for what you sell. Is there a market for it? Your investors want to know. You need to know. This chapter will help you analyze the marketplace for your business and offerings.

The Marketplace

A marketplace is an actual or virtual area where goods and services are exchanged, typically for coin of the realm. Santa Fe has a marketplace, as does Baghdad. There are even virtual marketplaces like eBay. At each, sellers present their wares—oranges, falafel, classic comic books—to buyers. If the buyer and seller agree on the price, a sale is made and products or services transfer.

Your business operates within one or more marketplaces, depending on the type of business. A small retail store will operate within a geographic area that is convenient to buyers, such as a downtown or a shopping mall. A wholesaler sells to clients within a geographic region or an industry. An Internet business sells to the world, or at least as much of the world as the product or service can be delivered to.

Throughout history, marketplaces had geographic limits. Merchants set up a stand with other merchants and hoped that customers would visit. Today, millions of merchants operate virtually. The toaster you buy online may be ordered through an online clerk in Syracuse, New York, restocked by a wholesaler in Canada, and manufactured in China with parts from four other countries. Consider how your small business can take advantage of virtual world trade.

What is your business' marketplace? Is it limited physically? Is there a virtual marketplace for what you sell? Are you able to compete within it? These are a few of the primary questions you must answer as you identify and analyze your business' marketplace.

Your Marketplace

Before you begin selling any product or service, you must understand the marketplace in which you will be operating. Who will be buying from you? How do they buy your type of product or service? Can you make buying easier or more convenient for them?

Selecting an appropriate business from the available opportunities is critical to the success of your enterprise. In addition, choosing your marketplace is important. One location may be more convenient to your residence but not to the majority of your potential customers. To serve your customers, you must be located where they want to buy. Physical locations for businesses must be selected based on buyers' preferences.

Define your business' geographic marketplace. It may be limited to a small area of your community, such as for a coffee kiosk, or only be limited to English-speaking Internet buyers who are serviced by freight trucks. You can then determine whether the physical location of your business is a critical component to success in your marketplace.

Here is an example from Appendix A of a paragraph about locations:

Widgee World projects the opening of three storefront operations in each of the first three years of operation. All will be located in the greater metropolitan area, and in locations near middle- and upper-income communities and high retail foot traffic. We rely on economic census data to help target the three storefront locations.

Market Limits

All marketplaces have limits, even online markets. The limits may be linguistic, geographic, monetary, cultural, or governmental. Before developing your business, you must consider its limitations. For example, the market for a day-care center will be limited to people who consider your location convenient to their needs. Your wholesale business may be limited by terms of a franchise or other agreement.

Market limits may also be dictated by your finances. For example, your widget store would fit perfectly in the new megamall going in, but initial profits just won't allow you to afford the rent. However, your business' long-term plans may include a move to the mall in three to five years. If so, explain that to your investors in the market-analysis section of your business plan.

Virtual Marketing

Billions of dollars in products and service are being traded over the Internet every year. Online selling has made world marketers of small, specialized businesses. For a relatively small investment, a business can join the millions of online sellers.

Therein lies the problem: There are millions of online sellers, all competing in the new virtual economy. Unless your product or service is unique and you understand the vagaries of online marketing, your target customers will be unable to find your virtual business. However, if you *do* have unique products or services and learn to market on the Internet, it is a relatively low-cost method of setting up a profitable business.

FACT

Statistics on Internet traffic and marketing are available through numerous online resources. A leading service is eMarketer (*www.emarketer.com*), which offers Internet usage and demographics data. It also offers a free daily e-mail newsletter on Internet marketing trends. Additional data and reports are available by subscription.

For many small businesses, the virtual market is secondary. That is, they operate a physical store selling antique and collectible books or other products and supplement income with online sales. Hard-to-find books are not commodity products that can be purchased at millions of outlets, so competition, even worldwide, is relatively small. This opportunity offers the physical store a broadened marketplace for books they find locally, enhancing their sales opportunities.

Market Experience

If your business plan is based on an existing business or your extensive experience within the marketplace, you have valuable knowledge that can help you analyze opportunities. For example, if you're the manager of a successful restaurant in the area, you already know who the competitors are, who your target market is, and have a sense of what marketing opportunities are available to you. Combine this with your daily management experience and you have priceless knowledge of the local marketplace. You can supplement this experience with your own surveys of market conditions and opportunities.

Make sure that your own business experiences, direct and indirect, are factored into your analysis of the market for your business. Include your credentials in your analysis. Your investors will want to know what training and experience give you insight into the marketplace.

Market Analysis 101

Market analysis is a complex field with a simple goal: find out what customers want. At the professional level, analysts use statistical math and computers to forecast future purchases. You can use them, too. Statistics is a mathematical science that collects, analyzes, interprets, and presents data that can help in making decisions. You can apply a simplified version of the statistical market-analysis process to your retail store without a PhD or MBA. Here's how:

- Collect data (factual information) from observations of and interviews with your customers.
- Analyze the nature and the relationship of the data collected; how does it fit?
- Interpret or explain the data in clear and useful terms that relate to your store.
- Present the data as actionable steps: do this, buy that.
- Make decisions based on the data gathered, interpreted, and made actionable.

Analysis Resources

Once your business' marketplace is defined, you can analyze it. An analysis is an examination of components. For example, a market analysis is the assessment of who your customers are, why they buy, when they buy, and who they currently buy from. It is a look at all of the elements that contribute to the buying process within your selected or target market.

Analysis requires factual information, called market data. Where can you get the needed data to analyze? Fortunately, there are abundant sources of market data for all industries and marketplaces. Some are available for free, other sources have a cost, and many can be built or supplemented with your own efforts. The types of data you need include industry, competitive, and economic.

FACT

Want to know more about basic statistics and find a few easy tools? Visit *www.statserv.com*. It lists and describes dozens of statistical software programs, some of them free, that can help in gathering and analyzing all types of data, including retail. One of them, XLStat (*www.xlstat.com*), is an add-on to the popular Microsoft Excel spreadsheet program.

Industry Analysis

What industry is your business in and what can you learn about it? First, identify the industry that your venture is in. The easiest way is to identify it by its NAICS code. You can then use this code to search economic databases to learn more about the size, sales levels, and major components of the industry.

QUESTION?

What is an NAICS?

The North American Industry Classification System was introduced in 1997 as a method of classifying industries in the United States, Canada, and Mexico. The six-digit number identifies the sector, subsector, industry group, industry, and country. For example, 339941 identifies a pen and mechanical pencil manufacturer in the U.S. NAICS replaces the older four-digit Standard Industrial Classification (SIC) in use since the 1930s. Business data is compiled based on NAICS and or SIC industry numbers.

Online resources for industry information include *www.business.gov* and *www.census.gov*, two extensive government resources offering free or low-cost business data. For additional information, search online for trade groups that serve your business' industry, such as the Gift and Home Trade Association (*www.giftandhome.org*) for gift-shop owners. Many offer broad industry statistics for free and will furnish more specific data for a fee or to members.

Competitive Analysis

Whatever marketplace you operate in, you will have competitors. Who are they and how can you compete against them? To find out who they are, become a customer. If your competition will be a national widget supplier, set up an account and buy a few widgets. You will soon learn more about their business and may find opportunities to profitably compete with them.

If you want to know more about a competitor's financial data, become an investor or a franchise candidate. Publicly held companies encourage new investors, offering extensive financial data that can help you analyze your defined competition. If the competition is a franchise, becoming a candidate can bring you valuable information as well. However, they probably won't give you their trade secrets.

Economic Analysis

Economics is the study of the production, distribution, and consumption of goods and services. In addition to understanding your industry and competitors, you must know its economics.

In addition, there are local resources that can help you analyze the marketplace. Chambers of commerce often have data on the local economy, based on research studies and tax information. Local government offices can also tell you about car and pedestrian traffic for specific locations in your area. Shopping-mall management firms will share economic data with prospective lessees, including sales levels for the major stores in the mall.

Your business plan must include a definition and analysis of your business' marketplace. Statistics and observations are blended into a concise review of who will buy what you're selling.

Available resources for your research and analysis include Market-Research (*www.marketresearch.com*) and Hoovers (*www.hoovers.com*). Both offer reports on a variety of business markets and players, typically identified by NAICS codes.

Following is a market analysis from a business plan:

There are approximately 140,000 residents living within three miles of Serendipity Mall. Approximately 22 percent (31,000) are between the ages of five and nineteen. Fifty-six percent (78,000) are between the ages of twenty and fifty-four. Blosser City has one of the strongest youth athletic programs in the country. There were 11,255 children participating in the sixteen various sports programs throughout the year. In addition, through the YMCA and other nonmunicipal sponsored leagues and programs, there are an additional 3,591 child participants. This does not include the residents of neighboring cities like Smallville and Baechtel, which are within the market area and have an additional 3,500 participants. Blosser City has forty-two public parks, of which the six largest are devoted solely to athletics. The three-mile radius has three high schools, four middle schools, and twelve elementary schools in the public school system. There are an additional six private schools and two new schools planned for the next two years. Blosser City is a young, active community, with outdoor sports played year round. The need for cold-weather boots and shoes does not exist, therefore, athletic shoes are worn year round.

The residents of Blosser City are in the upper income brackets, with an average income of approximately $74,000 per year. Sixteen percent of the area's population earn in excess of $100,000 per year. In the next three years, that percentage is expected to increase to 22 percent. These affluent, active residents are willing to buy the latest in athletic footwear, if the service and assortment are strong.

Our target markets are the athletic adult and athletic-participant children. The top two ACORN Consumer Groups determined by ABCD, an international information technology corporation, within three miles are: Prosperous Baby Boomers (30.7 percent) and Baby Boomers with Children (17.4 percent). By serving these customers well, the balance of the less-active community will identify Foot Loose as their athletic-footwear headquarters.

Market Segments

Most businesses don't sell in only one marketplace. In the Foot Loose example, athletic shoes are sold to both young people and adults. In addition, the market segments include the various communities in the surrounding area, each with its own unique market and competitors.

FACT

In defining market segments, you want to know what individuals have in common, their homogeneity. If older couples frequently buy from your business but young individuals don't, that's a market segment. In defining these segments, look for patterns. What do your customers have in common? Residence? Workplace? Needs? Interests? Attitudes? You can then define and analyze them in groups or segments to help them find what they're looking for.

A market segment is a portion or component of a marketplace; the smaller subgroups of a market. In the example, Serendipity Mall's marketplace has 140,000 residents. Not all of them are customers for athletic shoes. The owners of Foot Loose will identify, analyze, and attempt to draw customers from two primary buying groups. They will also draw from secondary markets, such as neighboring towns. By becoming a major source for athletic shoes in the area, they will also draw tertiary market segments, like people traveling through the area who stop at the mall.

How can you identify the segments in your marketplace and select those that are most appropriate for what you sell? Analysis. Through your research and common sense, identify the general traits of those who will buy from you. Then analyze and reach out to them. The most common methods of segmenting marketplaces are by geography, demographics, psychographics, and behavior.

Geographic Segmentation

Geography is a study of the earth's surface. Geographic segmentation is the study of economic and cultural information about people who live or work in specific areas. Geographic variables in marketplaces include:

- **Country:** USA, Lebanon, Argentina
- **Region:** Pacific Northwest, Atlantic Coast
- **State or province:** North Dakota, Quebec
- **Climate:** hot, cold, rainy, humid, temperate
- **City:** Chicago, Prescott, Camas
- **Zip Code:** 90210, 20500
- **Neighborhood:** Rancho Del Rio, Prune Hill

Before you establish a brick-and-mortar business (one with a physical location customers visit), analyze the geographic segments and opportunities within that marketplace.

Demographic Segmentation

Demographics studies people. Within a geographic marketplace, there may be people with lots of money and people with little. Some will have families and others not. There will be men, women, college grads, high-school dropouts, and people of various ethnicities. These population features will impact what you sell and how.

To better understand your marketplace, research the demographic variables of your chosen geographic location. You may discover that your business will be more successful somewhere else. Or you may find that a change in your business concept can reach a more profitable market. Demographic variables include:

- **Age:** 12–21, 35–48
- **Education:** college grads, technical-school grads
- **Family size:** no children, 2.4 children
- **Gender:** male, female
- **Income:** $25,000 annual, $250,000 annual
- **Language:** English, Farsi
- **Occupation:** white collar, blue collar
- **Race/Nationality:** Euro-American, Latino
- **Religion:** fundamental Christian, Baha'i
- **Sexual orientation:** heterosexual, homosexual

Each of these segments, if appropriate to your business plan, can be further analyzed. For example, what income group most often buys widgets? Or what are the income levels of the majority of shoppers at Serendipity Mall? You can discover the answers to these and other vital demographic questions using the resources offered earlier in this chapter.

Psychographic Segmentation

Psychographics study interests, attitudes, and opinions of individuals and groups. Your customers can be studied as psychographic segments; doing so will help you better understand their needs and how they make buying decisions. Psychographic variables include:

- **Attitudes:** positive, judgmental
- **Interests:** saving money, learning
- **Lifestyle:** sedentary, active
- **Opinions:** conservative, moderate
- **Personality:** humorous, serious
- **Values:** honest, self-centered

There are hundreds of other variables within psychographics. Some will relate to your customers and others will not be as important. To analyze your business' marketplace, you need to understand the behavior—the psyche—of your target customers.

Behavioral Conditions

Most people have variable psychographics, another term for behaviors. That is, in one situation your personality may be serious while in others it is humorous. There are so many variables that predicting what a customer group will do under certain conditions can be difficult. Behavioral variables include:

- **Benefits perceived:** easy to use, relatively low cost
- **Brand loyalty:** Coke, Pepsi
- **Current financial resources:** affluent, broke
- **Decision mode:** receptive, argumentative

- **Product end use:** new benefits, replacement
- **Readiness to buy:** needed, unneeded

Understanding customer behavior is important to selling. However, it is a condition that you can impact with the design, presentation, and promotion of your business. With an attractive website, you can help customer groups identify a need and increase their readiness to buy. You cannot change their current financial resources, but you can help them understand the value of what you offer and hope that your efforts earn a review of those resources.

SWOT Analysis

In analyzing your business concept and the marketplace, you must consider their strengths, weaknesses, opportunities, and threats—commonly called SWOT analysis. It is a strategic planning tool first used four decades ago to analyze business ventures. It continues to be a useful tool that can help you develop your business plan. Chapter 11 will expand this analysis into a marketing strategy with tactics.

Strengths

A strength, in business analysis, is an internal attribute that will help achieve an objective. These are the good things about your business. These are the attributes that make it stronger than competitors. Strengths for a business can include:

- **Brand:** established, recognized
- **Competition:** knowledge, assets
- **Costs:** inventory, employees
- **Creativity:** new products, services
- **Employees:** knowledgeable, credentialed
- **Resources:** location, financial

Your business plan offers a good opportunity for you to list the specific strengths of your venture. What brand, competitive, cost, creativity, employee, and resources strengths does your business venture have? Listing them will help you analyze your business. CuppaJoe is a fictional business concept based on the opportunity for an Internet cafe. It serves well as an example of SWOT analysis for a business plan.

Strengths are important to the definition of your business. Following is one that illustrates how they help identify your plan:

> *CuppaJoe has a valuable inventory of strengths that will help it succeed. These strengths include a knowledgeable and friendly staff, state-of-the-art computer hardware, and a clear vision of the market need.*

Weaknesses

A weakness is an internal attribute that can be harmful to a business' objective. To identify weaknesses, consider the same categories as reviewed for strengths. Is your business name or primary brand unrecognized? Is the competition strong? Will your costs of inventory and employees make it difficult to be profitable?

Business opportunities also have weaknesses. Here's an example:

> *CuppaJoe must address business weaknesses including a dependence on quickly changing technology and the cost factor associated with keeping state-of-the art computer hardware.*

It may be easier to identify business strengths than weaknesses, but you must make the effort. Your competitors will be analyzing them carefully in order to retain or grow their market share. Look at your business concept as your competitors will. Focus on the internal weaknesses and analyze how you can overcome them. Be proactive.

Opportunities

An opportunity is an external condition that can help a business in meeting objectives. What unique opportunities does your business or the current marketplace offer? Following are common market opportunities:

- **Competitor:** downsizing or redirection
- **Economic changes:** growth, recession
- **Environment:** enhancements, reductions
- **Global influences:** availability, costs
- **Perceptions:** popularity, increased need
- **Technology:** greater features, lower cost

These and other opportunities can offer your business openings to start or grow. For example, the increased availability of widgets globally may allow your business to import widgets at lower prices and reduce local competition. The reduced cost of a technology that your business depends on can give your venture a pricing advantage.

Your business plan must also address opportunities, such as this:

CuppaJoe's strengths will help it capitalize on emerging opportunities. These opportunities include, but are not limited to, a growing population of daily Internet users and the growing social bonds fostered by the new Internet communities.

ALERT!

SWOT can be applied not only to your marketplace but also to your competitors. To analyze those businesses that vie for your customers, identify the strengths, weaknesses, opportunities, and threats that individual competitors face—from their perspective (Chapter 9). The more you understand them, the easier it will be to beat them.

Threats

A threat is an outside condition that may be harmful to a business' objectives. Each of the market opportunities available can become a threat to your business venture. For example, your competitor may be poised to expand operations or focus its business more on the customers that you hope to serve. The local perception of your business location may be a negative if the neighborhood is declining. You need to analyze and address this issue.

How will your business handle threats? Here's an example:

Threats that CuppaJoe should be aware of include the rapidly fall-ing cost of Internet access and emerging local competitors.

Developing a SWOT analysis for your business plan will guide you in defining a target market as well as establishing an effective marketing strat-egy (Chapter 11).

Your Target Market

Why should you go to all of the trouble of analyzing strengths, weaknesses, opportunities, and threats to your venture? The purpose of market analy-sis is to define your business' target market. You want to know who your business will serve and verify that it will be profitable. Businesses with only altruistic goals don't survive.

A target market is a definition of your customers. It combines the geo-graphic, demographic, psychographic, and behavioral characteristics of those who will most likely buy what you sell. It will include more than one group of customers and note what they have in common. The market analy-sis performed for this section of your business plan will help you define your target market(s).

Following is a definition of target markets for Foot Loose Shoe Store:

Active Family will be the focus of our nonrunning marketing effort. They give us the largest target, most opportunity for multiple sales, and allow us to gain further access into the community's numerous leagues. A typical active family would be described as parents in their late 30s and early 40s with two children. If the children each play two sports, that would require a minimum of two pair of shoes per year for each. If the parents are also active, that could amount to an additional two pair per year. With the need to purchase six pairs of shoes per year, we expect this family to make shoe purchases anywhere from three to six times during the year. They may visit the store an addi-tional three to four times for accessories or simply to browse while in *the center. For example, there are 12,000 participants in the Blosser City Youth Soccer Program. Every one of them needs a new pair of soccer cleats every year. Currently, they need to leave Blosser City to get a good selection of styles. This is a volume customer, but our goal is to have the entire family come along for the ride and through service and knowledgeable sales help have an additional sale consummated. This average sale will be approximately $42.00.*

The next most important segment will be the participant runner. The average sale for this customer will be $75–$110. This customer should always make an additional purchase when visiting. Running socks, running apparel, running accessories, or supplements should be added to this ticket. By capturing the Runner, the less serious runner will be attracted to the store to be able to associate with their more serious counterpart.

We anticipate that 75 percent of our annual volume will come from these two classifications. The balance will be sport-specific buyers and nonfamily participants.

Your research may suggest that there is a broader or narrower market for your business. Or it may tell you that the market is already saturated and that, to be successful, your business must find another marketplace. These are important reasons to analyze your market before investing your time and money—and that of your investors—in a business that doesn't have the greatest chance of success. With careful and accurate market analysis, your business plan can then identify and seek customers, the people and businesses who will buy what you sell.

CHAPTER 8

Customers

The movie *Field of Dreams* suggests, "If you build it, they will come." But that's fiction, and any resemblance to business is purely coincidental. You can plan and build for a year, but if you haven't done so with your customers fully in mind, you may not have any. At the least, you won't have as many as you could if you understood and planned to meet their needs. This chapter helps you identify, find, study, and keep customers for your business.

Selling to Individuals

Chapter 7 guided you through analyzing your business opportunity's market. You identified the industry, competition, economics, segments, strengths and weaknesses, and opportunities and threats. In the abstract, you know who will buy what you will sell.

But customers aren't abstracts. They are real people with common needs and problems. They are the individual components of your marketplace. If you understand and treat them as individuals rather than market components, your business will be more successful.

For example, your widget store serves a hundred customers a day. Your market analysis says that, on a given day, you will sell twenty-five automatic widgets, ten left-handed widgets, and two widget gift certificates. Those are the averages. One day, you may sell fifty left-handed widgets and nothing else. Why? Because markets don't buy widgets, individuals do. Customers are individuals.

Recognize Individuality

Your business plan must recognize the individuality of your customers. Think of your customers as a market segment of one. That customer will have many things in common with other customers, such as needs, economic status, when they prefer to shop, and so on. But you must still recognize them as individuals.

Many people who start small businesses are good customers for what they sell. For example, a life-long golfer may open a golf-equipment store, an experienced crafter will open a craft-kit manufacturing business, and a world traveler will decide to start an import business. You are an individual, as are each of your customers. See an aspect of yourself in those who will buy from you and you will better understand their needs. Understand the needs of your own best customer: you.

Analyze Individual Needs

Customers are individuals, but their needs aren't unique. Otherwise, your business would require a single unit of thousands of products or hundreds of distinctive services. Your customers will share common needs. It is your business' task to fulfill the needs of the greatest number of individual customers.

ALERT!

Never forget that customers are individuals. You can make generalizations about them to determine what they have in common and how to best reach them, but when they buy from you, they are unique people, each with needs and desires. Those needs and desires may be the same as thousands of others, but if you treat them impersonally you can lose them.

As you write your business plan, consider the needs of individual customers, some like yourself and others with similar needs. Why? Because the majority of your competitors don't. They see products, services, and even customers as commodities or articles of trade. The component lacking from many businesses—and many business plans—is customer service, or serving the customer's needs. To paraphrase *Field of Dreams*, "Include customer service as a vital component of your business plan, and they will come."

Make sure your business plan clearly identifies individual needs. Here's an example from Appendix A:

> *Widgee World knows its product lines exceptionally well, the pressures of pricing, and the need for a constant introduction of new, related product lines as they become available. Equally important is the need to develop a marketing strategy that puts the company name in the customers' minds in the right place at the right time. Finally, there is simply no substitute for excellent customer service, resulting in a high percentage of repeat and referred sales. Widgee World will serve individual customers with common needs.*

Selling to Companies

What about companies? They aren't individuals; they are groups. If your business sells primarily to companies rather than individuals, how should you plan to serve them?

Actually, your business customers are simply individuals who represent groups. The entire company doesn't show up at your office to plan a purchase. The widget buyer for ABC Stores is an individual, not a company. She is an individual with a job that requires her to buy widgets for a company. Your business should answer the needs of the individual who is representing the company.

In addition, you must understand the needs of the company. If you're meeting with the maintenance manager of a chain of restaurants about your janitorial services, you need to know how many of their restaurants are within your marketplace. By identifying them in advance, you will be helping your customer—the maintenance manager—recognize the greater need and your participation in the solution. No matter how large the company and the problems it faces, it all comes down to selling to an individual.

Who are the individuals to whom your business will offer solutions? How can you identify them? Where will you find them? How can you reach them? Once they are your customers, how can you keep them buying from you and not your competitors? These are all important questions to the success of your business and the development of your business plan.

FACT

If your business sells to companies, keep a two-tiered database of your customers: the companies and the individual buyers. As your business grows, you may get additional customers from the company's other offices or you may develop relationships with other buyers within the company. An interconnected database of contact information will help you keep track of your customers at various levels and develop additional opportunities.

Identifying Customers

Established name-brand retail stores have it easy. If they have a proven product and an ideal location, many customers will find them. Of course, they will strive to attract more customers, but the target market (Chapter 7) knows where they are and what they sell.

New businesses often don't have this opportunity. They must identify individual customers and strive to attract and serve them. Businesses who are trying to grow into new markets have similar challenges. What's the solution? New and growing businesses must identify individual customers by first determining who they are, what they want, how they prefer to buy, and what authority they have in the buying process.

Once your business is established, develop a focus group of your best customers. They can be labeled as Special Shoppers or Executive Customers or another creative title. Interview them when considering any major change in your business such as a new product line, new business hours, or other opportunities. Also ask them about their own buying needs that your business can fulfill.

Who Are Your Customers?

You've identified your marketplace and defined the groups of people who will buy from you, but who are the individuals? Are they like you? Do they have similar needs and problems? Consider them as individuals with whom you have commonality. Look to friends, acquaintances, business contacts, and other individuals to help you in putting the faces of real people in your business plan's marketing strategy (Chapter 11).

What Do Your Customers Want?

Interview people who you expect to be typical customers. What are the problems that your products or services solve for them? For example:

Their Need	Your Offering
Busy family needs help cleaning house.	Household cleaning service.
Department store needs wide selection of widgets for upcoming season.	Wholesale widgets.
Businesswoman needs to meet with clients in Paris next week.	Business-travel services.
Elderly computer user needs help understanding technology.	Computer-training service.

It will help you personalize your business to individuals if you give customers a face and a name. You can better visualize who they are as people rather than as a member of the left-handed widget-market segment. In addition to the obvious opportunities to increase profits, selling to individual customers rather than market groups offers personal satisfaction for what you do.

How Do They Prefer to Buy?

Basic marketing studies won't tell you much about how individual customers prefer to buy; that requires your firsthand knowledge as well as your observation skills. Your business plan will be enhanced by a deeper understanding of how the people you will serve actually buy. How can you find out these preferences? By asking individuals. Question topics include:

- What facts do you need to make an informed buying decision?
- What buying authority do you have (covered in next section)?
- How do you prefer to make your purchases?
- When do you prefer to buy?
- How important is service after the sale to you?
- What other conditions are helpful in your buying process?

To go beyond what your competitors do for customers, go beyond the questions they ask. Find out from individual customers how they prefer to buy.

What Buying Authority Do They Have?

Not everyone who shops buys. There are many reasons for this, including that there is no current perceived need. In addition, the shopper may not have the authority or the money to buy. For example, a husband may love the new-model cars but, by agreement, won't buy until the couple is mutually committed to the purchase of a specific car.

What authority is required to make a purchase? The authority to decide on and pay for a selection. It may be implied authority: a young woman orders a hamburger. Or it may be deferred authority: a family lets junior decide where they will have lunch. Or it could be cooperative authority: the couple must agree on a lunch location. Market research and analysis may not tell you much about the buying authority of your customers. You will need to do your own research with individuals to better understand how buyers buy. You'll learn how to ask customers later in this chapter.

QUESTION?

How can I determine what level of buying authority a customer has?

Ask. Some of the questions that can help you discover buying authority include: Is there anyone else who needs this information before a purchase can be made? Does your manager/spouse/lender need to help with this decision? Would you like to discuss this purchase with anyone else before making a decision? Similar questions, based on what you are selling and to whom, can help you identify buying authority and direct your selling efforts.

In addition, you need to understand how people other than individual customers participate in the buying decision. Some are initiators who make the suggestion but don't make the purchase: "I think those shoes would look lovely on you." Others are influencers: "If you don't buy those shoes right now, I will." Still others are permitters: "Buy those shoes if you like them." As you study individual customers, you will learn not only how they buy, but also what authority they have and need to make buying decisions. These facts are important to your business plan as well as how you will sell.

Finding Customers

Market research and analysis (Chapter 7) will also tell you where to find groups of customers. It may identify them by zip code, income levels, commuting hours, or hair color. However, these are still groups and not individual customers. To plan your business, you must know your customers as individuals. Where should you look?

Find Individuals

Actually, you can begin with your market-analysis reports. Read and understand them thoroughly. What groups have they identified as potential buyers? Then, go a step farther and meet some of these individuals. If identified by zip code or neighborhood, drive these areas, find friends and acquaintances who live in the market, ask for referrals to other individuals who are within the target market group. If you're planning a retail store in the local mall, spend some time at that location, observing, interviewing, and doing your own analysis of the individuals who may become your customers. If your customers will be hardware stores, attend a regional or national hardware trade show and interview the individuals who may buy from you.

Find Influencers

Again, not everyone who shops buys. However, many who make the decision to buy do so with the help of initiators, influencers, and permitters. Who are they? Interview prospective customers to find out.

- Do you typically buy widgets by yourself or with others?
- When you buy widgets, does someone help you make the decision?
- Did anyone suggest that you buy this widget?
- Have you suggested to others that they buy a widget?

In addition, many types of transactions have influencers that you may not recognize as such. For example, someone may buy a brand of toothpaste or a car because an influential person buys it. Celebrity endorsements are popular for this reason. In many communities, there are local influencers who are respected for their knowledge and authority. It may be the local mayor or city official, a member of the clergy, or a minor celebrity. In developing your business plan, finding and interviewing these influencers can help you build your venture with minimal effort. An endorsement in your business plan can influence lenders and investors.

How can I find local influencers?
Start with the most influential people and businesses that you know. If your newspaper is a significant influence in your community, interview its editor or publisher, asking for referrals to other influential individuals. If there is a primary business in town that you hope to get as a customer, get an early commitment so that your business and marketing plans can mention this fact. Also ask the chamber of commerce manager and other association executives for guidance and referrals to local influencers.

Asking Customers

There are two primary methods of determining what customers want: ask them and watch them. Of course, before your business opens its doors, you don't have customers to ask or observe. An existing business that wants to grow does. Start-up companies, however, can study a competitor's customers to determine what they want. You can station yourself at your competitor's store and observe their buying habits. If possible, you can even interview some of your competitor's customers in an exit poll. If done carefully and from public property, such as a sidewalk, the worst that can happen is that the manager asks you to desist. Meantime, you can discover much about the needs and buying habits of your future customers. Most of this is observable data.

If you do get the opportunity to interview future customers on their choices and wants, make your interviews measurable. Standardize the questions you ask. For example, "What do you like about Mary's Widget Store?" is an open-ended opinion question that can take the interview off into a dozen different directions. However, "Do you ever purchase hydraulic widgets?" is a quantifiable question answered with either yes or no.

The key to getting good market data from customer interviews is to ask a few important and quantifiable questions. Define what you want to know before you write your questions and start asking them. For example, if your survey goal is to determine whether your store should add a line of designer widgets, your interview questions could be:

- What brands of widgets do you prefer?
- Have you seen ads for Yadda Widgets?
- Yadda Widgets are priced between $45 and $75 each. Do you frequently purchase widgets in this price range?
- If Bob's Widgets carried Yadda, would you consider purchasing them?
- What do you think about designer widgets?

That last question, obviously, can't be answered by yes or no. It's an open-ended question designed to get the interviewee to talk more. Not all survey questions should require closed, multiple-choice responses. Sometimes you can learn more of what the customer wants with an open-ended question than with a dozen closed questions. They're just not as easy to quantify and most interviewers save them for the last questions.

Want to know what your customers are thinking? Ask them! To remove the confrontational element, ask for their help. "I need some help, please. Can you tell me why you chose the electric widget rather than the hydraulic model?" Most people will answer and you will learn more about your customers and your business. Everyone wants to help others.

Quantifying Responses

By standardizing your customer survey and primarily using closed questions, you can soon develop a relatively accurate report on the survey topic. How many prospective customers should you interview? The more you get the more accurate your survey will be. The higher the price of what you will be selling the more surveys you should take. If they are short surveys and uncomplicated, you can give one in less than a minute.

Survey says: Among 105 customers interviewed, 78 percent have heard of Yadda Widgets; Yadda is preferred two-to-one over Bubba brand; customers are willing to pay the higher price for Yadda; and, if available at Bob's Widgets, they would consider buying them. Overall, interviewees like the new designer widgets, especially for gifts, and Yadda is the favorite of the majority. That is the type of actionable data your retail store can use as you add profitable lines.

Keeping Customers

Once your new or growing business attracts customers, how will you keep them? Your investors want to know. You need to know. Customer retention is a vital component of business success. For example, if you calculate that it costs you $100 in advertising and other promotions to earn a single customer and just $20 to retain that customer, it's a smart business decision to invest in retaining your existing customers.

That's why business experts suggest that you "lose a sale if you must, but never lose a customer." If a customer needs something that you don't have, make it your goal to satisfy and retain the customer by making a referral, even to one of your competitors. You may lose $5 in profits on the sale, but you will probably retain the customer, who will come to you first for future purchases. Lose the sale, but don't lose the customer.

Make sure that your business plan includes a design for how you expect to keep customers once you've earned them. Will it be through price, service, selection, or convenience?

FACT

If you don't know where to start in determining how you will keep customers, look first to your competitors. How are they retaining customers? Then determine what method will work best for your business depending on whether you want to avoid or beat your competitors. Also anticipate future competitors as well as redirections from current competitors. Stay ahead of them to stay in business.

Retaining by Price

Individual buyers and market groups often buy commodity products based on price. ABC Stores has Crust Toothpaste at $2.95, but XYZ Mart offers it at $2.75. If your business plan is developed to offer a commodity, be prepared to sell it based on competitive pricing. Any one of your competitors can cut its price and take some of your business away.

Most small businesses don't attempt to retain customers based on the lowest price. They often cannot compete with large competitors who buy millions of items and can sell it for less than a small store must pay at wholesale. Chapter 12 covers pricing your products and services in greater detail.

Retaining by Service

Service is helping others. Whether your business sells a product or a service, service is involved. Representatives of your business—yourself or employees—directly or indirectly assist customers in the selection of your products or services. This can range from signs that indicate location of specific merchandise to consulting selling of complex services, such as investments.

> One of the greatest assets that small businesses have is flexibility. You can change the way you market your business faster than a big store can train a new manager. If you see new opportunities for your business, you can take quick action while competitors are still analyzing. Make sure your business retains this competitive advantage.

What type and how much service your business will offer customers should be analyzed and documented in its business plan. It should answer what level of services you will provide to your customers, whether some customers receive additional services and by what criteria, as well as how you will promote and provide those services. For many businesses, service is value added. It is what differentiates one business from its competitor (Chapter 9). However, services cost labor that adds to the price of doing business. As much as possible, plan for your business to add value through cost-effective service to your customers.

Retaining by Selection

Many businesses capture and retain customers by offering a selection of products or services that is wider than available from competitors. For example, a hobby shop may carry more radio-controlled aircraft than are available from all other local sources combined. An investment service may be developed as a one-stop resource for all types of investment, from stocks and mutual funds to grain futures and gold.

Many of these businesses are niches, or specialized businesses within specialties. Small businesses often start up in this category. The primary reason is diversity. If a well-funded competitor enters the market and takes some of your customers, you still have segments of your business that can be expanded to compensate. In addition, many of your customers will appreciate the wide selection and buy from you even though your prices may be higher than price competitors. Identifying and analyzing your individual customers can help you determine the best ways to find and retain your best customers.

ALERT!

As you identify and analyze your business' customers, consider whether they attempt to gather and retain customers by price, service, selection, or convenience. You may discover a niche market based on one of these customer retention methods not successfully used by your competition.

Retaining by Convenience

In some markets, your small business must be all things to all people. A grocery store in a rural area, for example, doesn't have to compete on price, service, or selection. What it offers customers is convenience. Milk prices are higher than at the supermarket in a nearby town, but the convenience has its price.

Even so, smart business plans include elements of the other categories: price, service, selection. Customers always have a choice. If the perception is that your higher prices are so because of value—worth greater than price—customers will buy from you. Make sure that your customers recognize the value of what you sell and you will retain them. And be sure that your business plan reflects your knowledge and commitment to customers as individuals.

CHAPTER 9

Competition

Competition can be a good thing, although it may not seem that way when a big-brand competitor is taking your customers and your profits like a bully demanding your lunch money. How do you win against bullies? You outsmart them. This chapter shows you how to include competitors in your business plan and your success. At the end of this chapter are competitive analyses for a product and a service business.

Identifying Competition

Free enterprise is a two-edged sword. It gives you the right to build a business and your competitors the right to take it away. That's the nature of business. Your job is to identify your competition and develop a plan for responding to their threats. Once your business is successful, you will continue to face the challenges of competitors. You need to have an action plan for competition, and your investors need to know what it is.

Many new businesses simply ignore their competitors. They don't identify, analyze, and attempt to defeat their competition. Then they wonder what happened to all of their customers. To be successful in business, you must know who your competitors are and what they are up to.

Competitors are two or more organisms vying for the same resource. Two runners striving for first place are competitors. So are five hungry puppies at feeding time. If they all want the same thing, they are competitors.

So who are your business' competitors? Any other businesses (organisms) contending for the same customers (resources) as your business. Actually, the definition is even broader than that. Any person or business who may get one of your customer's dollars instead of you is a competitor. If your customers must decide whether to buy something from you or anything from someone else, you are in competition. The resource in this case is the dollar.

As you develop your business plan, begin a list of all potential competitors to your business concept. Once the list is complete, you will analyze it and eliminate those who are less significant. For now, fill up that list. JIT Tax Service, for example, may develop an initial competitor list like this:

- Heather's Tax Service
- Skylar Luedemann, CPA
- Mega Online Tax Preparation Service
- AARP Senior Tax-Aide Service
- Turbo-Tax Software
- *Do Your Own Taxes* book

A prospective customer with a need that your business fills has several options. In the example, the customer can use another tax preparer, an accountant, a free or low-cost service, an online service, a software program, or the directions in a book. All of these are competitors to the hypothetical JIT Tax Service. Whether they are significant competitors will be determined later, in analysis.

How can I identify my business' competitors?
Think like your prospective customers. If you needed your product or service, where would you go to buy it? Where else? What if costs were a forceful issue? What if they were not and you had a large budget for the purchase? Could you get it online? Is it available in a nearby town? Where else would you spend your discretionary income? To find your competitors, identify the need and follow the dollars.

Analyzing Competition

Every business or organism that may get a customer's money instead of you is a competitor. However, many of these competitors aren't significant bullies; you won't have to worry about them stealing your lunch money. Even so, you need to consider who they are and how they impact your business plan.

FACT

Want to know how your competitors are enticing your target customers? Become one of your competitor's customers! Get on their mailing or e-mail lists, visit their store or website, make testing purchases, watch for their ads. The more you know about how they market to your customers the easier it will be to keep your customers.

Products and Services

To be competitors, businesses must offer products and or services that offer customers a similar solution to a specific problem. In the example of a tax service, the customer has many options. If your tax service will focus on busy middle-income families within a local geographic area, you can begin analyzing and eliminating some of the businesses on your long list. Few prospective customers in this market will use a book or a free service for senior tax filers.

QUESTION?

I operate an online business. How can I identify my direct competitors?
Become a customer. Use a search engine to find sites that rank highest for your company's keywords. What search phrases would your customers use to find you? Then get on competitors' newsletter and e-mail lists. Believing you to be a potential customer, they will gladly share competitive information with you.

Pricing

In further analysis, you may discover that some competitors price their products or services significantly higher than your pricing structure. For example, a certified public accountant may charge two or three times what your tax service charges for the same preparation and filing. In addition, most middle-income families won't trust volunteer tax preparers to do the work.

Following is an example of pricing verbiage from the Widgee World Retailers business plan (Appendix A):

> We have conducted extensive investigations into the pricing for competitors' products throughout the metropolitan area. Our pricing is defined as competitive. Some items will be priced slightly higher and others slightly lower. Ultimately, we are very similar to most competitors in pricing. We look to make customer service and loyalty as the most defining distinctions between Widgee World and the competition. And we will work to promote the "made in the USA" recognition.

> It is imperative to note these price comparisons serve to establish the range within which each product category is to be found. In most instances, Widgee World will open storefronts where most competitors are not located.

FACT

If your business sells internationally using debit and credit cards, your merchant account provider will do the math needed to exchange foreign currencies. However, you should verify that they are doing so accurately. You can find the current exchange rates for currencies worldwide at *www.x-rates.com* and *http://finance.yahoo.com*. Your banker can also provide current exchange rates.

Customer Service

Two competitors in the tax example depend on technology for service: the online tax-preparation service and the software program. These can be significant competitors to your business, depending on how comfortable your prospective customers are with using technology to prepare and file their taxes. An advantage that JIT Tax Service has over these competitors is customer service. It will meet with customers and answer questions face to face. Many customers will prefer this approach, especially if you point the advantages out to them.

Make sure that your business plan includes an analysis of significant competitors. By identifying and scrutinizing them, you will not only discover what they are doing to succeed, you will be able to plan ways of beating them in the race for customers.

ESSENTIAL

Don't know what your customers want? Ask them. Rather than develop a market analysis plan, simply ask random customers about their buying experience with you. Encourage honest responses. The results may not be scientific, but they can be informative.

Competitive SWOT

Chapter 7 introduced SWOT: analyzing your business' strengths, weaknesses, opportunities, and threats. You can now apply this process when analyzing your primary competitors.

Focus your SWOT analysis on businesses you've identified as primary competitors. These are the bullies who are more adept at stealing your lunch money, your customers. Identify them by name or by a number if confidentiality is critical. This exercise cannot only help you combat competitors, it will also help you enhance your business plan.

Competitor Strengths

Just like your business venture, your competitors have strengths, real or perceived qualities that give them an advantage. It may be a brand or franchise name, lower inventory or employee costs, greater creativity, more knowledgeable employees, or financial or location resources. To successfully compete, you must know what these strengths are.

As you did with your own market analysis (Chapter 7), scrutinize your competitors' strengths. Use the industry tools offered in that chapter to study these businesses. In addition, use your own creative skills to study and learn from these competitors. Become a customer. Learn these competitors' strengths and include them in your business plan.

Competitor Weaknesses

Competitors aren't perfect or infallible; they have their own problems and shortcomings. It is your job to know what these are and, as appropriate, exploit them. Your goal is to serve their customer better than they do. You can do this only if you understand your competitors' weaknesses, where they don't provide what their customers need and want.

Again, use business-analysis resources and your own observations to identify potential competitive weaknesses. The best way to do this is to become one of their customers. However, be realistic about expectations. What you perceive as a possible weakness may simply be a misunderstanding of the competition. Remember that a competitive weakness suggests a strength to be built into your business.

Competitor Opportunities

Opportunities are external conditions that help a business. In the case of a competitor, these opportunities are typically external conditions that not only offer opportunity for the competitor but also for your business. The opportunity may be a change in the marketplace, economic growth or recession, global influences, perceptions, or opportunities available through new technologies. Your competitors can benefit from these external conditions and so can your business—if you identify and act on them.

Competitor Threats

A threat is an external condition that can negatively impact your competitor and possibly your own business. For example, if your business plan is for an independent bookstore and your primary competition is another independent bookstore, both you and your competitor will be impacted by the threat of a major bookstore chain coming into the market. In any case, you must understand the threats that your competitors face.

ALERT!

Don't get behind when tracking your competition. What you learned about them six months ago may not be true today. And the difference can impact your business. Continue to watch your primary competitors and always look for secondary competitors who could take some of your customers. Your business requires that you stay current.

Take a look at the following example from Widgee World Retailers business plan (Appendix A):

We actively researched our geographic market, visiting retail outlets that sell widgets and widget accessories. The research has resulted in the following observations:

- *Competitor #1—contains colorful displays of imported widgets and accessories. Imported widgets cost less and retail at discounted rates, not a particularly attractive choice for the consumer seeking a well-made widget.*
- *Competitor #2—a family owned operation that offers little variety and no accessories.*

- *Competitor #3—clearly our most contentious competitor, selling most of what Widgee World offers, but lacking good customer service.*
- *Competitor #4—offers most of what we sell, but lacking in the diversity of widget accessories. The interior is quite appealing to the type of target customer we seek. Customer service is rated above average when compared to all the other competitors above.*

Defeating Competition

Your research and analysis of competitors' strengths, weaknesses, opportunities, and threats will help you develop a clearer plan of action for defeating competitive advantages and increasing your competitive opportunities. That's the primary purpose of this exercise.

Chapter 11 offers methods of developing marketing strategies that can help defeat the strengths and benefit from the opportunities of your business' competitors. Take your competitors seriously. Yes, some can be bullies, but you can outsmart them—and take their lunch money!

Your plan for defeating competition should be in your business plan. The following is from Widgee World Retailers business plan (Appendix A):

Widgee World stores will meet the competition in the following ways:

- *Widgee World will be the first and only location to offer all of its inventory as "made in the USA."*
- *Few of the competitors offer an interior that is appealing to the typical widget customer. Widgee World, specializing in widgets, will place much emphasize on interior layouts and designs that will put the customer at ease, possibly even provoking impulse buying from the passerby.*
- *Widgee World's complete compliment of widgets and widget accessories allows for a much wider range of prices to meet the budget of practically any customer.*

- *Widgee World will start its storefront operation with the existing brand recognition created out of the familiarity and popularity of its kiosk located in the local mall.*

Here's another example of how Acme Time Management Consultants expects to defeat its competition (Appendix B):

Identifying competitors in this market was challenging. Four of the eleven professional organizers have no website, but are listed in the yellow pages. The remaining seven, higher-profile competitors are:

- *A Personal Organizers offers a broad range of services, including space planning, clutter control, filing systems, archiving, and photography.*
- *B Personal Organizers targets businesses and individuals, organizing their desks, filing systems, offices, and homes. It specializes in a one-hour, on-site seminar for businesses, with individual follow up for each employee.*
- *C Personal Organizers targets residential and business organizing, on-site workshops, and a booklet on eliminating clutter.*
- *D Personal Organizers targets organizational systems analysis, ergonomics, checkbook reconciliation, accounts payable/ accounts receivable scheduling, income tax summary, medical claim submission, and wardrobe coordination.*
- *E Personal Organizers promotes consulting, training, and hands-on organizing for your office, home, and life. They specialize in home offices, clutter control, closet organizing, and residential space management, paper, and time management for individuals and small business.*
- *F Personal Organizers offers services that include training and consulting, product sales, business computer set-up, merchandising, seminars, and other services.*
- *G Personal Organizers focuses on setting up paper-flow and clutter-control systems, paper and desk management, and a "finding" system; seminars and guest-speaking engagements.*

For lack of industry data, having a majority of local competitors on the Internet with websites affords the valuable opportunity to itemize general observations, leading ATMC to develop a strategy of advertising and promotion. Some of the following observations are unqualified, but we are confident they present a relatively accurate image of the competition:

- *The overwhelming majority appear directed to home-based businesses.*
- *Most appear to be one-person operations.*
- *Most websites are affiliated as subsites, not wholly owned sites, of web-hosting services.*
- *Several use before-and-after photos to demonstrate their space organization work.*
- *POWR and NAPO are the dominant affiliations.*
- *No pricing is listed at any of the sites.*
- *Space organization and employee organization are the most prevalent service offerings.*
- *Those offering seminars primarily address employee organizational issues, but the sites offer no details of seminar content.*
- *The majority appear to have been in business for one year or less. Only two note personal organizing experience of several years.*
- *The longer-standing, older companies extend their services to well-known corporate clients.*

The website observations support the assumption personal organizing is a new industry sector in our geographic market. None of them boasts certification or educational experience. There is also a strong tendency to draw on alliances with associations, chambers of commerce, and apparently reputable online sources for professional legitimacy.

CHAPTER 10

Analyzing Risks

Business is legalized gambling. No matter how much of a sure thing a business opportunity seems to offer, there is always a chance of losing some or all of what you invest. This chapter guides you in analyzing, understanding, and minimizing risks in your business with smart planning. It can help you develop a risk/reward structure that is tolerable. In business, no risk equals no reward.

Understanding Risk

As you plan for a new or growing business, you know that you're taking some kind of a risk, but what does that mean exactly? And how can you keep the risk to a minimum? Your investors want to know the answers, and so should you.

Risk is the likelihood of loss or injury. In business, risk is the possibility of loss of value. Understandably, you don't want to risk everything you have on a business venture that may not return the invested value plus a reward for accepting the risk. The chances of losing money in an insured savings account, for example, are infinitesimal, so the reward is a small rate of interest. The stock market offers greater potential gains and losses than savings because the risks are greater.

As you develop your business plan, you will discover that there is typically no heading called "Risk." Why? Because though risk is an underlying factor within all businesses and business plans, it isn't labeled as such. Instead, there will be numerous statements regarding risks and rewards throughout the plan. In fact, you could title the document "The Risks and Rewards of XYZ Business."

ALERT!

Most businesses profit from what they know about customers, products and services, and the marketplace. Modern businesses record their knowledge on computers. Make sure that your business has an adequate security and backup system. Without frequent backups, yours could be out of business in an hour.

Operating any business is about managing risk. That means you need to understand the value of what you are investing, consider the potential gains and losses, and make a decision. You will do so as you invest time and money in your business plan as well as in the daily operation of your venture—from hiring employees to ordering inventory or raw materials. All these and hundreds of other business decisions require that you understand the risks involved.

Value

The greater the value of something, the greater the loss if you lose it. People buy health insurance to reduce the risk of major financial loss in the case of catastrophic illness. Other insurance services work on the same principle: someone accepts a portion of the risk of loss in exchange for something of value—your insurance premiums.

Your business will require an investment of money and time (value) that may be in jeopardy or be exposed to possible loss. You don't want to lose these things of value, so you do what you can to reduce risks to an acceptable limit. You act more conservatively in your transactions or buy insurance as needed. Whenever you make decisions regarding things of value in your business or life, you (hopefully) consider the risks.

How do you calculate risk? There are complex formulas used by engineers, accountants, and actuaries, but most are based on a simple formula:

$$R = P \times C$$

Translated: Risk (R) is calculated as the Probability of an event (P) multiplied by the Consequence of it occurring (C). To calculate business risks, you need to understand probabilities and consequences.

QUESTION?

How can I calculate probability and risk?
There are numerous software programs that can guide you in estimating business risks. They range from simple risk management to mathematical and statistical probabilities. Use your favorite search engine for searches like "probability calculator," "business risk calculator," and similar terms. Be aware that some are designed for engineering and actuarial probabilities rather than business.

Probability

Probability is the likelihood that something has or will happen. For example, what is the probability that your new business will celebrate its fifth anniversary? What is the probability that the new line of widgets will be profitable? These are important questions to your business' success. How can you answer them?

In some fields, probability is easy to calculate. Mathematics, for example, deals with probability in firm numbers that don't really change. Smart gamblers live by probability tables in making bets. Statisticians use probability based on historical data; a million people used widgets without mishap before an accident, so the probability of an accident is calculated as one in a million. In business, probability is more complicated to calculate, as there are often factors more difficult to measure, such as the probability your business will still be operating in five years. However, there is sufficient historical data to offer a degree of accuracy in calculating probability.

You will use probability in many ways in your business plan and its operation. As you do, seek the most reliable sources of proven or historical data, such as business research resources. Your business plan and activities depend upon the accuracy of these estimates of probability.

Consequence

Consequence is the result of an action. If the result of your business venture's success for five years is that you will have a million dollars in the bank, you will use this fact and the probability of it happening to determine the risk.

In business, quantifying consequences can be difficult, and you must rely on an estimate or judgment of approximate value. As with probability, you must consider all resources and use the most reliable ones. The accuracy of your risk calculation depends on how precise your consequence is stated. Estimates are defensible guesses.

Risks of Gambling

Las Vegas is financed by people who don't understand risks. They pay billions of dollars each year in rent, salaries, and electric bills. They often make emotional decisions rather than logical ones. "I feel lucky," they say. Luck, as professional gamblers know, has nothing to do with feelings. The pros know that if the odds (probability) and payoff (consequence) are within an acceptable range of risk, the bet is "smart."

Starting and growing a business is a gamble. You may win or you may lose. The smart bet is to understand the risks, accurately determine probabilities and consequences, then make your decisions based on facts rather than feelings. Yes, there is an element of luck (unknown circumstances) in all enterprises, but those who depend on luck to succeed usually discover how unlucky business can be.

Degrees of Risk

Risk is an important topic in planning your business. But the question of risk isn't answered by a yes or no. There are degrees of risk, and the degrees are relative; that is, they may be at one level today and another level six months from now under new conditions. How can you define the level of risk involved for various components of your business? With knowledge and research.

Identifying Risks

What are the important risks in your business venture? What internal and external factors offer significant risk to your business goals? Each business concept has a unique set of risks. However, most businesses share types of risks. The risks common to most small businesses include:

- Competition
- Distribution
- Financing
- Industry maturity
- Management
- Production
- Regulatory environment
- Technology
- Cost structure
- Employees
- Industry cyclicality
- Interdependence
- Natural catastrophes
- Profitability
- Suppliers

The underlying question of risk is: What can go wrong? The above list includes the most common things that can go wrong in businesses. Add to it any risks that are primary in your industry or venture.

Next, prioritize those risks. In some businesses, the greatest risk is that a new technology will adversely damage your business. In another enterprise, new regulations or loss of key employees could be a major problem that could impact the future of your business. Or competitors may be a foremost risk factor. Also, consider both the external and internal risks that your business faces. Some are outside of your direct control and others allow you more control of the conditions and the outcome.

Rating Risks

There are numerous ways of rating risk levels for an opportunity. The ratings can be on a numbered scale of one to five, on a predefined scale, or by a defining statement. For example, the risk of profitability for your business can be rated as a three, a Moderate, or "relatively high for the value."

Rate each of your primary business risks on whatever scale works best for you. Many use the four-step scale: lowest risk, moderate risk, higher risk, maximum risk. You can also rate risks by probability in percentage, such as 0, 20, 40, 60, 80, or 100 percent chance of loss.

Because risk ratings are often subjective, categories often work better than specific numbers. In addition, ask a trusted advisor to help you verify the risk factors and ratings before including them in your business plan.

ALERT!

Don't assume that you've identified and accurately rated all primary risks for your business venture. Share your risk analysis with a knowledgeable and trusted business advisor. Don't be defensive; listen. There may be risk factors you haven't considered or your ratings may not reflect all aspects. Ultimately, you will decide what goes into your business plan. However, the smartest business people consider the experience and opinions of others.

For example, your plan may state "The risk of a major competitor taking a significant portion of our sales is rated as low" or ". . . is rated as a 10 percent probability." You may later, through your management efforts, reduce this probability to a lower level. For now, however, you need to analyze the various risks of your business and rate them as accurately as you can. Once they are identified, ranked, and rated, you can develop plans to reduce or eliminate risks.

Weighting

Some risks are more critical to the success of your business. For example, your business opportunity may be subject to higher-than-normal risks from competitors, costs, distribution, employees, financing, industry cyclicality or maturity, interdependence, management, natural catastrophes, production, profitability, regulatory environment, suppliers, technology, or other factors. How can you factor these unequal risks into your business plan and management? You can use category weighting.

Weighting is setting the relative value of various elements. In business statistics, you can calculate that, of ten types of risks, some are more important to your success than others. For example, risk from competitors may be less than one-tenth or 10 percent, so you set it at 5 percent. However, changes in technology could have a greater impact on your business so you give it more than one-tenth, such as 15 or even 20 percent. You weight the risk factor.

FACT

If you are using a numeric scale for calculating risks, you can interpolate or combine risk factors. For example, if technology risk is 60 percent with a weight of 20 percent of the total risk, then technology risks comprise about 12 percent (.60 × .20) of the total risks that your business faces. That's significant.

Weighting is an educated guess; you don't know for certain that changes in technology will have three or four times the impact on your business as competitive risks can. However, weighting the risks can give you a more accurate picture of total risk than simply assigning equal value to all business risks.

Rationale

Why did you rate your business profitability risk at 65 percent? Why do you believe there is a 10 percent chance that a major competitor could take your primary customers and sales? What is your rationale?

A rationale is an underlying reason. A risk rating system can be useful and efficient, but sometimes it doesn't offer the completeness that an investor or manager needs to decide about the risks of your business venture. They need more information. Your business plan is an excellent place to explain your risk rating rationale.

The following example includes data as well as rationale regarding a perceived risk in pricing for an example company, Acme Time Management Consultants (ATMC). From Appendix B, the following pricing paragraph illustrates the rationale:

> *The cost for professional organizing services is based on several key factors including skill, experience, and the self-worth of the individual organizer. The fees charged in this industry are diverse. Hourly rates typically vary between $60 and $150 per hour, with several in the profession earning as much as $1,000 per day. Though personal organizing is a relatively new industry sector, demand for the service is growing. ATMC will offer introductory, discount pricing for the first six months of operation. Anticipating positive results, the price structure will then be increased to a more customary rate.*

Rationales should be included in your business plan for all primary risks that your venture faces. It is vital to your success and to your investors' understanding that you analyze, rank, rate, and, as needed, rationalize your decisions about the risks that it faces. You cannot rely on luck (unknown circumstances) to somehow converge to make your business successful and prosperous. Your venture may receive some luck, but you cannot depend on it, especially as you spend large amounts of time and money on starting or growing a small business.

Minimizing Risk

All of your efforts in understanding, ranking, rating, weighting, and rationalizing your business' inherent risks will now come to fruition as you discover what you can do to minimize them. Minimizing risks is a vital step in your development of a business plan that will answer questions raised by investors and managers. What are the primary risks of your venture and how will you respond to them?

Your business isn't unique. Somewhere out there is another business with the same customer group and nearly the same products or services. To help you minimize risks, identify similar businesses and watch how they reduce their risks.

To minimize business risks, you first need to determine what they are—the topic of the first part of this chapter. Once identified, you need to consider the causes and components of the primary risks, then look for ways of reducing the impact of those components. Finally, you need to continue watching primary risk components so they don't threaten your business' success.

Identify Risk Reductions

Once you've clearly defined a problem, solutions become evident. For example, to minimize the risks of loss due to competition, an independent retail store can:

- Specialize in merchandise that competitors don't sell
- Offer a superlative level of individual service to customers
- Identify weaknesses of specific competitors and respond to them

These and other solutions are available to your business and should be included in relevant sections of your business plan. For example, niche marketing will require that you clearly analyze your market (Chapter 7) and define your customer base (Chapter 8), then be reflected in your marketing strategy (Chapter 11). Most important, you will document ways to reduce identified risks in your plan section dealing with competitors (Chapter 9). Minimizing primary business risks requires smart planning.

Track Primary Risks

Once the primary risks are identified and solutions offered, your business must carefully track them to ensure that they are being minimized. For example, if you have a primary competitor who could, on short notice, capture a significant customer, you must keep an eye on that competitor. Who is it? What is it doing today? What is it planning for tomorrow? How can you further reduce the risks that it presents to your business?

Your business plan—"The Risks and Rewards of XYZ Company"—must identify and respond to the threats that your venture faces. It must maximize the rewards by minimizing the risks. Like the professional gambler, it must consider the odds and either bet or pass depending on which action has the greatest chance of ultimate success.

Risk Management

Once business risks have been identified and assessed, what can you do about them? How can you manage them? Your business plan should include specifics on risk management involving customers, competition, marketing, pricing, profitability, suppliers, and other vital categories.

Professional business managers use one of four primary techniques in managing risks:

- Avoidance
- Reduction
- Transfer
- Retention

These responses are available to you in your business planning and management. Following are some proven guidelines for risk management in small business.

FACT

For additional information on risk management, visit *www.risk-management-basics.com*. In addition, the Small Business Administration (*www.sba.gov*) offers online resources on risk management that focus on the problems faced in business start-up and growth. You can also find courses on risk management at colleges and universities.

Risk Avoidance

Everyone understands risk avoidance. A barking dog blocks your path and you walk around it. Some people carry risk avoidance farther, not flying in an airplane because it may crash. In business, risk avoidance can be effective. For example, if you believe that competitors can ruin your business, find a niche where you will have no competitors. Of course, you must also determine that it will have sufficient customers.

In planning your business, consider the primary risks that you've identified and consider whether avoidance is a viable option. What can you do to avoid these risks?

Risk Reduction

Risk reduction minimizes the chances of risky events occurring. For example, if you're concerned about barking dogs, you avoid streets where you know they live. That may limit where you can walk, but it will also lower your risks of being attacked by a dog.

This chapter has focused primarily on risk reduction—how to identify and lessen the potential risks to your business. In most business situations, it is the easiest path to lowering inherent risks. Identify and mitigate. If a warehouse fire is a concern, reduce the threat by installing a fire suppression and alarm system. If new technologies may challenge your business, find ways of reducing the challenge through absorbing some technologies to mitigate potential damage.

Risk Transfer

In some cases, you can make your problems someone else's—for a fee. The entire insurance industry is built on this premise. Concerned that a fire will wipe out your assets? Buy an insurance policy that covers this loss.

Insurance isn't the only way to transfer risk. You can also pass it on to customers, suppliers, landlords, and others with whom you do business. For example, if the cost of returned merchandise is cutting into your profits significantly, you can transfer at least some of the loss by changing your return policy with customers, requiring that a restocking fee be paid or demanding that your suppliers accept returns.

Risk Retention

In some cases, the best thing to do about risks of loss is to brace yourself. That is, if you expect that 5 percent of your inventory will become outdated before it is sold and that's the best you can do, then accept the loss as part of your cost of doing business. All risks that are not avoided, reduced, or transferred are retained.

CHAPTER 11

Marketing Strategy

Your business plan has defined what it sells, to whom, against whom, and at what risks. Now what? It's time to develop a marketing strategy. How are you going to offer your wares to potential customers? This chapter guides you in developing a comprehensive marketing strategy, positioning your venture, and tackling additional markets. It helps you document the how of your business success.

Comprehensive Plan

Every endeavor has a strategy for winning. Want to win at Scrabble? Texas Hold'em? Stock-car racing? Politics? Business? You need a strategy, a plan toward a goal. The word comes from the Greek term for "generalship," the guy who develops and carries out military plans. It suggests that the endeavor is a battle that must be well planned and executed for success.

Your business is a battle. You will be fighting for fiscal territory with the help of economic weapons and soldiers in service. You will win a few and lose a few battles, but your goal will be to win the business war and live to fight another day.

Actually, you will develop numerous marketing strategies for various components and tasks within your business. For example, you will choose the best methods of introducing your business, offering your products or services, and positioning your business in the marketplace. You'll also develop a strategy for repositioning your competitors ("the enemy") so that your business wins more battles.

You'll continue using strategic thinking in other aspects of your business in addition to marketing. For example, if you have an investor or lender to satisfy, you'll develop a plan or strategy for sharing profits or paying back debt as needed. If you someday choose to move your business to a larger facility, you'll need a strategy to ensure success.

Initially, you need a comprehensive strategy that plans many aspects of your business opportunities and challenges. You must step back from your business for a moment and make sure that its overall concept is viable. That exercise is one of the major functions of writing a business plan—to define and strategize. To develop an accurate comprehensive plan, you must ask and answer some fundamental questions about your business.

What Business Are You In?

The question seems so simple that many entrepreneurs don't bother with answering it—then have problems as they lose their business focus. Your business plan uses the executive summary (Chapter 3) to help you answer this vital question. As your plan is developed and you get new data, your business focus may change slightly or significantly. In any case, you must update and verify your business definition.

Large corporations call this defining the core business. AT&T sells communication. That's their core business. You should not expect them to begin selling cars or mutual funds. They clearly understand and focus on the core business. So should you.

Established businesses often have difficulty growing to the next level—or even maintaining the current level—of profits. In many cases, the cause is that the owners/managers have lost their understanding of the core business. They have reached out to markets in which they aren't able to be competitive. By refocusing on their proven core enterprise, many unprofitable businesses can regain and even grow market share.

Make sure that you understand and clearly define your core business as succinctly as possible. What is it your business does uniquely to earn a profit?

What Market Segment Do You Want to Reach?

No business can sell to everyone. The marketplace is limited by geography, economics, product selection, service availability, competitive, or other restricting factors. So each business must define the market segment that it can best reach. It may be a local market or a niche online market or one that is defined by the income of customers. In each case, these segmentations must be clearly defined so a comprehensive plan can be strategized.

What Distribution Channels Will You Use?

Another seemingly obvious question to be asked in developing a comprehensive plan is: How will you get your product or service to the intended customer? Your answer is critical. Will you sell through a retail store, wholesalers, jobbers, brokers, door to door, online, mail order, party plan, or another proven distribution channel? Yes, you can eventually use more than one channel, but one must be primary. Which one?

A related question must be asked and answered: Is this the best distribution channel for your product or service? As you develop a comprehensive business and marketing plan, are you certain that the selected channel offers your venture the greatest chance of success? If it's retail, should it be wholesale? If you're planning to sell online, are you convinced that it is more profitable than selling through the mail or using party plans? There is no right answer for all businesses. Your job is to ensure that the selected distribution channel is the right one for your business concept.

What Share of the Marketplace Do You Expect to Capture?

As you analyzed the marketplace for what you're selling (Chapter 7), you determined not only the economic size of the market but also who your primary competitors are. If your business is entering a marketplace with $10 million in annual sales, how much of that can you realistically expect to earn? Can you get a 20 percent share of this market? How quickly? Will your share then grow? Will the growth be from market expansion or by earning it away from your competitors?

Your marketing strategy depends on how you define your business' position within the marketplace both now and in the future. This definition requires some defensible data. You can use industry studies, market research, and expert advice to help you calculate your business' market share. Most businesses will plan growth in part by increasing their share of the available market. If they expect to have 10 percent of the market on their first anniversary, they may aim for 15 percent or more on their second anniversary. Your marketing strategy must reflect these goals with a specific plan.

FACT

Want to know more about your competitors' market share? If the company is publicly traded, purchase token stock and get on every available mailing list. Search their website, if available. They will often tell you how much of the market they believe they own. Of course, many businesses embellish this figure, but it can give you an idea of the market size and their position in it.

Product/Service Strategy

Some products and services (Chapter 6) have longer periods between resales than others. For example, if you're selling wholesale candies to convenience stores, you may expect to service customers once or even twice a week. What you're selling is a short-term product that will soon need replenishment. If your business is tax preparation, your service is longer term and you'll be helping the majority of your customers annually. If your business sells houses, the lifecycle may be three to five years before you sell another home to the same customer.

The repurchase term of your product or service is important to your marketing strategy and comprehensive business plan. It will help you develop a plan for ensuring that your customers have what you offer when they need it.

Sustaining Sales

Many businesses ensure themselves against erratic selling cycles by offering secondary products or services that help maintain income during the off season. Tax preparers offer year-round recordkeeping services. Real estate agents develop referral business to supplement repeat-customer sales. Product-based businesses offer related services that customers need.

What strategy should your business use to sustain sales? Will you develop an automatic reorder system? Will you contact existing customers during slower seasons and seek additional or referral sales? Your business plan should include the specific goals and steps needed to ensure that what you sell is being offered to the greatest number of prospective customers.

Strategizing SWOT

Chapter 7 covered SWOT analysis, considering the strengths, weaknesses, opportunities, and threats that you business and your competitors face. As you develop your marketing plan, you should review this analysis and develop specific strategies for taking advantage of these internal and external business factors. Following is a SWOT analysis from Appendix B:

The development of a marketing strategy for Acme Time Management Consultants must begin with a SWOT analysis (Strengths, Weaknesses, Opportunities, and Threats).

Strengths:

- *Owner's varied organizational experience in corporate and residential environments*
- *Owner's acquaintance with many individuals in the local corporate world*
- *ATMC office strategically located in the geographic market*
- *Low operating overhead*
- *Competitive pricing structure*

Weaknesses:

- *Start-up company with no track record*
- *No individuals, as yet, identified to fill Office PO positions requiring specific organizational skills*

Opportunities:

- *Professional organizers are a relatively new professional in the targeted geographic market*
- *The Internet is increasingly becoming a primary source for seeking goods and services*
- *Population and economic census data indicate existence and continued growth of the specific types of office and residential clients ATMC will target*

Threats:

- *Some competition may react with lower price ranges*
- *Competitors will promote existing client base and experience*
- *Continued recession in the region may cut into total potential client base for all competitors*

As you can see, Acme Time Management has a viable plan for managing its strengths, weaknesses, opportunities, and threats. Make sure your market analysis considers the SWOTs of your business and that of your competitors. With it, you can proactively prepare for your business' marketplace.

Positioning

Wouldn't it be great if your business didn't have any competitors? You could charge whatever you wanted and not worry about another business taking your customers. However, in the real world, all businesses have competition (Chapter 9). If someone does come up with a unique business, chances are it will have competitors popping up by tomorrow afternoon. That means you must accept the fact that your business will face competition. But you don't have to be passive about it.

Positioning is the process of comparing your product or service favorably with that of your competitors. It is how your target market sees your business. Your market strategy should include specifics on your business' position within the market in comparison to your competitors in reality and through perceptions.

You may find a market research report available on your industry and geography that can help you target your marketing efforts. Check online resources like *www.marketresearch.com* and *www.forrester.com*. The reports may seem expensive, but they are less than the cost of custom reports.

Reality

In identifying your competitors, you've determined which are primary and what market share they currently have. If your position among competitors is strong, you can market your product or service by comparing it to a known, your competitors. For example, if your new widget store is growing faster than the established widget chain store in your marketplace, you can say so: The Fastest Growing Widget Store in Anytown!

Positioning also can be geographic. You can locate your new business near a known business, competitive or not, and draw from its position. Shopping malls are built on the premise that small businesses benefit from geographic proximity to big businesses. Your marketing strategy may include a relative comparison with your major competitor or the success of an established business.

Perceptions

Reality is what is true. Perception is what is believed to be true. It is an observation or conviction, often one that is suggested through advertising or other promotion. Politics, especially, relies on perceptions over reality. Each candidate and cause attempts to position itself as the appropriate answer to the current question. Perceptions often depend on emotional messages to sell their position: Everyone loves our new line of widgets.

Perceptions can be effectively used in positioning your business, especially if reality positions aren't successful. Your business can suggest that it offers the friendliest service in town, for example. This is a comparative perception. Your marketing strategy may develop one or more competitive positions based on favored perceptions. These should be documented in your business plan.

Differentiation

Your business should not only position itself well against competitors, it should also make sure that the marketplace knows the difference. Brand X is better than Brand Z. Who says so? Brand X, of course! However, if it is frequently repeated it becomes a perception. Your market strategy will benefit from a clear differentiation.

Differentiation can be used to favorably compare products, services, brands, competitors, and other business components. The differences can be in quality, price, design, features, benefits, distribution, availability, popularity, service, or other specifics. In each case, the differences are emphasized to draw attention to a specific advantage that will benefit the customer. Differentiation is an especially useful marketing strategy in defining and promoting niche markets, specialties within specialties. How is your product, service, or business unique? What's the difference between you and your competitors? What can your business offer that others don't?

Repositioning the Competition

Repositioning can be an effective counter strategy for your business. For example, you can strive to change the perception the marketplace has of your competitors. This strategy can be more expensive to implement, requiring additional advertising and promotion to be effective. In a sense, you are building your business' market position by reducing that of a competitor. If your marketing strategy includes opportunities for repositioning the competition, make sure they are documented in your business plan.

QUESTION?

How can I actually reposition my competitors?

By comparison and contrast. In advertising and promotion, you can either identify or anonymously refer to your competitors in relation to your own business. You can favorably compare your business to a well-known competitor: "Lower Prices than XYZ." Or you can compare your business to a group of unnamed competitors: "Best Service in Anytown!" By doing so, you are developing a perception that differentiates your business yet favorably compares it to established competitors.

International Marketing

Geography is a vital consideration in selling products and services. It is inherently easier to offer your wares to people who speak the same language, spend the same money, and function within the same culture. However, some business opportunities are so saturated in one marketplace that you must look to international marketing to earn customers. Thousands of businesses, small and large, use international marketing to start or grow their profits.

Be aware that international marketing often requires different strategies than domestic marketing. Though Western culture is prevalent in most of the world, the majority of world consumers prefer their own culture and appreciate business' recognition of it. Please your customers.

Language

More than 37,000 languages and dialects are spoken in the world, though most of its inhabitants speak one of thirty primary languages. English is the de facto language of international business, but twice as many people speak Mandarin as English. If your business will serve international markets, make sure you have the resources needed to speak your customers' languages.

If you don't know your customers' primary language like a native, hire one to speak for you. There are numerous business translation services available to assist you. Preferred are those with extensive experience communicating in English as well as the target language. Don't rely on dual translations, such as Farsi to French to English. Something will certainly get lost in the translation, and it could be your customers.

ALERT!

Make sure that your marketing message translates well. The classic example is Chevrolet's new (in 1962) compact car, the Nova. A nova, the marketers reasoned, is a star that suddenly increases its light output. A good name. However, in Spanish-speaking countries, the car was popularly referred to as *no va*; translation: "doesn't go!" This story emphasizes the importance of understanding the languages of your marketplace. By 1979, the Nova was no more.

Culture

A culture is a structure of the knowledge, beliefs, and behaviors of a specific group. It's how that group sees itself and others. It is comprised of art, music, religions, history, and other factors that influence how people act and react.

QUESTION?

How can I learn more about the culture of my international target market?
Start with the U.S. Department of State (*www.state.gov*). It offers extensive information for business on cultures and travel in other countries. Then visit the official websites for these countries, for example: *www. gov.ph*, the official website of the Republic of the Philippines, available in English and Filipino languages. If possible, plan a visit to meet with prospective customers and/or suppliers. To sell to customers, you must understand them.

Many cultural differences have been diluted by contact with more pervasive cultures and even businesses. The culture of Indonesia, for example, is impacted by McDonalds, CNN, *American Idol,* and other Western icons. Cultures are dynamic rather than static.

If your business will attempt to market to cultures other than your own, research and recognize how your prospective customers perceive cultural differences. Don't try to sell hamburgers in a vegetarian society.

Currency

Money is money, right? Not really. Money is relative. For example, a U.S. dollar may be worth more or less than a Canadian dollar or a Euro. The difference can make or break your international business. Depending on the foreign exchange rate or FX (*www.exchangerate.com*), your product or service may be a bargain or overpriced for a consumer in another country. It's smart business to know as much as you can about the currency of your target markets, whether you're selling in Afghanis (AFN) or Kwachas (ZMK).

FACT

If your business requires staying knowledgeable about global marketing conditions, subscribe to *Business Week* (*www.businessweek.com*), *Forbes* (*www.forbes.com*), or the *Wall Street Journal* (*www.wsj.com*). Also search the Internet for publications that are specific to your geographic or economic marketplace.

Be aware that the foreign currency exchange is a marketplace. That is, investors buy and sell world currencies based on various factors, similar to how stocks are traded on the New York Stock Exchange, and with as much volatility. There are even foreign-exchange futures, guesses at the exchange rate at a future date. If your business sells in a foreign currency, you will need to manage when and how you transfer money because timing is important to value. Consult with an international business advisor if you will be entering this marketplace.

Needs

In addition to the language, culture, and currency differences in international marketing, there are specific customer needs. These require analysis as much as any marketing component. The needs can be real or perceived and are subject to opportunities and competitors, just as in your domestic marketplace.

Many businesses that decide to market internationally have already identified a need, opportunities, and competitors within a specific foreign market. However, with the power of the Internet, many businesses are entering international markets without even being aware of it. The *lingua franca* of online business is English, and the exchange rates are automatically calculated by many merchants. Until it's time to ship product, you may not know whether the buyer is in Boston or Brasilia. Even so, as you intentionally direct your business internationally, make sure you consider the needs of your customers. They can make or break your business.

CHAPTER 12

Pricing for Profitability

Once your business plan answers questions about its structure, customers, and competitors, it needs to focus on profitability. Can it make a profit? A major component of this question is establishing a pricing structure that balances costs and opportunities. This chapter guides you in establishing your business' pricing methods. It also covers profitability and how you can increase it as your business grows.

Pricing

Many businesses believe that pricing is the most critical component of their new venture. It isn't; it is one of many. Without a clear identification of customers and competitors, pricing can be erroneously set and either repel customers or attract competitors.

A price is the amount or conditions required to consummate a transaction. If the price for a tube of toothpaste is $2.99, that's what you must pay the owner (store) to make it yours. If the price for a new car is $25,000 plus your old car, that's what it will cost you to complete the transaction. Some purchases have additional conditions, such as approval of a law, lender, or other authority. You cannot purchase alcohol, for example, unless you are of the legal age in your state.

It is critical that your business plan includes specifics on how you will price your products and or services. Yes, your lenders want to know your pricing structure; however, you also need to define it. Without appropriate pricing, your business may not be profitable. You need to establish pricing guidelines, make certain they are competitive, and make pricing easy to implement while being adjustable to meet changing business conditions.

Pricing Guidelines

Business schools teach the four Ps of marketing: product, promotion, price, and place (location). Three of the four are expenses; only price generates revenue. Pricing can be critical to the success of any business, though the most successful ones focus on value-added service so that price is less an issue.

How can you establish an effective pricing policy for your business? You must consider all the consequences of pricing to your business success. In the early history of business, keystone pricing was done at all levels because it was easy to calculate. It simply doubles the price you paid. For example, a shopkeeper would set a retail price that is double the wholesale price. A wholesaler would double the manufacturer's price. Easy pricing. However, as business has become more sophisticated, so has pricing. Following are some of the most common methods of computing a selling price:

- Break-even point
- Cost-plus pricing
- Rate-of-return pricing
- Demand pricing

Each has its own advantages and disadvantages. Depending on the type of business you are starting or growing, one may be more common than others.

Break-Even Point

The break-even point is when the income covers the expenses. If your retail store has to sell 120 widgets to cover the wholesale and overhead costs of a 400-widget order, that's the break-even point. Your profit will begin when you sell the 121st widget. Break-even calculations are more common to retail stores that buy large wholesale lots, such as dollar or bargain stores, though a break-even analysis can be calculated for any product. Chapter 19 will cover break-even calculations in greater detail.

Cost-Plus Pricing

Cost-plus pricing is more common among smaller businesses. Products are priced at a predetermined percentage above the direct costs to achieve an expected gross margin. To understand this method, some terms need to be defined.

The gross margin is the relationship of the profit to the cost. A widget with a wholesale cost of $6 is sold at a retail price of $10. Calculate: (10-6) / 10 = 40%, the gross margin.

The markup is the relationship of the profit to the selling price. It's the percentage added to the cost to get the retail price. Consider another widget with a retail price of $5 and a wholesale cost of $2. Calculate: (5-2) / 2 = 150%, the markup.

In the real world, most retailers use a variety of gross margins and markups. Primary merchandise may have one gross margin or markup while an impulse department or one that has less local competition may have a higher gross margin or markup.

Should your business use gross margin or markup? They are two ways of looking at cost-plus pricing. Many businesses prefer using markup; it's easier to calculate. For example, if the wholesale cost is $4 and the markup is 100 percent, simply add 100 percent of the cost to the cost to get a retail price of $8. Margins and markups are explained further later in this chapter.

Rate-of-Return Pricing

Your business plan will help you calculate a rate of return on your initial investment (ROI, Chapter 4). For now, let's use a rate of return of 12 percent. That means a $100,000 investment should pay back $12,000 a year or $1,000 a month in interest from the profit. The same method can be used to calculate a price as long as all other fixed and variable expenses, including payroll and your salary, are already factored in.

Retailers and wholesalers with large sales volumes, such as $1,000,000 a year or more, frequently use ROI pricing. It's also more common with stores that require an extensive initial investment in land, fixtures, and other costly components. Many service business, too, use ROI pricing.

QUESTION?

My business is seasonal. How can I establish profitable pricing?
Though your business operates seasonally, it will probably have overhead costs during the off season. These costs must be factored into your overall costs so that your business will still be viable when the next selling season arrives. As you establish prices, calculate annual overhead costs including any ongoing labor needed to keep the business in operation.

Demand Pricing

Airlines are notorious for demand or yield pricing. Buy the ticket well in advance and the price is lower than if you walk up to the counter on the day of the flight. Retailers, wholesalers, and service businesses can't use this method as easily unless they sell hot/cold merchandise. If your store gets the hottest new widgets in and everybody knows that supplies are initially limited, your price can be high—maybe even higher than the manufacturer's suggested retail price (SRP). When supply catches up and the market is saturated with these widgets, prices will slide until they hit the clearance table at prices barely above wholesale.

There are many other types of pricing methods. As you research and develop your own business, you will find ones that are most popular for your venture. Remember that the key to pricing is profitability more than ease of use. That's why there are hand-held business calculators and software to do the figuring for you.

Competitive Pricing

Many businesses begin by simply pricing their products or services at levels below that of their competitors. That's okay, if your costs are lower or you are willing to make a lower profit in order to build your business. To establish competitive pricing, you must know what your competitors are paying to buy or produce what they sell. That isn't always easy. If you have been employed by your competitor or in a similar business, you may have some insight into their costs and pricing structure.

Need an example? Following is the Competitors' Pricing summary for Widgee World Retailers (Appendix A):

> *We have conducted extensive investigations into the pricing for competitors' products throughout the metropolitan area. The following table represents the average pricing for all four of our competitors.*

COMPETITORS' AVERAGE RETAIL PRICE POINT		
Widgets	**Accessories Category 1**	**Accessories Category 2**
Small—$2.50	Small—$1.60	Medium—$4.99
Medium—$3.25	Medium—$2.35	Large—$5.45
Large—$4.00	Large—$2.50	Commercial—$21.95
Extra Large—$10.00	Extra Large—$4.00	
Commercial—$31.95	Commercial (Regular)—$4.95	
	Commercial (Large)—$11.95	

Our pricing is defined as competitive. Some items will be priced slightly higher and others slightly lower. Ultimately, we are very similar to most competitors in pricing. We look to make customer service and loyalty the most defining distinctions between Widgee World and the competition. And we will work to promote the "made in the USA" recognition.

It is imperative to note these price comparisons serve to establish the range within which each product category is to be found. In most instances, Widgee World will open storefronts where most competitors are not located.

Smart businesses don't get caught in the "I'll beat any competitor's price" trap. A competitor with deep pockets or a special purchase can drain your profits by setting up a few products that are offered at under cost—called loss leaders. Instead, sell your products and services based on perceived value.

Perceived Value

How much is a house worth? Whatever a buyer and a seller agree it is worth. On a specific day, the price may be $200,000. The perceived value a year later may be higher or lower, depending on market conditions that impact the buyer and seller. A seller may be in a hurry to get rid of the home or the buyer may see an investment opportunity that can lower the perceived value of the house.

FACT

You can test perception pricing by offering a few products or services at higher prices and tracking results. Do the higher prices drop off sales for those items? Do the increased profits cover the lower sales levels? Let your customers help you establish the most profitable pricing for your business.

Perception is a belief based on outside influences. Perceived value is what someone believes the worth of a product, service, or benefit is. Commodity products, such as toothpaste, are sold by price, though the manufacturer attempts to increase perceived value—our brand is better than their brand—through advertising. Services are priced based on the relative value of benefits to the buyer. If the service will save the buyer $1,000, the service price will be set at a fraction of that. An intelligent buyer won't pay $2,000 to save $1,000, for example.

Be sure that your business plan considers the various ways that products and services are priced, and establishes a pricing structure that offers long-term profitability.

Service businesses define pricing differently, as illustrated in this example from Appendix B:

> *The cost for professional organizing services is based on several key factors including skill, experience, and the self-worth of the individual organizer. The fees charged in this industry are diverse. Hourly rates typically vary between $60 and $150 per hour, with several in the profession earning as much as $1,000 per day.*
>
> *Though personal organizing is a relatively new industry sector, demand for the service is growing. ATMC will offer introductory, discount pricing for the first six months of operation. Anticipating positive results, the price structure will then be increased to a more customary rate.*

PRICING STRUCTURE		
Type	**Discount**	**Customary**
Business—Single	$30	$60
Business—Group	$165	$200
Residential	$25	$50

> *Group rates are noted in the table above to represent an approximate median of the range from $150 to $175 hourly for 3–10 individuals. The exact price charged within the group rate depends on the number of participants and materials used to provide the service. For ease of calculations, the group medians listed in the table above are implemented in the financial projections.*

Margins and Discounts

A margin is the measurement of a difference. In business, you'll be using price margins, gross margins, profit margins, and other margins. Pricing is the task of establishing a price difference between what you pay and what you charge for products and services. Gross margins and markups have an impact on pricing and profitability.

First, understand that margins are different depending on what type of business is being discussed. A retail business, for example, will use one level of margins or buy/sell differences while a wholesaler, manufacturer, and representatives use another. In addition, you must consider the approximate profit margins of your buyers as you establish prices. For example, a wholesaler selling to retailers must know what margins its customers use so the wholesale price margins can remain competitive.

A gross margin is the amount of income left after paying for the goods sold. If your business sells $1,000 in merchandise that cost you $600, the gross profit or margin is $400. More useful is to calculate gross margin as a percentage of revenue. Simply deduct costs from sales, divide the result by sales, and convert it into a percent. In the example, divide the gross margin of $400 by the sales of $1,000 to get 0.4, then state it as a percentage: 40 percent. In the example, the gross margin is 40 percent.

What does gross margin have to do with pricing and profits? It can help you establish profitable prices. If you buy $600 worth of products and you want to establish a price that offers you a 40 percent gross margin, you can divide the cost (600) by 1 minus the GM (1-4 = .6) or $1,000.

Another common pricing term is markup, which is just another way of looking at gross margin. The difference is that it is a markup based on cost rather than sales. Products that cost $600 that you will sell at $1,000, as in the example, will have a markup of 66.67 percent—the selling price is the cost times 1.6667. The "1" is the cost and the ".6667" is the markup.

Whether your business is retail, wholesale, product, or service, gross margins are an important tool in pricing. Gross margins and other ratio analysis are covered more completely in Chapter 19.

Discounts

Pricing also involves discounts, a reduction from the standard price. If a sale offers 25 percent off, that's the discount. The standard price is sometimes called the list price, the one listed or suggested by the manufacturer, referred to as the manufacturer's suggested retail price (MSRP or SRP). The effective or market price is the one the customer actually pays.

Why would your business want to offer discounts to customers? Many reasons. The primary ones include:

- Increase short-term sales
- Move out-of-date stock
- Reward valued customers
- Motivate customers to buy

Businesses of all types and sizes—from hot dog stands to aircraft manufacturers—use various discounts and allowances to increase profitability. They include:

- Discounts for noncredit payments
- Quantity discounts
- Functional discounts (for the buyer taking over some function of the transaction, such as warehousing or service)
- Seasonal discounts
- Promotional discounts
- Trade-in allowances

Your business plan should outline any primary discounts and allowances that you will offer to customers, and explain why and how. In addition, make sure that such discounts and allowances don't have a negative effect on profitability. To be cost effective, discounts must increase profits sufficiently to make up for potential losses.

To illustrate, following is the Promotional Offerings summary from Appendix B:

A 15 percent discount will be granted to any client who uses $500 of our services (including purchases). Each time a client reaches this amount, this discount will be automatically subtracted from the total cost of their next purchase/request for our services.

How can you determine what discounts and allowances will work for your business? Take a look at your competitors. What discounts do they offer customers and why? Also look at similar businesses for discount structures that you can profitably apply to your business. Just make sure that they meet their intended purpose: to increase overall profitability.

Costs

The price at which you sell your products and service greatly impacts your business' profitability. However, it isn't the only factor. Costs are critical, too. A cost is what you pay for something. It could be the wholesale cost of products you sell at retail, the employee costs required to provide a specific service, or the cost of raw materials used in manufacturing.

Cost typically includes more than just the purchase price. For example, a retailer will buy products at cost, then have the products shipped to the store and prepared for sale by an employee. All of these are costs.

In business, costs are typically segmented based on whether they are fixed or variable. The following further explains calculating business costs.

Fixed Costs

A fixed cost is one that doesn't change in proportion to business activity. A retailer or manufacturer, for example, must pay rent, utility bills, and some salaries regardless of whether sales levels are high or low. Fixed costs are not typically included in the costs of goods sold.

Chapter 16 on income statements will expand on this topic. In the meantime, figure that your business has fixed costs that will impact your profitability and pricing.

Your new or growing business should continually search for lower costs on your primary products and services. However, don't lose quality or value because it can reduce profitability. Instead, search for current and prospective suppliers who can help you earn discounts on what you already buy.

Variable Costs

A variable cost is one that changes in proportion to business activity. Typical variable costs for a business include the cost of goods sold, materials, and production costs. A manufacturer who buys parts only does so as they are needed to make things, hence it is a variable cost and considered part of the costs of goods sold.

QUESTION?

Who set the rules of accounting?
Accountants. The guidelines for business accounting are referred to as Generally Accepted Accounting Practices (GAAP) and are established by consensus within countries. The United States uses a slightly different structure from Canada, and the UK has another structure. The primary difference is based on taxation laws within the countries. Small businesses don't need to worry about the complex rules. Your accountant will know which apply to your business.

Defining variable costs can be tricky for some businesses. The factory needs electricity for some lights and security whether or not there are employees present; that's a direct expense. However, Monday morning arrives and the electric machinery is started for production; that electricity is a variable expense. Smaller companies don't differentiate, but large companies do.

Cost Accounting

Cost accounting is the process of tracking business expenses, primarily those involved in producing something. Factories use cost accounting to account for every nut and bolt used to make something. They must know to the penny what something costs to manufacture because profits are in the pennies.

Your business may not require detailed cost accounting of every component, but it will need general accounting of all income and expenses to establish prices and determine profitability.

Profitability

Profitability is the bottom line. It is why you will spend time determining the appropriate pricing for what you sell. If your business isn't profitable, you won't be able to serve your customers for very long.

Profitability is the ability to make a profit; profit is income less expenses. Sell $500,000 worth of widgets with expenses (including costs of goods sold) of $400,000 and your profit is $100,000. The primary purpose of your business—any business—is to make a profit for its investor(s).

Of course, calculating a profit isn't quite that easy. Before taxes or after? Which taxes? Are there tax credits available? Is the profit retained by the business or passed on to the investors? You don't need the answers to all of these questions for your business plan, but you do need a basic understanding of the types of profits you'll be earning. Chapter 16 covers income statements that are used to calculate gross, net, and similar profits.

Gross Profit

Gross profit is the difference between revenue and the cost of providing a product or service before deducting overhead expenses and taxes. A retailer calculates gross profit by deducting the costs of goods sold from total sales. A manufacturer deducts materials and consumables needed to make the product.

Depending on the business, gross profit is also called sales profit or gross operating profit. It typically doesn't include expenses of operating the business, called indirect or overhead expenses.

Net Profit

Net profit *does* deduct overhead from gross profit. It is the amount of money left over after all fixed and variable expenses are paid, except one: taxes. Net profit is also known as pretax profit; once taxes are paid, the amount becomes profit after taxes. If no profit was made, it is loss after taxes.

Increasing Profitability

As your business grows, you will discover opportunities to increase profitability. You will find cost-effective ways to increase sales, reduce overhead, reduce costs of goods sold, and offer profitable discounts and allowances. Anything that increases your gross margin—the difference between sales and costs—offers potential profitability.

Your business plan should include ideas for boosting profitability, especially if the business is established but not sufficiently profitable. How can you increase profitability? The three primary ways are to increase turnover, reduce costs, and adjust pricing.

Increase Turnover

Turnover is change. In business, turnover typically refers to changes in inventory. If a specific widget model sells one unit every month, the turnover—or "turn"—rate is said to be twelve a year. Assuming that your business makes $10 for each one sold, increasing the turn rate to fifteen units a year will increase sales by $30. Costs of goods sold will increase with higher turnover, but fixed costs—rent, salaries, etc.—will not, and your business will increase profits.

Retailers and wholesalers often attempt to increase inventory turnover by offering discounts, allowances, and incentives that build sales and still leave profits. Service businesses strive to increase the number of customer-service units turned. If the turn rate for a carpet-cleaning business is fifty rooms a month, they will strive to increase the turn rate to sixty to increase profitability.

What should inventory turnover be for my type of business?
The answer depends on your business. However, your accountant can give you an approximation, based on industry resources and other factors. In addition, your business may have different turnover numbers for different departments. Ask your accountant and your primary suppliers.

Reduce Costs

Reducing fixed and variable costs can also help your new or growing business increase profits. If a widget costs your company $100 to manufacture and you find a way of reducing that cost by 10 percent, you are also increasing your profits. In fact, if you only make a $10 profit on a unit and you now earn a $20 profit, you have doubled profits.

All product and service businesses benefit from reducing costs. Because service businesses rely on the efforts of employees, many attempt to cut wages and related costs. However, they often find out that the quality of service diminishes and sales are lost. Instead, find ways to reduce costs by increasing employee productivity. Analyze how you can make your employees more effective by using training and technology to get more from their time.

Adjust Pricing

Pricing is an important issue in your business plan. Your pricing policy should include measurements to ensure that products or services are priced for profitability. If your competitors lower prices, you may need to adjust yours. Or you may decide that the gross margin on these products isn't sufficient, so you refocus on offering products with higher margins.

In addition, you will continue to use cost accounting to know what your products or services are costing you to produce. As needed, you can adjust pricing to remain profitable. Include your pricing policy within your business plan.

CHAPTER 13

Advertising
and Promotion

A significant challenge among new and growing businesses is getting the word out that you are open for business. Your business plan must address this challenge and offer readers a clear explanation of how you expect to present your business to potential customers through advertising and promotion. This chapter outlines how successful businesses use the mass media to sell their businesses.

Using the Mass Media

As you analyze your business' markets and opportunities, you must consider the best methods of reaching these markets. Do your customers watch television, listen to the radio, read newspapers or news magazines, see billboards, read pop-ups, or click on links? More important: How can you cost-effectively reach them with your message at the point where they are considering a purchase of your product or service?

Media is the plural of medium, something in the middle position—such as between you and potential customers. Mass media are mediums of communication designed to reach the mass of the people. Mass media include television, radio, newspapers, magazines, billboards, and the Internet. In addition, there are target media or specialized communication mediums that focus on specific groups. A local radio station, for example, is a medium designed to reach a specific group of people, such as eighteen- to thirty-two-year-old males living in Columbus, Ohio. A website, such as *www.FixItClub.com,* is focused to reach do-it-yourselfers with instructions (and ads) on household repairs.

The primary business goal of the media is to make a profit by delivering advertising messages to prospective buyers. The media does so by offering these buyers something they want: news, information, data, music, entertainment, or other benefits. Most small businesses use newspaper, shopper, broadcast, and other media to present their messages to potential customers. Your marketing analysis and business plan should consider the most effective media for delivering your message.

Newspaper Advertising

The task of a newspaper is to make money for its publisher. It does so by developing a relationship of information and trust with its target readers. In fact, it will have numerous target groups, each developed in order to sell advertising to businesses that want to reach them. The paper's sports section offers one target group, the classifieds another.

Newspaper advertising is sold by the column inch or other space measurement. Take a look at your local newspaper. Most have between four and eight columns of text to a page. An advertisement that is one column wide and one-inch long is one column-inch (1 c.i.).

The more space you buy at a time, the lower the advertising rate. That is, the column-inch rate for a quarter-page ad is lower than the rate for a 1 c.i. ad. In addition, buying a specific number of column inches in advance, for use over a month, a quarter, or a year, earns your store an even lower rate.

FACT

Newspapers sell advertising space by the column inch or c.i. You can determine the cost of newspaper advertising by asking the paper's ad representative for a rate card. It will show you standard rates, discount rates for multiple insertions, color surcharges, and deadlines for each edition. It will also describe the paper's market, circulation, and special features.

Once you've identified the local newspaper and section of the newspaper that best reaches your target customers, contact the paper's advertising department and meet with an ad rep to get a rate card and discuss campaigns. Remember that ad reps are typically commissioned salespeople who get paid more when they sell more. Make sure that your ad rep is willing to develop a long-term relationship with you rather than sell whatever is hot this week.

Shopper Advertising

A shopper is primarily an advertising publication. Most don't attempt to be objective news sources. Their function is to bring as many buyers as possible together with sellers. Regionally, shoppers are also called penny savers.

One of the big differences between newspapers and shoppers is how they are distributed. Though most newspapers are delivered by carriers, they must limit advertising to qualify for cost-effective USPS second-class postal rates. Shoppers, because they are primarily ads, don't get this low distribution rate and are distributed either at retail stores or by more expensive third-class postal rates.

Because newspapers are purchased by consumers and shoppers are not, newspapers are considered more desirable media for advertising.

People are willing to pay for them; shoppers simply come in the mail or are handed out free. However, the advertising rate (also measured in column inches) is typically much lower than that of area newspapers. As with newspapers, contact your local shopper publications and ask for a rate card and sales rep to learn more about their market and advantages.

If your new business will do a lot of advertising, consider hiring an advertising agency to help you place ads at the best rates. Typically, ad agencies are paid a percentage of your ad budget, but you can also hire them on an hourly basis to design an advertising program for you. Check local telephone books for ad agencies in your marketplace.

Broadcast Advertising

Radio and television have revolutionized advertising, bringing sound and moving images to the sales pitch. Each type of broadcast media has its advantage. Radio is more portable, found in cars, stores, homes, and devices. Television is more visual, offering additional sensory messages to the advertising process. However, in most markets, television advertising is too expensive for small businesses. A thirty-second advertisement (called a "spot") can cost thousands of dollars to produce and require thousands more in advertising fees to make a significant impression on viewers.

Radio stations play specific types of music or offer news and talk on definite topics for one purpose: to draw a defined audience to listen to ads from their sponsors. The audience for sports talk radio will be different than a hip-hop or an oldies station. Considering the local population, radio stations position themselves to reach—and to sell to—a defined audience that isn't otherwise being reached efficiently.

The point to remember about radio advertising is to select what your customers want rather than what you want. You can be a big fan of PBS, talk shows, or classic rock, but if these local stations don't focus on delivering your message to your prospects, don't advertise on them. Spend your money where it will bring you more money; advertising must be an investment. Your advertising representative can help you write your store's ads and advise you on whether talent (announcers) or you should read them.

FACT

Radio and television stations have rate cards that report the price of thirty- and sixty-second commercials (called spots), program sponsorships, and other advertising opportunities. Your spots can be purchased within a popular show or they can be set up as run-of-schedule (ROS) ads that are spread throughout the broadcast day. ROS ads have a lower rate or price than specific placements.

Magazines

A magazine is a focused periodical. It is published on a regular basis (weekly, bimonthly) to be read by a specific target market, such as local upscale buyers or contractors interested in news about residential remodeling. Your ad in a magazine has readership as long as the issue is in print; once it is replaced by a new issue, your ad has effectively expired.

Magazine advertising makes sense for niche businesses, those that are focused toward a readership that is similar to that of your target customer. It may be a geographic magazine or one defined by an industry or special interest. Your business plan should identify any magazines and trade (industry) publications that are read by your target market.

Magazine advertising is typically sold by the full or partial page. A two-page ad is called a spread. You can request a rate card through the magazine's advertising department or your advertising agency.

Magazine ads are purchased as fractional pages, such as quarter-page, half-page, etc. Rates decrease for the space used as the size goes up. A half-page ad typically costs less than two quarter-page ads. Frequency also earns a discount. An ad in two issues, as a rule, costs less than twice the single-issue rate. You can save advertising dollars by purchasing a longer-term contract for the most effective size of ad for your business.

Other Media

Once you open your business, you will be inundated with media sales reps offering everything from yellow pages advertising to vanity ads. There will be placement ads in regional directories, reps for bus-bench ads, pitches for ads in shopping carts, direct-mail campaigns, and many others. Which should you consider? Any that will profitably bring you new customers. How can you know if the medium is profitable for your business? You can't.

The easiest way to determine where you can profitably advertise is to carefully study your best competitors. They know. They've probably spent many thousands of dollars on advertising that doesn't return a profit. Follow their lead. Eventually, you will discover profitable media that they are missing, but don't try to reinvent business advertising just yet. Follow the leaders.

Promotion

Once your business is ready for operation, you obviously want to let as many people as possible know about it. That requires promotion. Promotion is the distribution of information about a product or service to those who may use it. Some business promotions, such as advertising, are more obvious than others, like news stories. In fact, advertising is often called above-the-line (more obvious) promotion, and news stories are part of below-the-line (less obvious) promotion.

How your business plans to use promotion is called its promotional mix. In addition to advertising, some businesses will use public relations, endorsements, sponsorships, product placements, or trade shows to promote their offerings. So can you.

Public Relations

Newspapers, broadcast stations, and some other media thrive on information. For example, a newspaper must fill approximately 50 percent of its pages with "news." It may be about a recent crime, fire, or scandal. But it may also be about your store's grand opening or a new line of products or services. Your news probably won't make the front page, but it can be somewhere in the paper, attracting readers who are looking for "news."

FACT

Most daily newspapers have a business editor who is looking for anything newsworthy from the local business community. Contact these papers and introduce yourself as someone starting or growing a local business. Then ask what the editor is looking for in news stories. Also ask for a direct phone, fax, or e-mail address. Make sure you know in what issue(s) business news is published and what the deadlines are.

Many new and growing businesses hire a public-relations (PR) firm to help them identify and design promotional opportunities. You establish a promotional budget and hire the agency to help you develop a cost-effective campaign.

QUESTION?

How can I find a public-relations firm that will fit my promotional budget?
Start with your local chamber of commerce, mall tenant association, or other business group. Some agencies will be members as well. Ask other members about their PR experiences and whether they can make recommendations. If your budget is small, some PR agencies can assist a group of similar clients (neighbors, related products or services, etc.) pool their resources and cooperate in promotional campaigns.

What kind of "news" can you promote?

- Grand opening
- New product line
- Celebrity visit
- New-employee introduction

- Changes in technology that impact customers
- Special sales events
- Business anniversaries
- Holiday promotions
- Customer-appreciation events with prizes

The list of promotional opportunities for your business is endless. Read your local newspapers and shoppers, and listen and watch local radio and television to identify promotional opportunities that your business plan can mention to impress its investors.

Endorsements

Wouldn't it be great if local celebrities used and recommended your products or services? It would be a newsworthy opportunity to bolster your business. Endorsements are used by national brands, but they can also be useful to local businesses. Think of the restaurant visited that had signed autographs from national entertainment or sports figures. Your business can have a signing wall as well. If you sell books, consider a writer's wall with titles and signatures from local writers. If you sell sporting goods, ask local athletes to sign a wall or bring a sport photo in for display. If you have numerous visitors from other cities or countries, display a map and encourage customers to put a pin up for their hometown.

Endorsements can backfire on sponsors. Many have invested millions of dollars in endorsements by celebrities who get negative publicity that hurts the sponsors' image. Make sure that any endorsements you purchase are immune from negative publicity.

You can also attempt to gain endorsements from other local businesses. You can display an ad, menu, poster, or other promotional collateral from other businesses (with their permission) in your store. Offer reciprocal endorsements or offer a gift certificate in your store to other businesses that will allow you to be promoted in their store. Creative endorsements don't have to be expensive.

Sponsorships

Local businesses, especially, have opportunities for community sponsorships and related promotions. For example, your business name can appear on youth sports uniforms, baseball-field outfields and scoreboards, car-show trophies, charity prizes, local stock cars, and a dozen other promotional opportunities.

Which sponsorships are right for your business? The answer depends on your specific business. Which sponsorship opportunities are available in your marketplace? Which ones draw the type of people you like to call your customers? Look for sponsorship opportunities that cost-effectively promote your business and make sure that you mention a few of them in your business plan.

Product Placements

Big business spends big money buying what are called product placements. They want to make sure that when actor Ben Affleck is drinking a soda in his next movie, the soda is clearly their brand. And they pay the movie studios thousands of dollars to make sure that it is.

You don't have to spend thousands for local product placement, but it will cost you something. For example, if your business rents and maintains decorative plants for doctor's offices, make sure that your business information is prominently displayed on the product or nearby. If your business sells used cars, try to get a product placement at local banks who, in turn, will get placement and mentions on your car lot. Include product-placement opportunities in your business plan to impress your investors with your promotional skills.

Trade Shows

Some small businesses benefit from trade shows. A trade show is an event that attracts people of similar interests or needs. A small furniture store can promote itself by participating in a local home show or bridal fair. A number of local car dealers can sponsor an auto fair to draw buyers in.

A similar promotional event is built around businesses in a specific location, such as a downtown merchants event or one in a shopping mall. The events are promoted through local media and typically feature local entertainment (artists, musicians, writers, broadcast celebrities). There is usually a cost for participation, but it can be less expensive than an advertising campaign while offering better results. However, to take full advantage of shows, you must make sure that it will draw prospective customers and build your brand name.

QUESTION?

How can I tell if my trade has a trade show?
The best opportunities can be found by reading newspapers and magazines that serve your trade. Also, trade associations often sponsor trade shows. In addition, check online resources such as Trade Show News Network (*www.tsnn.com*).

Media Planning

Advertising and publicity are primary components in marketing your new or growing business to customers and prospects. Because this phase of marketing takes time and money, it's important that you develop a media plan so you can get the most value for your assets.

Media planning includes identifying objectives, developing a strategy, and establishing a preliminary media schedule. These components should be included in your business plan.

Media Objectives

An objective is a goal; it is something you want for yourself or your business. Including your business' media objective in your business plan can help you toward that goal. It doesn't define how you will reach that goal, it just puts it out there. For example, media objectives for a small business may include:

- Gain awareness of Bob's Widgets among widget buyers in metropolitan Trumania.
- Establish a professional image for Acme Time Consultants, Inc. with business executives and professionals in the Southeast.
- Maximize efficiency in manufacturing and marketing electronic widgets that feature our patented technology.

To be actionable objectives, they should also be measurable. For example, Bob's Widgets may establish an objective of building brand awareness in the market until a shopper survey rates the business as one of the top two in local brand awareness. Acme Time Consultants may establish a goal of at least 25 percent of the regional market for time consultants.

Make sure that the media objectives your business establishes are clear and measurable. Include them in your business plan.

Media Strategy

Media objectives are the "what." A media strategy is the "how." How, for example, will Bob's Widgets gain buyer awareness? Give away business cards stapled to $10 bills? Hire airplanes to pull advertising banners? Place ads in local media read by widget buyers? The owners of Bob's Widgets can waste a lot of money attempting to reach an objective if they don't first have a viable strategy.

How can you develop a media strategy for your business? First, you need to determine what media is available to you. Who reaches your potential customers? Local newspapers or shoppers? Radio or television stations? Billboards? Other media? Sponsorships or endorsements?

Once you've identified the most viable media for your message, you need to prioritize them by value. Will the local shopper bring you more new prospects than billboard ads? For this exercise, you'll need to speak with representatives of the primary media. It will be a good education. It will also help you analyze the best media values in your marketplace.

Preliminary Media Schedule

Timing is crucial in business. It's especially important in promoting your business to prospects and customers. You can't have a Christmas sale in

August. Actually, you can, but you'll be wasting lots of money attempting to attract prospects when they aren't ready to buy.

That's the key to media scheduling: Attract buyers when they are ready to make a decision. That's the best time to reach them. Second best is before they make a decision, but not so early that they forget your message before they're ready to buy.

Your business plan should include a preliminary media schedule, listing the primary media you will use, when, and what your budget will be. You don't have to place orders for the media yet, but you should select the most appropriate vehicles and know how best to use them for gathering valuable prospects.

Capabilities Brochure

Prospective customers and investors will be impressed if you have at least the preliminary design for a capabilities brochure for your business. What is a capabilities brochure? It is a document (printed or on a website) that outlines your business' capabilities. It will include a mission statement that's rewritten for customers, an overview of what your business is capable of doing, and what benefits it will bring to customers.

A capabilities brochure is your business' defining profile document. You will give it to potential investors, larger customers, potential employees, and suppliers. It tells them, succinctly, why they should be doing business with you. It is an important component of your media plan and can help you sell your business plan.

CHAPTER 14

Sales and Distribution

Your business offers products or services to customers. How do customers know about your offerings? How do you convince them of the benefits? How do you get your products or services to the customer? These are business-plan questions answered in this chapter on sales and distribution. No matter what your business offers—from cell phones online to hypnosis services—you must find an effective way to sell and share.

Sales Basics

Your business plan must address two primary questions: Who are your customers? and How are you going to persuade them to buy from you? Your business' customers were defined in Chapter 8. This chapter offers recommendations on how your business plan can document how you sell and distribute to your customers.

A sale is an exchange of goods or services, typically for money. Selling is informing the customer of the features and benefits of the product or service and, as needed, persuading the customer to make the purchase. Persuasion is the skill of guiding people toward making a decision. The job of a seller in any business, then, is to inform and persuade.

What does it take to become a good seller?

- Product knowledge
- Knowledge of competitive products
- Knowledge of product features
- Knowledge of benefits to customers
- Communication skills
- Listening skills
- Persuasion skills
- Professional skills (presentation skills, recordkeeping, etc.)
- Ethics

Persuasion is a vital component of selling. Whether your business sells homes, widgets, consulting services, or time shares, persuasion can help you get your message across and, possibly, accepted by another—a transaction. You can persuade others by appealing to their reasoning, emotions, or both.

Appeal to Reason

Reason is a description or explanation. It's the facts. When buying a product or service, purchasers want to know what it is, how it works, and what benefits they will derive. You, as a customer, want to know this; your customers do, too. Depending on what you are selling, you can appeal to others by using various types of reasoning, such as logic, rhetoric, and proof. Following are some examples to illustrate:

- **Logic:** "You want something that will clean stubborn stains on enamel, and XYZ has been proven in scientific tests to clean enamel easier and better than any other stain cleaner."
- **Rhetoric:** "XYZ is the best stain fighter available."
- **Proof:** "Let's test XYZ on this stubborn stain."

These simple examples offer three ways you can appeal to a person's reasoning to help you convince them of the validity of your facts. You probably recognize these phrasings from the thousands of ads that bombard you daily. That's because advertising is built upon the foundations of persuasion.

Appeal to Emotion

Emotion is a strong human feeling, such as love, hate, anger, fear, and compassion. Salespeople and other persuaders often use emotional appeals to help make a sale. Should they? That depends on what is being sold. Selling real estate, for example, involves the buyer's reasoning, of course, but it is also an emotional purchase, so it's appropriate to use emotional appeals to help sell a home. It isn't an appropriate tactic for selling industrial control valves.

Emotional appeals are frequently used in advertising, religion, propaganda, and sex. For example:

- "Imagine living in the nicest home on the block."
- "Find full acceptance at our church."
- "Immigrants are taking over our country."

Many consumers still consider appeals to their emotions as primary elements in their decisions to buy. However, a growing number of educated consumers expect salespeople to only use emotional appeals when they are appropriate to the product or service, and they will stop buying if the appeal is inappropriate.

Sales Channels

How will you get your product or service to customers? This is a critical question for all businesses, especially start-ups and those ready to grow. It should be included in your business plan. Select a less effective channel and your business will suffer. Find the most appropriate sales channel and it can bloom and surpass your competitors.

There are numerous types of sales or distribution channels available to entrepreneurs, depending on how directly the seller and buyer interact—direct, with a distributor, or through an agent. There are complex versions of each of these channels, but all are based on how the seller and the buyer interact.

> **ESSENTIAL**
>
> If you are not a trained salesperson and your new business requires that you persuade customers to buy, read *The Everything® Sales Book* by Dan Ramsey. You can also spend a few hours watching the direct-sales channels on television: QVC, Home Shopping Network, etc. You'll quickly identify primary techniques used to sell products to a broad audience. These techniques can be used, with variations, in all types of sales.

Direct Sales

Direct sales present goods and services directly to the end user. It's a broad term that covers many selling methods. The purest definition of direct sales involves the producer and the ultimate user of a product, such as a farm vegetable stand where customers can select produce grown nearby. It can also cover retailers who sell their products to store customers, though retailing really is a component of dealer sales. The difference is perspective. The widget retailer is selling directly to users; the widget manufacturer is selling through a distributor to a dealer, the retailer.

Direct-service providers, such as a tax accountant, work directly with the end user, called a client. Many other service businesses use direct sales channels to distribute their services.

Distributor Sales

Some businesses use distributors to get their products or services into the hands of buyers. A distributor is a business that buys for resale. Wholesalers are distributors to retailers. If your business produces a product or service and doesn't sell directly to end users, it will probably use a distributor or sales agent to reach end users.

If your business is a distributorship, make sure you include the primary facts in your business plan. For whom will you distribute? Do you have a contract or other agreement? Does it involve an exclusive territory and, if so, what are the parameters? To whom will you be distributing? Will your business at any time own what you are selling? Your investors want to know.

Agent Sales

A sales agent offers goods or services produced by others. In most cases, the agent is independent and is paid a commission on the transaction amount. A travel agent, for example, doesn't own the airline ticket or hotel reservation at any time. Instead, the agent brings the buyer and seller together to earn a fee or commission.

Many small businesses benefit from establishing sales agents rather than hiring sales employees. Costs can be more controlled, as commissions are only paid if sales are made. The downside is that the agent may also be selling for your competitor; if the commissions are higher, the agent may be working harder for the competitor than for you.

Dealer

A dealer is typically the last business in the distribution channel and transacts directly with the end user or ultimate buyer. Retail stores are dealers, also known as resellers. The majority of small businesses operate as retail dealers, either with physical (called brick and mortar or B&M) stores or online as virtual stores.

Exactly where some businesses fall within primary distribution channels can be confusing. To clarify, identify your business' relationship with the end user. Do you sell direct, through a distributor or agent, or through a dealer? Also consider that the final end user may not be your primary customer. If you are a manufacturer, your customer may be a wholesaler. If you are a service provider, you may use an agent to sell your services.

FACT

If your business depends on sales skills—and most do—subscribe to one or more popular magazines. They include *Sales Magazine* (*www .salesmagazine.com*), *Sales Pro Magazine* (*www.salespromagazine .com*), *Selling Power* (*www.sellingpower.com*), and *Agency Sales Magazine* (*www.manaonline.org*).

As your business begins or grows, consider what other distribution channels may be open to you in the future. Many successful wholesalers have branched out to operate retail stores and some have become manufacturers of what they sell. Continually seek new opportunities.

Following is a sales strategy summary for a furniture store: Key to the sales strategy is direct sales calls on all market segments targeted in this plan, with the exception of interior designers. These sales calls need to be made by the owner to take advantage of his background and knowledge of the products and competitors. Experience has proven that the more time he devotes to sales, the more sales result. A full-time team member needs to be found and added as soon as possible. Without this person, too much of the owner's time is deflected away from his major task of selling.

Forty-four specialty retailers have been identified, as well as sixteen unfinished furniture retailers. With proper geographical planning and appointment scheduling handled by a competent team member, three or four sales calls could be achieved in a day. This would mean that the owner could pay a visit to all sixty prime prospects over a three-week period.

Sales Management

Whether your business is manufacturing, wholesale, retail, or services, sales is an integral component of your success. Without sales, no products or services get distributed and no profit is made. You don't have to be part of the sales staff, though in a small business you probably will be, but you do need to know how to manage salespeople (including yourself) toward productive transactions.

The steps to productive sales management include planning, tracking, reporting, and adjusting the system for better results. The steps are the same whether you are selling widgets or whale-watching cruises.

Sales Planning

Your business plan should include specifics on how you will sell your product or service. Your investors will want to know that you've thought about this topic and developed a workable plan. More important, you will want to summarize your ideas on how to approach the vital topic of selling to customers.

Many small businesses are started by someone who has had experience buying what they want to sell. A long-time golfer will sell golf equipment. An experienced contractor will sell home-inspection services. As customers, they already know how they want to be treated by sellers. They realize that the selling experience is critical to a transaction.

In addition to how your business will sell, you must plan how much it will sell. Sales forecasting, covered later in this chapter, is a critical component of your business planning. It will require setting sales goals and tracking results.

Sales Tracking

Once sales goals are established, they can be compared to actual results, called sales tracking. There are numerous tools developed for tracking sales results against goals. Smaller businesses often use spreadsheet programs such as Microsoft Excel and OpenOffice Calc. Excel is a component of MS Office; OO Calc is free from *www.openoffice.org.*

Tracking sales requires milestones. For example, your new business may establish a goal of $1 million in sales within five years. To arrive at that goal, your plan can have secondary goals or milestones at one, two, three, and four years. It can also break the first year's milestone into smaller units: expected sales within the first three, six, or nine months. Once the milestones are established, you can use sales tracking to determine if your venture will meet them and make needed adjustments.

Be aware that there is a difference between sales tracking and revenue tracking. For example, your company may have revenue goals of $10,000 a month and calculate that it will require five sales of $2,000 each during the month. Each sale, in your estimation, requires presenting your message to ten prospects. Your sales goal, then, is to make fifty presentations each month ($50 / 10 \times 2,000 = 10,000$). You must make and track these presentations or other sales functions to meet your revenue goal.

FACT

Many professional salespeople use portable electronic devices called personal information managers (PIMs) to track customer contacts. Popular PIMs include ACE (*www.goace.com*), EssentialPIM (*www.essential pim.com*), Heiler (*www.heiler.com*), KDE PIM (*pim.kde.org*), RiverSand (*www.riversand.com*), and many others. In addition, contact-management programs like ACT! (*www.act.com*) offer versions for PDAs.

Sales Reporting

In a small business, sales tracking and reporting are the same because the salesperson is the sales manager. As your business grows, the function may expand, so it is important that you plan now, in the development stage of your business concept, toward a system that offers clear sales reports.

What should be included in sales reports? Whatever helps management reach specific sales goals and milestones. For example, a travel agent's sales reports will include incoming and outgoing customer contacts; whether they are prospects, new customers, or existing clients; and the results of the contacts. In addition to keeping management apprised of sales activity, it can help determine which sales activities are most productive. What is the value, in sales, of calls to new versus existing clients? Your business plan may not require this level of detail, but your operating or growing business should.

How often should sales reports be developed? The selling cycle is different for various businesses. A retail store may sell products the same day they are received and the transaction will take only moments. Daily or weekly reports are appropriate. A remodeling service may work with a customer for weeks or months before the sale is made; the project completion can take months or even years. Weekly or monthly reports to management will be sufficient.

If you are responsible for managing salespeople, especially ones that are not at your business location, establish an integrated sales-tracking system. It can help you not only know what is being sold, but also who is most effective at selling, and who isn't. Many of the sales-tracking systems include reporting and sales-management features.

Managing Results

So what? Your future sales reports may indicate that sales in one territory are markedly off or that a new service isn't selling well to the target market. What should you do? The answer is beyond the scope of your business plan (and this book), but you do need to design a process for acting on what you learn from sales reporting. Who is responsible for reaching sales goals? How will they manage the people and assets needed to meet specific goals? Include your preparation for managing sales-report results in your business plan.

Commissions and Incentives

How will your new or renewed business compensate salespeople? The answer can be critical to your sales forecasting and may be of interest to your investors. What are your options?

Compensating your salespeople requires determining how to best motivate them while offering sufficient financial security to keep them working hard for you. The options include wages, salary, partial or full commission, bonuses, and other incentives. Again, your business plan doesn't have to go into specifics, but it should address the issues of sales and other employee compensation, especially for key employees and job titles.

In your business plan, consider how similar businesses compensate employees involved in the sales process. Do they pay wages, salaries, commissions, bonuses, or offer other incentives to encourage productivity? Also consider whether your business should compensate differently than your competitors in order to attract employees who prefer the security of salaries or the opportunities of commissions.

Wage or Salary

Salespeople are compensated in various ways, depending on how much of their time is spent on developing relationships with customers and presenting your products or services. A retail clerk, for example, may have duties receiving and stocking merchandise, handling transactions, and other responsibilities. Face-to-face persuasive selling may be only a small or no component of their workday. They may be most motivated by an hourly wage or a weekly or monthly salary. In determining wages, consider whether your business will pay a living wage.

QUESTION?

How can I determine what a living wage is in my business community?

A living wage is wage sufficient to provide the necessities and comforts essential to an acceptable standard of living. Specifically, it is the cost of living in your community based on the size of the living group (one adult, two adults with one child, etc). If you've decided to pay your employees a living wage, visit *www.livingwage.geog.psu.edu* to calculate what that amount is for your location.

Commission

For wholesalers and other salespeople, the primary part of their job will be persuasive selling. Many employees, especially those with advanced persuasive skills, often prefer to be paid at least a portion of their income based on the value of the sale, called a commission. A commission is a fee based on a percentage of the value of the sale. The commission formula may be based on the sale total, the gross margin, or per unit. Commissions typically range from 3 to 15 percent of the sale total (excluding taxes) or 10 to 30 percent of the gross margin. To be eligible, commissioned salespeople must accurately track their sales or the employer must have a trustworthy system for tracking the source of all sales.

FACT

To establish a fair commission rate, first determine whether there are nonsales functions to the job that should be paid by a wage or salary. Then research competitors to learn how they pay. Your business competes with them for employees as well as sales, so the specifics of pay may be difficult to obtain. Ex-employees can be helpful.

Bonus

A bonus is based on either individual, department, or store sales totals for a period. For example, a retailer may offer a bonus of 5 percent if monthly sales exceed a specified level. Some retailers offer yearly bonuses and split it among all employees based on the number of hours or days they worked. Others use bonuses as incentives to wage and salary workers who can impact sales levels.

QUESTION?

How can I find out what types of bonuses and incentives my competitors offer to employees?
Your competitor's employees may come looking for a job. You can't ask them to divulge competitive information, but you can ask what their previous salary or wages and bonuses were. To attract the best sales employees, you probably need the best sales incentive program.

As with other forms of compensation, consider how your competitors are paying key employees. To attract better employees and get more work out of them, you may want to offer performance-based bonuses. Just make sure that the system is perceived by employees as equitable. Otherwise productivity in nonbonused employees may slip.

Other Incentives

Not all employees want taxable incentives. Some prefer the personal use of a company car, better health insurance, bonus vacations, extra days off, or other work incentives and rewards. Consider these and other incentives for compensating key employees in your business, including primary salespeople.

Before establishing an incentive program, talk with a tax advisor. Some business incentives are considered compensation and will require that they be reported to taxing authorities and that taxes be paid on them, typically by the receiver.

Forecasting Sales

Forecasting the level of sales is an important component of your business plan. Forecasts are predictions of future conditions based on historical and new data. The weather forecaster can predict tomorrow's high temperature based on what it is historically as well as data about weather entering the area. Your business must know what sales are coming in to be able to anticipate expenses and work toward profits.

How can your new or growing business forecast sales income? Cautiously, based on historical and new data. In your planning, you may have learned from industry sources that annual sales for your type of business are approximately $250 per square foot of sales-floor space. If your store's sales floor is 1,500 square feet in size, you can start with a forecast of $375,000 in annual sales. Because your business is new, this may be your goal for the second year of operation, and you estimate that the first year will average 60 percent of that amount or about $225,000.

Alternately, you may elect to forecast sales based on the average price of whatever you sell. If you are a widget wholesaler offering left-handed widgets that wholesale for $10 each and your market analysis (Chapter 7) projects a first-year sales level of 50,000 units, sales can be forecast at approximately $500,000.

An example of sales forecasting helps illustrate how it's included in a typical business plan:

In the first year, CuppaJoe anticipates having two drive-thru locations in operation. The first location will open in the third month of this plan and be fully operational beginning on the 1st day of September. The second drive-thru will open six months later. CuppaJoe is building in a certain amount of ramp-up for each facility while commuters become familiar with its presence. The drive-thrus will generate 288,000 tickets in the first year of operation, or approximately $558,000 in revenue.

In the second year, CuppaJoe will add two more drive-thrus, and in the third year, CuppaJoe will add an additional nine drive-thru facilities. The addition of these facilities will increase the revenue from drive-thrus to a total of over 1,000,000 tickets or $2.35 million in the second year and 2,675,000 tickets or just over $6 million in the third.

In addition to the drive-thrus, CuppaJoe will deploy one mobile unit in the fourth quarter of the first fiscal year. CuppaJoe expects this mobile unit to generate 10,000 tickets each, at an average ticket price of $2.45, which will generate gross revenues of approximately $24,500.

In the second quarter of the second fiscal year, CuppaJoe will deploy a second and third mobile unit. CuppaJoe expects all three mobile units to generate 150,000 tickets, or gross revenue of $375,00 in the second year. In the third fiscal year, with an additional fourth mobile unit deployed, CuppaJoe expects to see 264,000 mobile unit tickets, or $673,200 in gross revenue.

CuppaJoe is also showing revenue from the commerce portion of our website, where it will sell CuppaJoe T-shirts, sweatshirts, insulated coffee mugs, prepackaged coffee beans, and other premium items. CuppaJoe is not expecting this to be a significant profit center, but it is an integral part of the marketing plan—as a function of developing our brand and building product awareness. CuppaJoe expects revenues from this portion, to begin in the second fiscal year, to reach $26,000 initially and $36,000 in the third fiscal year.

Total first-year unit sales should reach 298,402, equating to revenues of $558,043. The second year will see unit sales increase to 1,177,400 or $2,348,900. The third year, with the addition of such *a significant number of outlets, we will see unit sales increase to 2,992,000, equating to gross sales revenue of $6,022,950.*

FACT

The key to accurate sales forecasting is frequent adjustment. If you forecast annual sales at the beginning of the year and forget about it, you may not even come close to your goal. However, if you look at the forecast monthly or even weekly and adjust your sales efforts, you have a much better chance of hitting your sales-forecast targets.

Various business-plan software programs, such as Business Plan Pro (*www.businessplanpro.com*), include tools and questionnaires for developing accurate sales forecasts for a variety of businesses. Professional business-plan developers can also assist in accurate forecasting. In addition, you can do your own sales research using resources in the chapters on market analysis (Chapter 7) and marketing strategy (Chapter 11). For supplementary examples, refer to the sample business plans included on this book's CD.

Your sales forecasts will not only help your investors understand your business' profitability, they can guide you as you start up or grow your business opportunity toward success.

CHAPTER 15

Suppliers and Resources

Your business needs suppliers. Some will provide raw material that you use in manufacturing or primary products that you resell to retailers or consumers. Your identification of and relationship with these resources can make or break your business. This chapter covers developing profitable relationships with suppliers no matter what your business is about. It covers primary and secondary suppliers, franchises and territories, as well as affiliations with original-equipment manufacturers (OEMs). Business planning isn't only about how you sell; smart planners also know how to buy. Your business plan must document this.

Finding Suppliers

Whatever your business model, you will depend on suppliers to furnish you with needed products and or services to offer to others. For example, an auto-repair service requires parts suppliers, tool suppliers, and other primary components. A widget importer needs international widget manufacturers and exporters. A restaurant needs food purveyors and equipment suppliers.

Your business planning should address your need for primary suppliers. You don't have to spill everything to investors, but you do need to make them comfortable with your selection and planning in this critical business area. They typically want to know that you've researched the most effective primary suppliers, know how to develop or have already developed a relationship with them, and are ready to work with suppliers toward success. Remember that investors don't have to know every detail of your business operation, but they do want to know that you know.

Find Effective Suppliers

For every business imaginable, there are dozens and possibly hundreds of primary suppliers awaiting the start up or growth of your new business. Who are they? You have probably identified a few of them in your market analysis and research into competitors. However, for your business to be effective, you don't need the closest nor the most prominent suppliers; you need the best suppliers. That's going to take a little research on your part.

First, review your executive summary (Chapter 3) to identify the focus of your business. (If it has changed during your subsequent plan development, modify it now.) Know what business you're in. The executive summary is the best synopsis of your business concept. For example, if you're planning a high-end coffeehouse, your primary supplier should be a purveyor of quality coffees and possibly teas. Another primary supplier will be the best in coffee and espresso-brewing equipment. Everything else—cups, napkins, condiments, and so on—will come from secondary suppliers. Your business must get the most appropriate primary suppliers for what you offer . . . or change what you offer.

Second, look closer at your competitors. Who are their primary suppliers? Your competitive research (Chapter 9) identified your principal competitors and possibly revealed their major suppliers. You may elect to use the same suppliers or suppliers that compete with your competitors' suppliers. If your competitor is Starbucks, you may choose to buy coffee beans from Peet's, Seattle's Best, or other well-known suppliers.

FACT

The Internet is a powerful resource for finding suppliers for anything you want to sell. Use search engines such as *www.google.com* and *www .yahoo.com* for initial searches, using your primary products as key words. However, the resources that come up first on the search aren't necessarily the biggest or the best. Be a smart buyer to enhance your opportunities as a smart seller.

Third, look to industry associations and publications for additional suppliers. For example, coffeehouses often belong to the National Coffee Association of the U.S.A. (*www.ncausa.org*). In addition to coffee-consumption research and coffeehouse manuals, the association is a resource for finding primary suppliers of coffee and related beverage products and equipment. Trade associations are covered in more detail later in this chapter.

Develop a Relationship

Most wholesale and materials suppliers are inundated with requests for information on how to buy directly and cut out the middleman. To protect their customers' business, most make it difficult to set up a wholesale or dealer account with them. That's understandable, as once your business is established you don't want your suppliers to sell directly to your customers. You want to develop a strong business relationship with your primary suppliers.

Suppliers make relationships difficult to begin but easy to continue. They often do this by requiring an application from you before they will tell you much about discounts and opportunities. The application process usually runs off any people who aren't serious about developing a business relationship. So, once you've identified your business' primary suppliers, request and complete an application with as much specificity as you can. If asked, offer the name and location of your business, its projected revenues, and other information, typically found in your executive summary.

Feed the Relationship

Depending on how critical primary suppliers are to your business' success, you may want to establish and develop a relationship with them even as you are developing your business plan. For example, in a competitive coffeehouse market, your success may depend upon being able to get an exclusive territorial relationship with one or another primary supplier. If you can't, you might reconsider your business plan.

What motivates your suppliers to give you the best prices and service? The same things that motivate you to offer these to your own customers. Analyze your own business and personal needs to develop more profitable relationships with your suppliers.

As you begin working with a primary supplier, you will probably be working with one or two salespeople who will service your account. Your relationship with these individuals can be critical to your success. If you match well personally, your supplier's rep may help in your education, possibly saving you from problems or costly operating errors. That rep is betting on your success.

Use the Relationship

If you have been successful at identifying and securing business relationships with primary suppliers, you can count your efforts as an asset. Your business will benefit from it, if you use it. For example, a working relationship with a primary coffee supplier can help you calculate what level of inventory you should have as your business starts or grows. Your sales rep cannot give you data about your competitor's orders, but the rep can make suggestions based on experience. "Based on your store setup, I suggest that you initially purchase 100 pounds each of our three most popular blends." If your relationship is trustworthy, that advice can increase sales and reduce expenses, enhancing profits.

Again, depending on your business structure and the detail needed in your business plan, you may not identify primary suppliers and develop profitable relationships with them before you approach investors for funding. However, if you can, your efforts will impress investors as well as offer you guidance toward success.

Secondary Suppliers

All businesses use secondary suppliers for essential but noncritical components. A coffeehouse needs cups and napkins. An office needs paper and folders. An auto shop needs work clothes and shop rags. All of these and other supplies can come from one of a number of secondary suppliers. You don't need to identify them before you develop your business plan, but you should select them before you start your business.

For example, if your business is built around an effective office, you will need office supplies. You have numerous choices ranging from Staples, Office Depot, and other franchise stores to independent stationery stores in your community. In addition, you can purchase office supplies online from Quill, Reliable, and other Internet and catalog resources; all have similar products. Why choose one over another? If your business is locally oriented and is attempting to fight franchise competitors, select secondary suppliers who are local. If not, choose the supplier who offers you whichever you need: either lowest price or best service. You may decide to use one supplier over all others or share your orders among different secondary suppliers. Whatever you decide, do so based on whatever is best for the profitability of your business. You don't have to include secondary suppliers in your business plan, but planning for them can help assure your lenders that you've considered your options.

Business Relationships

Your new or growing business can benefit from developing close relationships with larger and better-known businesses. You will not only have a proven supplier, you can also attract investors and customers based on the name value of your supplier.

There are various names for these business relationships, depending on their structure, requirements, and restrictions. They include OEM relationships, joint-marketing agreements, third-party supplier agreements, VARs, and franchises. These and similar business relationships can benefit small businesses. Your business concept should consider such relationships as you plan your opportunity.

OEMs

Original-equipment manufacturers (OEMs) are established suppliers who offer both things your business needs and benefits from name association. For example, an independent auto-parts store can develop a business relationship with the National Automotive Parts Association and become a reseller of NAPA auto parts.

Most OEM agreements are with manufacturers of automotive, electrical, or computer equipment. One manufacturer supplies branded components for another manufacturer. A widget manufacturer may use Bosch motors in their electric models. Depending on the agreement between the two companies, a widget manufacturer may be able to benefit from the widely known Bosch brand.

Joint-Marketing Agreements

A joint-marketing agreement is usually made between two or more businesses who have relatively equal brand status. They agree to cooperatively market their products or services. Bob's Widgets may team up with Mary's Widget Covers to cross market their complementary products. Or Smith's Widget Services can develop a joint-marketing agreement with either or both of the widget businesses.

Normally, joint-marketing agreements are not made between direct competitors. The businesses usually have similar acceptance in the marketplace for related products or services. As you develop your business plan, consider what joint-marketing agreements you can profitably develop. Your investors will want to know about them.

If you develop a joint-marketing agreement with another business, make sure you use an attorney with experience with the legal aspects of these relationships. Their hourly fees will be high, but it can be well worth the investment, especially if a problem occurs later in the relationship.

Supplier Agreements

Your business may also benefit from signing an agreement with a primary supplier. For example, your widget store may agree to purchase all of its widgets from Acme Widget Wholesalers. In exchange, Acme may agree to give you a higher discount rate, reduced shipping costs, or other benefits. Acme knows you won't be shopping around among its competitors and may reward you for your commitment.

If you do sign an exclusive supplier agreement, make sure that it sufficiently benefits your business. Continue checking with the supplier's competitors to ensure you are getting the lowest pricing or best services from the agreement. Supplier agreements can benefit both parties as long as they continue honoring the terms.

Where can I find VARs for my type of business?
Start with your competitors and their suppliers. Depending on your type of business, you may find that they also produce or distribute unbranded products or services that you can modify and rebrand. Alternately, read industrial and distribution magazines in your field for ads offering VARs.

VARs

A value-added reseller (VAR) is a business that resells another company's products or services as its own. It is a common agreement in the computer industry, especially among software developers who write an application that can be included on a computer system or resold under a different brand. A computer manufacturer may sign an agreement with a business software developer to market a combined product, such as a computerized point-of-sale (POS) system. The POS system could be marketed by the computer company, the software company, or even a third party who develops an agreement independently with the computer and software companies.

Service companies, too, can be VARs. For example, a training service can agree with a major training developer to rebrand and resell their services within a specific territory or industry. If the perceived value of a product or service is increased by a reseller, it is a VAR. Consider how your business venture can benefit from VAR agreements either now or in the future.

Franchises

A franchise is a licensed privilege. If you want to open a McDonald's restaurant and benefit from the name brand and marketing privileges, you must first be licensed by the franchisor. You'll have to pay fees for the privilege, conform to their requirements, and get training at McDonald's Hamburger University.

QUESTION?

Where can I find out more about business franchises available to me?
Two online sources include *www.franchise.com* and *www.franchise .org*. In addition, look to marketplaces similar to yours in other areas. For example, if you're starting a coffeehouse, visit other cities and neighborhoods to look for franchised coffeehouses that aren't in your area yet. Also read trade magazines for franchises and less-expensive business opportunities.

Small businesses can benefit from franchises and business opportunities. Typically, a franchise is more expensive to establish and operate than a business opportunity. However, the name value and training that comes with a franchise can help your business become profitable quickly. If you are establishing a franchised business, the franchisor will assist you with developing a comprehensive business plan.

Additional Resources

Your new or growing business will need more than primary and secondary suppliers. In addition, it will need a variety of resources to help it succeed. For example, a new trucking business will need to join a trade association, hire a consultant, or develop professional contacts within key industries that use trucking services.

For every conceivable business concept, there are dozens and sometimes hundreds of additional resources that can help the business succeed. Your job, as you develop your business plan, is to identify resources that can impress your investors and improve your bottom line. These include professional resources, trade associations, consultants, and other valuable contacts.

Professional Resources

A profession is a professed knowledge or skill in a specific trade. A lawyer, certainly, is a professional, but so are restaurant managers, travel agents, educators, and others who have advanced knowledge that is useful to others. Your Internet retail store, bed-and-breakfast business, or widget manufacturing venture all require professional management and professional advice.

Your business plan must identify the professional resources that are available to its management team. For example, a trademarked information service business needs professional help to develop valuable information, but it also needs help protecting its trademark rights. You may not be able to name all professional resources available to you, but you at least need to identify what professional resources are critical and how you will go about selecting them. You can start right now by brainstorming to determine what professional resources your business will need. For example, a sports bar may need the following professional resources:

- Marketing-survey service
- Sport-licensing service
- On-call cable-television repair service
- Cleaning service

- Noncompeting sports bar (for advice)
- Employee background-checking service

Each of these professional resources can enhance your business by offering you information or advice that helps you understand your customers and your opportunities better. As your business develops, you will identify specific resources, but your business plan will benefit from considering them now.

QUESTION?

How can I find out what trade associations serve my business sector?
Start with your local trade associations, your chamber of commerce. In addition to membership, they can often direct you to national associations that serve specific trades and professions. In addition, you can find listings in magazines and periodicals that serve your industry. Also, find out what trade associations your competitors are members of.

Trade Associations

All businesses are served by at least one trade association. These professional associations are both resources and advocates for their members. Local trade associations include chambers of commerce and businessperson associations. National trade associations are built around the type of business (retail, wholesale, restaurant) as well as the products or services sold (fast food, tax services, auto parts, etc.). There are more than 8,000 national trade associations in the United States and Canada. Following are just a few:

- Air Conditioning Contractors of America
- American Beverage Association
- American Resort Development Association
- Book Industry Study Group, Inc.
- Council on State Taxation
- Fantasy Sports Trade Association

You get the idea. The benefits of membership in an appropriate trade association can be invaluable to your new business. Not only do trade associations watch pending legislation for problems and opportunities, many also conduct extensive surveys of members. Membership can give you rights to learn how others in your field are finding and keeping good employees, building the local marketplace, and promoting their business.

Consultants

An expert is someone who knows more and more about less and less. An expert who shares knowledge for a fee is a consultant. In this diverse world, there are consultants who know more and more about anything under the sun. Want to sell solar panels to people who live in RVs full time? Need to determine the most popular brand of wine in your area's marketplace? Hire an expert consultant!

The problem can be finding and assessing the appropriate consultant. The Internet makes finding a consultant easier, as you use search engines to identify candidates: "wine consultant Houston," for example. Unfortunately, anyone who has imbibed may establish a wine-consulting service.

FACT

You can find an extensive list of business consultants—and thousands of other types of resources—online at the Open Directory Project (*www. dmoz.org*). Start with the primary categories on the main page and work through the listings until you find the resources you need for virtually any type of product or service.

Determining that at least one of the candidates can help you can be more difficult. You will need to develop a list of specific questions that you want answered and interview the consultants with the best credentials for answering your questions. Of course, the consultant doesn't want to work for free, but you can often get a preliminary question answered as a free initial consultation to determine whether the candidate will be useful in answering further questions. Because specialized consultants can be expensive—

$150–$500 or more per hour—make sure your questions are well considered and succinct.

Other Contacts

Your small independent business is not a turnkey franchise. You don't sign a thousand pages of contracts, write a big check, and someone hands you the keys to a moneymaking business. With the help of suppliers and resources (including this book), you're going to have to figure it out yourself.

Your business plan may not include all of the valuable business contacts you've developed to start or grow your business. In fact, you don't want to include everything you know in this document. If a copy falls into the hands of another smart person, you may have an instant competitor. What you know has value; give your investors no more information than you need to entice them to invest in your business.

Other valuable business contacts include newspaper editors, radio-news directors, community leaders, friendly competitors, elected officials, law enforcement, lawyers, accountants, and others who can teach you something about your business, its opportunities, and its pitfalls. Without including specific names, your business plan can note that you have developed resource contacts that will help you start or grow your business.

CHAPTER 16

Income Statement

The goal of your new or growing business is to bring in more money than you pay out. The difference is the profit. It is vital as you plan your business to establish a trustworthy system that tracks and manages income, expenses, and profits. This chapter introduces the first and most important financial document your business will develop—the income statement. You'll see why successful businesses of all sizes and types rely on their income statement to ensure profitability.

Profit and Loss Basics

Profit is the excess of income over expenses. If you buy something at $2 and sell it for $3, your profit is $1. If you sell it for $1.50, your loss is fifty cents. You know that.

Your business is planning to make a profit. However, you also want to know if it is operating at a loss, and why, so you can make adjustments. That's just good business.

For now, you want to ensure that your business is planning to be profitable. You want a document that shows you and your investors where the income is expected, what expenses need to be paid, and how much profit is left over. Both now and in the future, you will rely on the income statement to keep you informed.

Income Statement

An income statement is a financial document that shows how gross income (income before expenses) is converted into net income (income after expenses). Gross income or revenue is sometimes called the top line and net income is the bottom line. Because the statement considers profits and losses, it is also referred to as a profit and loss (P&L) statement. Seemingly to make business more confusing, some entrepreneurs and accountants refer to an income statement as an operating statement or an earnings report. There are slight differences between these reports, but the terms are often used interchangeably. For consistency, use the most accepted: income statement.

Don't know accounting from aardvarks? There are numerous good books on basic business accounting available at larger independent, chain, and college bookstores. In addition, check out AccountingCoach (*www.accountingcoach.com*), which includes hundreds of clear articles explaining accounting terms.

Following are examples of two income statements for start-up businesses to illustrate the components.

The first example is a Projected Income (Profit and Loss) Statement for a product business (from Appendix A):

	Year 1	Year 2	Year 3
Revenue			
Total Sales	426,000	821,000	1,215,000
Gross Revenue	426,000	821,000	1,215,000
Cost of Goods Sold			
Cost of Goods Sold	85,200	164,200	243,000
Total Cost of Goods Sold	85,200	164,200	243,000
Gross Margin	340,800	656,800	972,000
% of Net Revenue	80%	80%	80%
Sales, General, & Admin Expenses			
Sales & Marketing	50,000	50,000	50,000
Total Sales & Marketing	50,000	50,000	50,000
% of Net Sales	12%	12%	12%
Other SG&A Expenses			
Administration	225,180	407,585	639,760
Total Other Expenses	225,180	407,585	639,760
Total SG&A Expenses	275,180	457,585	689,760
% of Net Revenue	64.60%	55.74%	56.77%
Depreciation	33,000	66,000	99,000
Interest	5,000	10,000	15,000
Total Depreciation & Interest	38,000	76,000	114,000
Net Profit (Loss)	27,620	123,215	168,240
% of Net Revenue	6.5%	15.0%	13.8%

This income statement estimates gross revenue as the total of sales. If a business derives income from nonsales sources, it will be listed here as well. Some businesses opt to break down sales more, showing where sales are expected by department or category of product or service.

The cost of goods sold is the cost of buying any raw materials and producing finished goods. In retailing, the cost of goods sold (COGS) is the purchase price of wholesale products, such as store inventory. Depending on the business, the cost of preparing inventory for resale may or may not be included in COGS. Instead, some businesses refer to it as cost of sales (COS). COGS will be covered in more detail later in this chapter.

The gross margin, as defined in Chapter 12, is the relationship of the profit to the cost. A widget with a wholesale cost of $6 is sold at a retail price of $10. Calculate: (10-6) / 10 = 40%, the gross margin. Your income statement can document the gross margin for your business. Gross margin is discussed later in this chapter.

The operating expenses are then listed. In the example, the business sells a product and the expenses include sales, general, and administrative expenses. Your business plan may include more or less detail, depending on size. Operating expenses are described in more detail below.

Finally, the income statement shows how much the business sets aside for depreciation and to pay interest on debts. Depreciation is the reduction in value of an asset due to age.

The bottom line on the example income statement shows projected net profits for the first three years of operation. They are projected because they haven't happened yet. Once the business is established, income statements will include actual net profits.

FACT

A projected income statement—and most other financial statements in your business plan—are also referred to as *pro forma*. Pro forma is Latin for "as a matter of form." Pro forma can also refer to reports that exclude unusual and nonrecurring expenses, such as transactions that adjust the purchase or sale of business property, but this definition is rarely used in small business.

Variation

The second example is for Acme Time Management Consultants. As you can see, it is a service business and doesn't calculate costs of goods sold because goods (products) aren't sold; advice, measured in time, is sold. In addition, the business planners decided to develop monthly projections for the first year. Note that both income and expenses are well detailed, which makes tracking the source of losses easier.

PROJECTED ANNUAL INCOME (PROFIT AND LOSS) STATEMENT FOR A SERVICE BUSINESS (FROM APPENDIX B):

Item	Jan	Feb	Mar	Apr	May	Jun	Jul	Aug	Sept	Oct	Nov	Dec	Total
Income													
Residential		1,200	1,260	1,323	1,389	1,459	1,532	3,216	3,377	3,546	3,723	3,909	25,934
Business/Individual		1,500	1,620	1,750	1,890	2,041	2,204	4,761	5,141	5,553	5,997	6,477	38,933
Business/Group		300	321	343	367	393	421	546	584	625	668	715	5,284
Total Income		3,000	3,201	3,416	3,646	3,893	4,156	8,523	9,102	9,723	10,389	11,101	70,150
Expenses													
Prof. Organizer Commissions								2,386	2,549	2,723	2,909	3,108	13,675
Recruiter	2,083	2,083	2,083	2,083	2,083	2,083	2,083	2,083	2,083	2,083	2,083	2,083	25,000
Taxes & Benefits	417	417	417	417	417	417	417	417	417	417	417	417	5,000
Mileage		319	340	363	386	412	439	468	500	533	569	607	4,937
Utilities	120	120	120	120	120	120	120	120	120	120	120	120	1,440
Advertising	1,100	1,100	1,100	1,100	1,100	1,100	1,100	1,100	1,100	1,100	1,100	1,100	13,200
Memberships	1,915												1,915
Office Supplies	30	30	30	30	30	30	30	30	30	30	30	30	360
Insurance	100	100	100	100	100	100	100	100	100	100	100	100	1,200
Maintenance	75	75	75	75	75	75	75	75	75	75	75	75	900
Legal and Accounting	100	100	100	100	100	100	100	100	100	100	100	100	1,200
Licenses	150								150				300
Telephone Service	200	200	200	200	200	200	200	200	200	200	200	200	2,400
Office Equipment Lease	175	175	175	175	175	175	175	175	175	175	175	175	2,100
Miscellaneous	30	30	30	30	30	30	30	30	30	30	30	30	360
Office Lease	1,000	1,000	1,000	1,000	1,000	1,000	1,000	1,000	1,000	1,000	1,000	1,000	12,000
Bank Loan/Line of Credit	136	136	136	136	136	136	136	136	136	136	136	136	1,636
Total Operating Expenses	7,631	5,886	5,907	5,929	5,953	5,978	6,006	8,421	8,765	8,822	9,044	9,282	87,623
Net Profit (Loss) Pretax	-7,631	-2,886	-2,706	-2,513	-2,307	-2,086	-1,849	101	338	901	1,345	1,820	-17,473

Cost of Goods Sold

What did it cost your business to sell your product or service? This is a critical question to determining profits. Also critical is that your business standardizes how the answer is measured. Does it include commissions? Overhead? Other expenses? Your accountant will help you establish an optimum income statement for your business plan and operations. However, you, as owner and de facto manager, need to know how COGS is calculated and profits are derived.

COGS

For most small businesses, the cost of goods sold (COGS) includes direct costs attributable to the production of the product(s) by the company. It usually includes the cost of raw materials and direct labor. A widget manufacturer, for example, will include the metals and plastics that are manufactured into widgets, the (depreciated) equipment used, and the labor costs of those who make the widgets. The manufacturer would not include the costs to ship widgets to dealers nor the salaries of the sales staff.

Retail COGS

Retail businesses don't always produce something. They may purchase products for resale. There may be direct labor costs in preparing those products, but they are typically minimal compared to the cost of the wholesale products. Restaurants and other more labor-intensive businesses will have higher costs to prepare products (foods) for sale.

Once a business is operating, COGS is often calculated by starting with inventory value at the beginning of the period, adding the total of purchases, then deducting the ending inventory level. If a business starts with $300,000 in beginning inventory, makes purchases of $100,000, and ends the period with $150,000 available for sale, the COGS for the period is $250,000 (300K + 100K-150K = 250K). Direct labor must be included in calculating COGS.

Note that you should deduct purchase returns and allowances from your COGS. If it was returned to your supplier, it obviously wasn't available to you for manufacturing or resale. Also, remember that not all businesses calculate COGS; service businesses don't technically have goods, for example.

FACT

If your business is a sole proprietorship, you will probably file your business' federal income tax using Schedule C. Part III on the back side is used to calculate your business' cost of goods sold. Identify whether the valuation is cost, market, or other basis. Ask your accountant for guidance.

One more point: A business doesn't include the cost of shipping product to customers in its COGS, but the customer does include shipping in its COGS. A widget store, for example, adds shipping costs as a direct expense of acquiring widgets from a wholesaler or manufacturer. Why is calculating COGS so important to many businesses? Because Income - COGS = Gross Profit!

Gross Margin

Calculating gross margin is important for developing an accurate income statement for your new or growing business. To better understand the gross margin, following is a more complete description.

Gross Profit

Gross profit is the difference between revenue (sales) and the cost of goods sold (COGS). If Bob's Widgets sells 120 widgets at a wholesale cost of $10 each, then sold them retail for $18 each, the gross profit would be:

Revenue $\qquad$ $12 \times 18 = 2160$
COGS $\qquad$ $120 \times 10 = 1200$
Gross profit $\qquad$ $2160 - 1200 = 960$

Gross Profit Margin

The gross profit as a percentage of revenue is termed the gross profit margin, or the gross margin. The gross margin is calculated like this:

(Revenue - COGS) / Revenue

Using the example on the previous page:

$$\frac{2160 - 1200}{2160}$$

The result is 0.4444 or 44.44 percent. That's the gross (profit) margin.

Why is the gross margin number so important to your business? Because it is used in determining how much to charge a customer for what you sell. That's important. If your business takes on a new product with a COGS of $100 and your gross margin is 44.44 percent, you can quickly calculate that the price you should charge the customer is $144.44. Chapter 12 covered gross margin and markup with further examples.

Operating Expenses

A big chunk of the costs of running your business will go to a broad category called operating expense. They're also called operating expenditures, operational expenses (or expenditures), or OPEX. It's the ongoing cost of running your business. Some examples can help you better understand operating expenses:

- Accounting expenses
- Advertising
- Attorney fees
- Insurance
- License fees
- Office maintenance
- Office supplies
- Property-management fees
- Property taxes
- Salaries
- Travel expenses
- Utilities
- Wages
- Warehouse repairs

In the example of a product business offered earlier in this chapter, operating expenses were grouped under a category called Sales, General, and Administrative Expenses. In the service business example, the operating expenses were much more detailed. How you break them out depends on the size and complexity of your business plan as well as the requirements of your lenders. Details can help lenders better understand your venture; however, some lenders can get lost in the details and miss the focus of the business.

Net Income/Loss

You and your investors all are interested in the bottom line. That's typically the last line of your income statement, the one that includes net profit (or loss) before taxes. In some highly taxed businesses, the net profit should be stated after taxes.

Taxes are the last thing you deduct from profit before calculating what your business really earned. Those taxes can make the difference between profit and loss. Make sure you use all available tax deductions. A professional tax accountant can help you identify opportunities.

Be aware that it's okay for your business plan to show short-term losses. For example, your income statement may indicate that the overhead and costs of goods will exceed revenues for the first few months or even the first year of operation. That may be acceptable to you and your investors if the plan shows offsetting profits in the future. Alternately, some businesses may operate at a seeming loss but still be profitable due to tax incentives. Your accountant can help you understand tax opportunities.

GAAP

With all the variables of business, how can you know that your accounting records accurately reflect both the realities and the opportunities of profit? Is there a standard for accounting?

There is no accounting standard like there is in manufacturing, where everything is precise and measurable. Accounting, instead, uses interpretable rules called generally accepted accounting principles, abbreviated GAAP. The larger and more complex your business the more closely you must adhere to GAAP. At the minimum, you must establish an accounting system that allows you to accurately report your income, expenses, and profit or loss for taxation purposes.

FACT

The Financial Accounting Standards Board (FASB; *www.fasb.org*) is developing standards for the accounting industry. However, they are primarily for large corporate and international accounting. Small businesses will continue to follow GAAP and standards within their own industries.

Only the simplest businesses, operated by trained and experienced businesspeople, can rely on management to also keep the books. Because there is tremendous detail to daily business activities, it's often more efficient to hire a bookkeeper, overseen by an independent accountant, to develop the records that management needs to operate an efficient business.

As your business grows, its accounting records will come under increasing scrutiny by managers and investors. Make sure that the accounting system you use is proven as well as invaluable. The best place to start is with an accurate pro forma income statement in your business plan.

CHAPTER 17

Cash-Flow Forecast

How can you make sure that, at any given point in your business, the money coming in is sufficient to cover the money going out? You can track and forecast the flow of cash in and out of your business. This chapter shows how smart business planners use cash-flow statements to make sure their business is liquid and that lenders know it.

Cash-Flow Basics

Cash is king! This axiom is especially true in business. Each year, thousands of profitable businesses fold because the profits are on paper and not in the cash register. A major supplier needs its cash before a major customer pays its bill. Businesses grow to become revenue rich and cash poor. Your job, as you plan your new or growing business, is to make sure that the cash flows as it should.

FACT

Many software programs available for developing business plans, as suggested in Chapter 2, include an interactive module that walks you through developing a cash-flow statement with specific instructions and examples. In addition, many of the sample business plans on the CD included with this book offer example cash-flow statements that you can follow.

Cash flow is the tracking of actual income and expenses as cash or other liquid assets. In earlier times, cash-flow statements were called statement of change in financial position and flow of funds statement. These titles help describe their purpose as records of where the money is coming from, where it is going, and when. Another way of looking at income and expenses is:

- Income = sources of cash
- Expense = uses of cash

Obviously, you cannot use more cash than you receive from sources. There are many types of cash flow, each depending on the prospective of the calculator. The most common are operational, investment, and financing cash flows. Following is an overview of each.

Operational Cash Flow

The day-to-day operation of your business develops and costs cash. That's the operational cash flow. Your business plan may include an operational cash-flow statement (now) or forecast (future) or both.

The problem with forecasting operational cash flow is that you may not really know exactly when specific bills will be paid by your customers. You can establish credit policies that encourage quick cash, but you may not be able to entice your largest customers to follow them. For example, you may offer a 2 percent discount if the invoice is paid within ten days, but the customer may not take advantage of the discount. Even if the sale terms are net thirty days, you may not get paid in thirty days. The customer, also under cash-flow pressure, may hold off paying the bill for forty-five, sixty, or more days.

Operational cash-flow events include:

- Payments to or for employees
- Payments to suppliers for goods and services
- Receipts from the sale of goods or services
- Tax payments

Operational cash flow events exclude:

- Amortization
- Deferred tax
- Depreciation
- Gains or losses from an asset sale

Your business plan should include an operational cash-flow statement or forecast. It can show investors that you plan to have sufficient cash to pay bills as they come in.

Investment Cash Flow

Once your business is up and running, it will invest in new products and services, maybe a new or expanded location, and other ventures. You and your investors will want to know if the cash flow from such opportunities will be profitable investments. Investment cash flow shows cash received or expended through capital expenditures, investments, or acquisitions.

The source of cash for future investments may be current profits. Or the source may be outside investors. Your business plan may need to include investment cash-flow futures for your business. Money that goes to repay investors also needs to be reported as part of investment cash flow.

Investment cash-flow events include:

- Expenditures for the purchase of land, buildings, and equipment
- Loans to other firms
- Receipts from sale of land, buildings, and equipment
- Returns from investment in other firms

FACT

Short-term cash flow doesn't always have to be positive. In some periods, expenses will exceed income. However, you must be able to cover the costs of running your business every month. If income is not the source, then a line of credit or other resource must pay them. Your business plan should indicate how negative cash-flow periods will be managed.

Financing Cash Flow

Your business may also decide to invest its cash in other businesses or purchases at a specific rate of interest. Financing cash-flow reports cash received or expended as a result of financial activities such as interests and dividends. If you pay out interest, it is reported as financing cash flow.

Financing cash-flow events include:

- Dividend payments
- Proceeds from issuing debt instruments
- Repayment of debt principal

Combining the Flows

Your business plan, and later, your business reports, may include all three types of cash flows, reported on the cash-flow statement. Depending on the size and complexity of your business, the various cash-flow calculations may not need to be extensive. However, your investors will want to know that you plan to have the money to pay all your bills, including profits to them or interest on them.

There's one more point to make: Cash-flow statements are about cash. They should not include noncash transactions like depreciation and write-offs where no cash actually flows. It's a statement of liquidity.

Cash-Flow Statement

Following is an example of an annual cash-flow statement for Widgee World Retailers, Inc. (Appendix A), covering its first three years.

	YEAR 1	YEAR 2	YEAR 3
Cash Flow from Operating Activities			
Net Income/(Loss)	27,620	123,215	168,240
Adjustments to Reconcile Net Inc/(Loss)	50,449	226,312	376,855
Add Back Depreciation Expense	33,000	66,000	99,000
(Decrease) Increase in Accounts Payable	3,753	6,793	10,663
(Decrease) Increase Other Current Liabilities	833	833	833
(Increase) Decrease Accounts Receivable	(5,175)	(8,377)	(16,001)
(Increase) Decrease in Inventories	(10,282)	(19,540)	(38,078)
(Increase) Decrease in Other Current Assets	(50,000)	(50,000)	(50,000)
Cash Provided By Operating Activities	50,199	345,237	551,513
Cash Flow from Investing Activities			
Purchase of Fixed Assets and Start Up Expenses	(165,000)	(330,000)	(495,000)
Cash Provided By Investing Activities	(165,000)	(330,000)	(495,000)
Cash Flow from Financing Activities			
(Decrease) Increase Long Term Payable	0	0	0
(Decrease) IncreaseEquity Investment	305,000	0	0
Cash Provided By Financing Activities	305,000	0	0
Net Change in cash Decrease/Increase	190,199	15,237	56,513
Cash at the Beginning of the Period	0	190,199	205,436
Cash at the End of the Period	190,199	205,436	261,949

Note that the statement has three sections:

- Cash flow from operating activities
- Cash flow from investing activities
- Cash flow from financing activities

At the bottom, it reports cash at the beginning and end of the period. Year-ending cash becomes year-beginning cash, called carryover.

Looking more closely, the operating section reports the net income (in this case, projected or estimated) that increases cash followed by the expenses and other decreases to cash. It also includes the cash provided by the equity investment of one or more investors.

As you can see, a cash-flow statement can be an invaluable tool in making sure the business is solvent for the periods planned. Of course, the numbers are estimates, but your business plan should support the claims of its cash-flow statements.

An alternate cash-flow statement example can be seen on page 274 in Appendix B for Acme Time Management Consultants, Inc., a services business. The example is a projection for the first year of operation, by month.

The example takes a simpler look at cash flow, offering an opening balance for each month, adding sources of funds, and deducting uses of funds to come up with net cash-flow figures. The result is deducted from the opening balance to become the ending cash balance. Those numbers will start the new year as the opening balance.

Which form should your cash-flow statement take? Whichever fits your reporting needs and those of your investors. A short and simple business plan can document cash flow with a basic spreadsheet. A more complex business with partners or other investors may require a detailed cash-flow statement to attract needed funds.

If your business has an excess of accounts-receivable (AR) money due to it, but little cash, do what major businesses do: factor. Factoring is accounts-receivable financing. It is selling promises to pay tomorrow for cash today. Of course, factoring businesses expect a discount, just in case some of the ARs don't pay. Ask your banker or accountant about factoring.

Statement Functions

Why project cash flow? If your business has more sales than expenses as well as a line of credit to tide it over, why do you need to go to the trouble of tracking and estimating the flow of cash?

Actually, there are numerous reasons to forecast cash flow. The cash-flow statement is intended to:

- Measure the business' liquidity and solvency
- Report on assets, liabilities, and equity toward making changes
- Offer comparative information on the operating performance of various departments or groups
- Identify the forecasted receipt of income and payment of expenditures for the business

Cash-flow documents are also important to companies that don't operate on a cash basis. Some businesses use the accrual method of accounting, reporting income and expenses when they are earned or incurred rather than when they are received or paid. Accrual businesses still have to know they will have the needed cash to make payroll.

CHAPTER 18

Balance Sheet

Starting and running a successful business requires balance. In addition to time, skill, and other intangible assets, you must manage the tangible assets your business owns. It must also balance the liabilities, or what your business owes. This chapter presents one of the most important financial documents your business needs: the balance sheet.

Balance Sheet Basics

In the world of finance, a balance sheet is a summary of assets, liabilities, and equity. If you've applied for a personal loan, the application included a simplified balance-sheet structure:

- What do you own (assets)?
- What do you owe (liabilities)?
- What is your net worth (assets minus liabilities)?

Your business will have a more developed balance sheet than you do personally. It will include more detail and require more verification. Your business' investors want to know exactly what they are getting into, and they'll want assurance that you know, too.

A balance sheet is also called a statement of financial position. It is a snapshot of your business on a specific date. It may be the first day of operation, the beginning of the third year, or on the date that you sell your business. It's called a balance sheet because the financial components on one side (assets) must equal the financial components on the other (liabilities and equity). Equity is also known as capital, net worth, ownership equity, and other terms. The term "balance sheet" is based on double-entry recordkeeping that always makes two entries for every transaction or event. The purchase of a building (asset) is offset by a reduction in cash and credit (liabilities). The difference is your business' equity in the building.

Simple Balance Sheet

Your small independent business will probably have a simple balance sheet. The balance sheet of large multinational companies can go on for pages. In addition, large businesses often prepare separate balance sheets for individual divisions or locations. A balance sheet for a small business may look like this (from Appendix B—Acme Time Management Consultants, Inc.):

Item	End of Yr. 1	End of Yr. 2	End of Yr. 3
Assets			
Cash	$6,199	$37,274	$123,314
Fixtures and Equipment	$2,000	$2,000	$2,000
Prepaid Expenses	$2,500	$2,500	$2,500
Total Assets	$10,699	$41,774	$127,814
Liabilities			
Initial Funding Loan	$16,672	$8,344	$0
Equity			
Common Stock	$15,000	$15,000	$15,000
Retained Earnings	-$20,973	$18,430	$112,814
Total Equities	$10,699	$41,774	$127,814

Note that the total assets equal the total liabilities and total equities, so the balance sheet is in balance. In fact, the equity is calculated by deducting the liabilities from the assets. Stated another way:

$$Equity = Assets - Liabilities$$

At any time, you should have an accurate balance sheet of your personal assets and liabilities. In addition to helping you manage your money, it is also useful when asking for a loan. The better your personal balance sheet looks, the greater chance you will get the loan.

Corporate Balance Sheet

A balance sheet for a corporation or any larger business is more complex. It may break down assets and liabilities into current or short term (less than a year) and long term (more than a year). It may also include deferred assets and liabilities that aren't available or due yet. The equity account, too, may be more complex to show shareholder earnings, retained earnings (kept in the business and not distributed), and other important financial data.

Following is a balance sheet example for Widgee World Retailers, Inc. (Appendix A):

	YEAR 1	YEAR 2	YEAR 3
ASSETS			
Current Assets			
Cash and Cash Equivalents	190,199	205,436	261,949
Accounts Receivable, net	5,175	8,377	16,001
Inventories	10,282	19,540	38,078
Other Current Assets	50,000	50,000	50,000
Total Current Assets	255,656	283,362	366,028
Intangible Assets	0	0	0
Less Amortization	0	0	0
Net Intangible Assets	0	0	0
Fixed Assets			
Property & Equipment	165,000	330,000	495,000
Less Accumulated Depreciation	(33,000)	(66,000)	(99,000)
Net Fixed Assets	132,000	264,000	396,000
TOTAL ASSETS	387,656	547,362	762,028
LIABILITIES & SHARHOLDER EQUITY			
LIABILITIES			
CURRENT LIABILITIES			
Accounts Payable	45,036	81,517	127,952
Accrued Liabilities	10,000	10,000	10,000
Other Current Liabilities	0	0	0
Total Current Liabilities	55,036	91,517	137,952
Line of Credit	0	0	0
Long Term Debt	0	0	0
Long Term Liabilities	0	0	0
TOTAL LIABILITIES	55,036	91,517	137,952
SHAREHOLDER EQUITY			
Equity	305,000	305,000	305,000
Paid In Capital	0	0	0
Distributions	0	0	0
Current Earnings/(Loss)	27,620	123,215	168,240
Retained Earnings	0	27,620	150,835
TOTAL SHAREHOLDER EQUITY	332,620	455,835	624,076
TOTAL LIABILITIES & SHAREHOLDER EQUITY	387,656	547,352	762,028

Your accountant will help you determine the level of detail needed for your balance sheet. If you have some knowledge of accounting, you can probably set up one sufficient for your business plan. The business-plan software programs available will walk you through the process of developing a balance sheet and explain terms in further detail.

Notations

Simple balance sheets are self-explanatory. The more complex the business the more notations may be required as footnotes on the balance sheet. Notations may include explanations of specific entries or details about them. If there is a line of credit, for example, the balance sheet may include a notation regarding its size and with whom it is established. Terms may also be included.

The point of balance-sheet notations is to answer important questions that may arise in the business-plan reader's mind as she reviews it. You don't want to put the process on hold while a reader makes calls or writes letters to get a question answered. A simple notation may clarify the question and allow the due diligence (investigative) process to continue.

Ratios

Some investors are looking for specific ratios as they peruse your business plan. They may only invest in businesses that have a 2:1 ratio of assets to liabilities, for example. If you know what these ratios are, you can include them in your plan.

Common business ratios include liquidity, debt, profitability, and market ratios. They are useful in comparing finances between industries, companies, time periods, and other business components. Chapter 19 includes more information on developing and using financial ratios in your business.

Break-Even and
Ratio Analyses

To effectively report on the financial components of your new or growing business, the business plan should include analyses of the break-even point and various financial ratios. In addition, your ongoing financial reports should use these reports to help you track how your business is doing and, as important, what is contributing to its condition.

19

Break-Even Analysis

To make a profit, a business must first break even. What does that mean?

Break even is the point where total costs are equal to total income. If your widget business buys 1,000 widgets for $5 and plans to sell them for $12.50, it must sell 400 of them to break even; the 401st widget sold becomes profit. Of course, there are other expenses to selling a widget, and all must be included in figuring a true break-even point.

FACT

A break-even analysis is also known as a cost-volume-profit analysis, a more descriptive term. The calculation can assist you in predicting the effect of changes in costs and sales levels on the profitability of your business or a product or service line within your business.

The basic formula for determining break-even points on business and products or services is:

$BE = FE + VE$

$BE = Break\ even$
$FE = Fixed\ expenses\ or\ fixed\ costs$
$VE = Variable\ expenses\ or\ variable\ costs$

To know the true break-even point, you must know the fixed and variable costs. Following is a closer look at these important components of business analysis.

Fixed Expense

A fixed expense is one that doesn't change as sales increase. Rent and overhead are typically considered fixed costs. So are executive salaries, interest payments, insurance expense, payroll taxes, and depreciation. These expenses must be paid whether you sell no products or a million of them.

Confused by accounting? It's the language of business. Consider taking a college-level course in basic accounting or studying a book on business accounting to better understand the terms that will become an important language of communication with investors and other financial people in your future.

As you calculate the fixed expenses of your business or a product or service, remember to make it as accurate as possible. If part of an executive's salary is commission based on sales income, only include the portion that is a fixed expense and doesn't change as sales increase.

Variable Expense

A variable expense is one that changes as sales increase. Inventory is considered a variable cost. Wages of workers who produce or prepare the products or services are considered variable expenses. Make sure you differentiate them when you calculate income and expenses.

QUESTION?

What if there are too many variables for me to calculate a reliable break-even point?
You can calculate different BE points, such as worst case, best case, and most probable. It will take a little more calculating, but it will give you—and investors—a broader understanding of the break-even element of pricing. Make sure that your summary includes how you arrived at each calculation so that you and other readers will better understand their value.

Your business play may have a break-even analysis for a primary line of products or services or it may have one on the entire business. For example, a consulting service must sell X hours of services each day or month to pay the costs of running the business.

Using Gross Margin

In calculating a break-even point for products or services, you may not have a viable estimate of variable expenses or costs. What can you do? You can use gross margin as defined in Chapter 12. Gross margin is the relationship of the profit to the cost. A widget with a wholesale cost of $6 is sold at a retail price of $10. Calculate: (10 - 6) / 10 = 40%, the gross margin.

Gross margin can be used in calculating the break-even point of a product or service like this:

$BE = FE / GM$
$BE = Break\ even$
$FE = Fixed\ expenses\ or\ fixed\ costs$
$GM = Gross\ margin\ expressed\ as\ a\ percentage\ of\ sales$

Here's an example. Bob's Widgets calculates that fixed costs for a new line of widgets is $5,000.00 and the gross margin is 20 percent. Plug these numbers into the formula:

$5,000 / 0.20 = 25,000$

The break-even point for this new widget line is $25,000.

Using Profit Goals

You can also add in a profit-margin goal when calculating profits. Your business plan may establish that the line must contribute a specific amount to profits, such as $10,000. The profit goal is added to fixed expenses:

$(5,000 + 10,000) / 0.20 = 75,000$

The calculation reports that to cover fixed costs and meet the profit goal with a 20 percent gross margin, the business must sell $75,000 in products or services. From this figure, your business plan can establish monthly sales goals, such as $6,250 a month (75,000 / 12).

Business Ratios

The language of business is math. Mathematics are used to measure income, expenses, profits (and losses), taxes, and every other aspect of conducting business. So it is no surprise that ratios are also important.

A ratio is the relationship of two or more measurable things. Ratios help you compare. Imagine that your business ratio of sales to profits is 10:1 (ten to one). Every $10 in sales earns $1 of profit, on average. You now want to know how that ratio compares to the sales-to-profit ratio for similar businesses. Going deeper, you may want to compare the COGS ratio or the sales-expense ratio for your business to others.

As important, investors and other financial people look to ratios to diagnose your business. They may decide to only invest in businesses with a specific earnings ratio or asset ratio. So it's important that your business, and your business plan, understand how ratios work. Following is a summary of common types of business ratios: liquidity, activity, debt, and profitability ratios.

FACT

Liquidity is one of the most important financial ratios for your business. It helps you answer the question: Does my business have enough immediate assets to pay immediate liabilities in an emergency? The answer can save—or lose—your business.

Liquidity Ratios

Liquidity, in business, is a measurement of how easy it is to convert your assets into cash. Land and buildings have low liquidity. Cash has the highest liquidity. Liquidity ratios measure the availability of cash to make purchases or pay off debt. Following is a short list of some of the more popular liquidity ratios in business:

- Current ratio = current assets / current liabilities
- Quick or acid-test ratio = (current assets - inventories) / current liabilities

- Receivables turnover ratio = net credit sales / average net receivables
- Inventory turnover ratio = cost of goods sold / average inventory

These and other ratios are selected to make tracking the business easier. By establishing an optimum ratio as a goal and adjusting the business to meet that goal, an owner or investor can more easily manage the many aspects of business success.

Activity Ratios

Activity ratios are often used for larger businesses, especially ones that rely on supplier and customer credit. For example, the average collection-period ratio can guide management in determining whether collections are getting behind. The formula is:

accounts receivable / (annual credit sales / 360 days)

A similar ratio can be set up for average payment period. Another useful activity ratio is the inventory-turnover ratio:

cost of goods sold / average inventory

The result can guide management in ensuring inventory is resold and replaced (turned over) frequently enough to be profitable.

Debt Ratios

Nearly all businesses borrow money or have other forms of debt. Investors and bankers are often interested in what the level of debt to assets is for the business. Debt ratios measure the business' ability to repay long-term debt. A couple of popular debt ratios are:

- Debt ratio = total liabilities / total assets
- Debt-to-equity ratio = (long-term debt + leases) / owner's equity

There are many other debt ratios useful in business. Your accountant and banker can suggest the best ones for your business.

Profitability Ratios

Profitability ratios are useful for ensuring that assets and expenses are well managed. Gross margin, discussed earlier in this chapter, is a profitability ratio. Other useful ones include:

- Net profit margin = net profits after taxes / sales revenue
- Return on equity = net profit / equity
- Return on investment = net income / total assets

Profitability is the lifeblood of business. Profitability ratios can help you quickly take its pulse.

Other Business Ratios

You can make a ratio out of any two numbers in your business. You can use a ratio of the people who visit your store in comparison to those who buy. You can establish a ratio of newspaper to radio-advertising dollars. The question is: Is it useful in measuring and managing your business? If it is, use it.

Find a noncompetitive business friend with whom you can exchange financial ratio information in confidence. The business friend may be in a similar business in another market or a noncompeting business in your marketplace. Comparing what you're learning about business can make your both better entrepreneurs, and your businesses more profitable.

You will find invaluable ratios for your type of business.

For example, you can develop a:

- Sales-per-customer ratio
- Units-sold-per-customer ratio
- Customer-visits-per-day ratio
- Department-sales ratio
- Credit-or-cash-transaction ratio

There are many opportunities for developing useful ratios to help you manage your new or growing business. What are the most critical measurements of success and profitability for your business? Turn them into measurable and trackable ratios.

Present Your
Business Plan

Your business plan is finished! Now what? Who gets it? How can you present it successfully? How do you get the money you need? How do you actually start or grow your small business? These are all good questions that are answered in this final chapter.

20

Choosing Candidates

Chapter 1, the first step in your business-plan process, discussed readership. Who will read your business plan? Now that you've developed a comprehensive plan, it's time to focus on the specific candidates who will assist you in funding and managing your business.

Depending on whether you're starting a new business from scratch or buying an existing business, candidates for reading your business plan include owners, lenders, investors, and suppliers. Each candidate has a unique prospective. An owner of an existing business, for example, may want to see how you plan to grow the business. A lender wants to make sure that you have sufficient experience to successfully manage the business. What they all have in common is that they want to know how they are going to be paid. They want to minimize risk and increase rewards, just like you do.

QUESTION?

When should I present my business plan to relatives who may invest?
At the same time that you present it to all potential investors. Friends and relatives are important in your life, but business is business. Treating some investors differently than others can make managing your venture more problematic. Help friends and relatives understand the business aspect of your relationship.

You may have a few versions of your business plan, focused to the type of investor as well as the needs of the individual. For example, an SBA lender may want you to follow the SBA business-plan format closely. A primary supplier may not need all the details and only want the executive summary and some supporting financial documents, such as sales forecasts. Until your business is in operation, your customers are those you hope will invest in your business plan.

Choosing Owners

You may be your own best resource for funds. Certainly, you are enamored with the opportunities this business venture offers; however, few businesses have a single owner. Most have a spouse, a partner, a relative who will invest some money or time, a manager who will operate all or a portion of the business, or a corporation that you will participate in. In each case, your business plan must effectively communicate the potential risks and rewards to another person. Even if you're the only reader of the business plan, you need to develop it to answer the questions important to success.

Now that you've developed your business plan, you may have a better idea of how you will finance it—or at least who will participate with you in self-financing and management. Make a list of these individuals and groups. Summarize their needs, concerns, and questions. What will it take to convince them that your business plan will lead to success?

ALERT!

Know your business plan's audience. Do any of its readers have a relationship, business or personal, with any of your competitors? Is there a chance that your business plans will be shown to competitors? How can you control plan distribution? Will aspects be unintentionally leaked in a conversation? Your business plan is a valuable asset. Make sure it is secure from loss.

Once you know who will be reading your business plan and what they want to know, consider how you can best approach them. For some, such as spouses or preliminary partners, this may be an easy task. For potential managers or a new corporation it will be more difficult, as you may have to select from a variety of candidates.

Even if your business plan is written for an existing business' owner, you will need to determine whether that is an individual, a couple, includes relatives, or will be read by members of a partnership or corporation. Know your readers!

Choosing Lenders

Few businesses are fully self-funded. Most small businesses need outside capital to start up and grow. Unfortunately, attracting a lender who will loan you a few or many thousands of dollars is typically a more difficult task than asking a relative or friend to make the investment. Lenders ask tougher questions. They want to know what your investment is in the business, how much is needed, what the return-on-investment (ROI) will be, and, most important, how you plan to pay back the lender. In most cases, the lender has others involved in the transaction who are asking similar questions. Your business plan must answer these and other lending questions.

Lenders are typically commercial banks and other traditional sources of business capital. You may be surprised who makes small business loans. Start with your own bank, savings and loan, credit union, or other financial institution. Some have progressive business centers and offer a simplified loan process, especially to existing customers. Others partner with lenders who work specifically with small businesses. If your business' financial needs are relatively small, you may opt for a signature loan or a home-equity line of credit (HELOC). As with all loans, compare rates and terms before signing anything.

FACT

Many small businesses are financed with a home-equity line of credit. If you use this secured resource, make sure that adjustable interest rates won't damage your business. Interest payments that jump dramatically can cause havoc in a new and barely profitable business. Also make sure that you plan to meet any balloon payments.

The Small Business Administration (*www.sba.gov*) offers a variety of opportunities to submit business plans to business lenders. Chapter 2 offers basic information about the SBA and Small Business Development Centers (SBDCs) that are established in metropolitan areas to assist potential business owners on how to write a business plan and find lenders. The SBA doesn't actually make small business loans; instead, they help match up qualified business people with preferred business lenders. Some programs go a step further and guarantee a portion of the loan. Working with the SBA to get a lender can save you time and interest.

Choosing Investors

You may already have some outside investors in mind for your business opportunity. As you've researched the plan, you may have identified other people, businesses, or corporations who are interested in reading your business plan for potential investment.

Lenders are adverse to risk. They will loan you money only if they're relatively certain that they will get it all back. Investors supply money to the business and accept some of the risk of its operation. The investor may get a very high rate of return or may lose the entire investment. Investors accept more potential risk and more potential reward. Investors will read your business plan to determine the risk level and if it is acceptable based on the potential rewards.

QUESTION?

How can I find out more about investors, venture capitalists, and angels?

First, contact your local SBDC for funding opportunities, especially private equity funds. Also contact vFinance, Inc. (*www.vfinance.com*), Funding-Post (*www.fundingpost.com*), or the Network of Business Angels and Investors (*www.nbai.net*). There are numerous reputable directories—and a few unscrupulous ones—available on the Internet. Proceed with caution and do your homework before presenting your business plan to any lender that hasn't earned your trust.

Not all investors accept the same level of risk. Venture capital is private equity capital, usually pooled from diverse investors looking for a greater profit from loaning their funds than they could get at the bank. Venture capitalists (VCs) that will consider higher risk ventures are called angel investors or angels. They typically require partial ownership or management of the business to maintain control on how the money is earned and spent.

Choosing Suppliers

Your new business will rely on suppliers of some type (Chapter 14). If your business is manufacturing, you'll need raw materials. If it is wholesale, you will buy from manufacturers, distributors, or importers. If your business is retail, your products will come from wholesalers, distributors, or others. Even if you're selling a service, you will need an office, equipment, and other components supplied by others. Significant suppliers may be a good source of credit or investment for your business.

Depending on the type and size of your business, you may rely heavily on one or two primary sources. To get your business going, you may need to get extensive credit from these suppliers. Other small businesses save cash by relying on suppliers to rent, lease, or loan them needed fixtures or to send them substantial inventory on credit terms. Suppliers who do so may need at least a peak at your business plan.

To make sure that your business plan answers the questions that important suppliers ask, you first need to identify these suppliers. Then interview each to determine their requirements. In order to offer you credit, do they need to read the executive summary, the income projections, or the entire business plan?

FACT

Your primary suppliers may only need a credit application from you, plus a pro-forma income statement. Don't give them more than they require unless you believe it will help you establish a more profitable working relationship with your suppliers. The wider you distribute your business plan the greater the chance that your competitors will get a copy.

Distributing Your Business Plan

How can you deliver your business plan to potential investors and other resources? Very carefully. You have invested many hours and dollars in developing a business plan that carefully outlines an opportunity that you believe will be profitable to you. Don't give all your hard work away to someone who will use it to become a competitor. Your business plan has significant value. Treat it as such.

Confidentiality

Before you submit a copy of your business plan to any potential investor or supplier, make sure you first get a signed Investor Application and Confidentiality Agreement. The agreement:

- Acknowledges the value of the business plan
- Requires the reader to keep information in it confidential
- Notes that the investor has no obligation to make an investment in the business
- Asks for verifiable financial references
- Requires your counter signature

A signed confidentiality agreement will not protect you against a competitor getting a copy, but it dramatically reduces the chances. It also offers you legal recourse if the document is distributed without your authorization.

ALERT!

You can further protect your business plan from being copied by printing it on paper that cannot easily be photocopied. If you are distributing electronic text files, such as Microsoft Word, you can make a small change to each file distributed so you can easily identify who got which version. You can also require a password to access the business plan. Protect the value of your business plan.

Here is a sample confidentiality agreement:

The undersigned reader acknowledges that the information provided by _____ *in this business plan is confidential; therefore, reader agrees not to disclose it without the express written permission of* _____.

It is acknowledged by reader that information to be furnished in this business plan is in all respect confidential in nature, other than information in the public domain through other means, and that any disclosure or use of same by reader may cause serious harm or damage to _____.

Upon request, this document is to be immediately returned to _____.

_____

Signature

_____

Name (typed or printed)

_____

Date

Formats

What format should you use to distribute your business plan? Whichever is most practical for your reader and offers you sufficient security. A printed copy is often preferred by investors but is the least secure. You can distribute text or word-processor files, though you should lock them with a password for security. Alternately, you can publish them on a website with password protection. Give the potential investor the site address and password.

QUESTION?

How can I protect text files with a password?
There are numerous software programs available that will lock text files and only allow access with a password. Some also log all accesses so that you know who is seeing your files. Take a look at FileShield, LockMyText, and FolderLock. These and other freeware and shareware programs are available through *www.qarchive.org* and other download sites.

As you distribute copies of your business plan, make sure that you keep track of who gets it, what their interest is, and how to contact them. If you are protecting the version with a password or changed word, make sure that you record the information so you can identify the source of any unauthorized copies.

Business Plan Follow-Up

As you distribute copies of your business plan, make sure that you also ask when the reader will make a decision. Should you check back in a few days, a week, a month, or later? If you have a deadline for investment, let the investors know what it is and when you will be contacting them for an answer. Record this information on your calendar and make sure that you follow up.

Contacts

What should you say to business-plan readers when you follow up? That depends on who the reader is, what the reader is looking for and why, and the time frame for a decision. For example, following up with a primary supplier may be as simple as getting a yes or no within thirty days. For major investors or lenders, you may need to contact them when the plan goes to the decision committee, check back weekly to answer any pending questions, and then wait for a call from a representative giving you a response.

Be prepared for turndowns. In fact, your business plan may be turned down by the majority of its readers. If so, remember to ask each one why the investment was not right for them. You can learn from this information and revise your plan accordingly. You can also ask to make needed changes and resubmit the plan.

Changes

In addition, your follow-up should include any notices or changes that potential investors need to know about. For example, if you've found full investment, be courteous to outstanding prospects and let them know that your business plan has been funded. You may be contacting these prospective investors again in the future, so maintain a professional working relationship.

Banking the Money

Your business plan has been funded! Congratulations! Now what?

First, make sure that you clearly understand the terms and conditions of all funding approvals. Not only might the fine print conflict with your understanding of the investment, it may also conflict with what other investors are requiring. You may be giving away rights that you don't intend to share.

Hire an attorney or accountant to review all investment documents, especially those required to get funding from investors or credit from suppliers. You don't want to give away your valuable business because you misinterpreted a clause.

Spending the Money

Monies from investors may come in various forms. If from a supplier, the investment will be in the form of credit. You will be able to order inventory or supplies on account and pay for them according to your agreement. If from a major investor, you may get monies deposited in your business account following a defined schedule, such as $10,000 on document signing, $40,000 within thirty days, $25,000 when the business opens, another $25,000 when it has been open ninety days. Or you may get a lump sum deposited to your business bank account.

FACT

Business banks are different from consumer banks. The bank that has your personal checking account may not be the best for your business account. Survey the local and regional banks in your marketplace for ones that offer the type of services that your new or growing business will need, including small business loans, factoring services, and letters of credit.

Make sure you have a plan for spending the money you receive from investors. Develop a cash-flow document (Chapter 17) that includes how and when investments and credits will arrive and how they will be used to build or grow your business.

Track Your Investments

The bottom line in business is ROI, return on investment. Make sure that what you and others invest in your business pays off. Continually update your financial records and report the results to primary investors, including yourself, so you can make needed adjustments. You may even be able to return unneeded investment dollars because you manage each dollar well.

Planning and funding a business is a big job. Fortunately, you're not the first person to do so. In fact, hundreds of thousands of small businesses will develop a start-up or growth business plan this year and many of them will be successful, if they clearly identify their goals and develop a well-considered plan for reaching those goals. They can succeed in developing a profitable business—and so can you.

Widgee World Retailers, Inc.
Business Plan

CONTENTS

I. EXECUTIVE SUMMARY

A. The Company

Widgee World Retailers, Inc. is a retailer specializing in the sale of widgets and widget accessories. The company was incorporated in the state of New York in 2005. It has been operating a retail widget kiosk in the local shopping mail since that time. The family ownership, highly experienced in the retail industry, consists of Mr. John Doe, CEO; Mrs. Jane Doe, COO; Mr. Joe Doe, CFO; and Ms. Janie Doe, Human Resources Manager.

It has been in an environment of excellent customer service that Widgee World has offered its widgets in a comfortable, relaxed setting. The fast-growing consumer demand for widgets, and now the inclusion of widget accessories, combined with our retail experience will result in a very profitable venture, including positive community relations with the contribution of 2 percent of sales in support of local charities and U.S. military family support programs.

B. The Industry: Widgets and Accessories

Widgee widgets and their accessories rank first among the most highly enjoyed widgets in the world. Overall widget sales have exploded in the U.S. with sales growth exceeding 8 percent nationally in 2008. More importantly, we are now tracking the same level of sales growth in our geographic target market. *Widget Magazine* has declared widget stores the retail-business model of the new millennium.

Widgee World will develop a fresh, new, and exciting retail concept. It is a new, creative approach to an underserved market. Widgets have been common throughout Europe for hundreds of years. Widgets have only recently experienced record growth in the past five years. We believe bringing widgets and their accesso-ries together in a singular storefront setting will be very profitable within a very short period of time.

C. Mission Statement

The mission of Widgee World is to develop a relationship with our customers by providing superior customer service and unique, quality widgets and accessories, resulting in much return business.

D. Goals

Our company goals for creating a unique widget retail concept will be accomplished by living our mission statement on a daily basis. To become the place to go for widgets and accessories we will:

1. Promote a healthy lifestyle by providing low prices and multiple accessory product lines.
2. Focus on an orderly, cost-conscious development of our first storefront, using the experience of this operation to better facilitate future storefront operations.
3. Constantly expand and revise our widget offerings, reflecting the desires and needs expressed by customer feedback.

E. Objectives

Widgee World intends to direct its track record of success from kiosks to fully functional storefront operations that are not subject to the ebbs and flows of cash flow and profit margins impacted by seasonal attendance and diverse, unrelated competitors associated with an amusement park. To that end, the objectives of our company include:

1. Secure capital financing in the amount of $305,000 to fund the start-up of the first storefront operation.

2. Open one store per year in the first three years of operation.

3. Secure gross revenues of $426,000, $821,000, and $1,215,000 in each of the first three years of operations.

4. Maintain a gross margin level of 80%.

5. Secure a net profit of 6.5% before taxes by the end of year one of operations.

USES OF CAPITAL FINANCING	
Category	**Amount**
Equipment & Machinery	$205,150
Initial Inventory	$15,000
Working Capital	$50,000
Other Start-Up Costs	$34,850
Total	$305,000

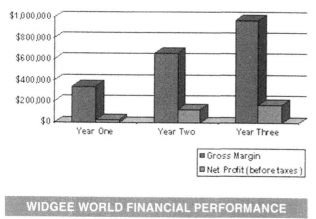

WIDGEE WORLD FINANCIAL PERFORMANCE			
Year	**1**	**2**	**3**
Gross Margin	$340,800	$656,800	$972,000
Net Profit (before taxes)	$27,620	$123,215	$168,240

Financial objectives above are detailed in Section VII (Financial Analysis).

F. Keys to Success

Widgee World indentifies seven keys necessary to fulfill its goals and objectives in this highly competitive industry:

1. Our management's retail experience and ability to develop employees who appreciate the quality of our products, take pride in the company, and excel at providing excellent customer service

2. Instilling employee loyalty to the company and the customers it serves

3. Securing storefronts in locales with high foot traffic and commercial areas in middle- and upper-income neighborhoods

4. Maintaining a quality of product and service equivalent to if not better than the best any competitor can offer

5. Creating a company image that can be emulated in eventual expansion activities

6. Pursuing the consistently successful industry trend of maintaining popular widget and accessory lines that encourage customer loyalty

7. Vigilantly monitoring cash flow, avoiding unnecessary expenses

G. Funding Requirements

To date, owner equity invested is $51,500. These funds were used to start and expand the company's existing kiosk operations at the local shopping mall. We now seek to commence more formal storefront operations, simultaneously phasing out the kiosk. The capital sought for this shift of operations is $305,000, in return for an ownership equity position to be determined at the time of negotiations.

II. COMPANY HISTORY

Founded by Mr. John Doe in 2005, Widgee World initiated its start-up on March 14th, 2005. It was converted from a proprietorship to an S corporation later that year. Operations began with the opening of the kiosk on Memorial Day, 2005 at the local shopping mall, a major retail landmark in this region.

Initially, Widgee World had positioned itself to open a concept store in conjunction with the kiosk, but personal equity investment was insufficient to expand beyond the existing operation. Ownership, as is typical of so many start-ups, deferred personal compensation to insure that retained earnings were invested into the expanded product offerings. In the first full year of operations, gross sales reached $165,000. In 2008, gross sales increased 80 percent to $297,000, well above the industry range of 6 percent. This is due, in great part, to a renegotiated contract whereby mall management's fee was reduced from 40 percent to 35 percent of gross sales.

Another critical factor of this growing success has been our cost of goods sold (COGS). Last year we were able to maintain COGS of only $31,000, or 18.8 percent of gross sales. COGS for this year are expected to be 11.5 percent of gross sales. It will be due to a 50 percent COGS reduction of several sale items.

Despite the success of the kiosk operation, Widgee World has decided it is time to start more traditional storefront operations to increase net profit. The mall kiosk offers limited financial opportunity due to seasonal tourism and periods of reduced hours of operation at the mall in this highly tourist-oriented town.

III. PRODUCT DESCRIPTION

In the world of business, the term "widget" is meant to reflect something universal, but generic. Widgee World gives the widget a more profound meaning of quality in craftsmanship and retail worth resulting from a highly competitive pricing policy.

According to a study conducted by the International Widget Association of America, widget consumers across America want:

- Competitive prices
- Various colors
- Brands they can trust
- Convenience of use
- Creativity in the expanding line of accessories compatible with the widget
- Quality craftsmanship
- Functional packaging

Our main focus is to provide the best of widgets and related accessories that meet the standards and desires noted above.

A. Widgee World Widgets

Widgee World widgets are unique in comparison to the alternative product offering on the market. They offer consumers something different altogether. Unlike many competitors, the seams will not separate if used repetitively for a long period of time at a single sitting, insuring the user the same quality of work remains from the first to last use.

We sell widgets that come in six different sizes, allowing for the selection of an accessory that fits the needs of the individual customer. They are fabricated, unlike so many other items, in the United States, and the unit cost is surprisingly low. Each size is reflected by the Category 1 accessories noted in the following section.

B. Widget Accessories Category 1

Widgee World is proud to offer the Widget Accessories Category 1 for every occasion. Our six signature category 1 accessories are made of some of the finest materials available in the marketplace, and they reflect practically every kind of need in the home or, if you like, the small office.

Item	Description
Small	From the least experienced to the professional do-it-yourselfer
Medium	Designed for medium use with any size of widget
Large	Not for a person new to the use of widgets
Extra Large	For medium-level use and endurance
Commercial— Regular	The lightweight accessory for those familiar with widgets
Commercial— Large	A heavy-duty accessory for the toughest job

C. Widget Accessories Category 2

Widget Accessories Category 2 is designed for the widget user who is seasoned in the use of accessories, but with the need to accomplish more tasks. Each size possesses the heavy-duty construction required for varied uses and long-lasting endurance.

WIDGET ACCESSORIES CATEGORY 2	
Item	Description
Medium	For small tasks
Large	Provides more options and more endurance
Commercial	Provides the most options with even greater endurance

As with the widgets and Category 1 accessories, these items are made of high-quality materials, made in the United States, and with amazingly low unit costs. What sets them apart from Category 1 accessories is that they allow for a more diverse use of the widget and provide more enduring performance.

IV. INDUSTRY ANALYSIS

Widgets have been available for sale in the United States for over two decades, not as long as or as popular as in Europe. However, the industry market research data indicates nothing less than strong sales growth in the United States for many years to come.

A. Industry Trends

The Widget Association of America indicates the strongest national retail chains selling widgets are:

- National Widget Retailer #1, ranked #2 among the fastest-growing retail chains, increased annual widget sales 29.8 percent to $4.8 million in 2007
- National Widget Retailer #2, ranked #9 among the fastest-growing retail chains, increased annual widget sales 27 percent to $1.24 million in 2007

1. Widget Magazine

Widget Magazine, the most respected publication in the widget industry, has provided much significant data associated with the U.S. sales of widget:

- Industry sales are projected to reach a record $511.1 billion in 2009, a 12 percent increase over 2007. It will also mark the 15th consecutive year of growth.
- Widget retailers are expected to increase annual sales to $142.4 billion, a 10.5 percent increase over 2009.
- Widget accessories have become more diverse in response to a more diverse consumer population with more uses for the widget.
- Nearly 75 percent of all Americans have used a widget at one time or another in their lives.

- More than 75 percent of widget retailers indicate their customers will be more value conscious in 2009, increasing the demand to offer competitive pricing.

Annual Change in U.S. Widget Sales

4.7% — 2003
7.4% — 2004
8.5% — 2005
10.2% — 2006

Most indicators suggest a very strong year to come for all sectors of the widget industry, from sales to new outlets and expanded work force. Furthermore, as the do-it-yourself consumer sector grows, so will widget sales.

2. Adjusting to Current and New Events

a. Challenges

The twentieth century's version of the industrial revolution (Information Technology), the Internet, 9/11, and its proceeding two-year recession and rising oil prices have directly impacted the widget industry.

In 2008, nearly half of all U.S. adults reduced the trips to and purchases at retail outlets as a direct result of the increased gasoline prices. In recent months, prices have fluctuated up and down, and it is anticipated this will continue for the foreseeable future. Therefore, retail pricing of widgets and widget accessories must be very competitive with alternative items providing the same uses.

b. Signs of Sustainable Growth

In brief, the U.S. economy is projected to show a potpourri of positive and negative economic performance, the end result being a net gain. The key is to identify trends of opportunity and make conservative decisions in matters that could otherwise adversely affect gross sales, gross margin, and net profit.

B. Who Buys Widgets?

According to *Widget Magazine*:

- Adult males age thirty and above most commonly purchase and use widgets
- Middle- and upper-income households have a widget
- Most widget accessories are sold on the weekend, indicative of the do-it-yourselfer

Therefore, Widgee World has a specific niche group to target for its advertising and promotional strategies.

C. Competitors

We actively researched our geographic market, visiting retail outlets that sell widgets and widget accessories. The research has resulted in the following observations:

- Competitor #1—contains colorful displays of imported widgets and accessories. Imported widgets cost less and retail at discounted rates, not a particularly attractive choice for the consumer seeking a well-made widget
- Competitor #2—a family owned operation that offers little variety and no accessories
- Competitor #3—clearly our most contentious competitor, selling most of what Widgee World offers, but lacking good customer service

- Competitor #4—offers most of what we sell, but lacking in the diversity of widget accessories. The interior is quite appealing to the type of target customer we seek. Customer service is rated above average when compared to all the other competitors

There are other retail outlets in our target market, but the four listed proved to be the most challenging to what Widgee World endeavors to accomplish.

D. Competitors' Pricing

We have conducted extensive investigations into the pricing for competitors' products throughout the metropolitan area. The following table represents the average pricing for all four of the competitors listed.

COMPETITORS' AVERAGE RETAIL PRICE POINT

Widgets

Small $2.50
Medium $3.25
Large $4.00
Extra Large $10
Commercial $31.95

Accessories Category 1

Small $1.60
Medium $2.35
Large $2.50
Extra Large $4
Commercial (Regular) $4.95
Commercial (Large) $11.95

Accessories Category 2

Medium $4.99
Large $5.45
Commercial $21.95

Our pricing is defined as competitive. Some items will be priced slightly higher and others slightly lower.

Ultimately, we are very similar to most competitors in pricing. We look to make customer service and loyalty the most defining distinctions between Widgee World and the competition. And we will work to promote the "made in the USA" recognition.

It is imperative to note these price comparisons serve to establish the range within which each product category is to be found. In most instances, Widgee World will open storefronts where most competitors are not located.

E. Competitive Advantage

Widgee World stores will meet the competition in the following ways:

- Widgee World will be the first and only location to offer all of its inventory as "made in the USA."
- Few of the competitors offer an interior that is appealing to the typical widget customer. Widgee World, specializing in widgets, will place much emphasize on interior layouts and designs that will put the customer at ease, possibly even provoking impulse buying from the passersby.
- Widgee World's complete complement of widgets and widget accessories allows for a much wider range of prices to meet the budget of practically any customer.
- Widgee World will start its storefront operation with the existing brand recognition created out of the familiarity and popularity of its kiosk located in the local mall.

Widgee World knows its product lines exceptionally well, the pressures of pricing, and the need for a constant introduction of new, related product lines as they become available. Equally important is the need to develop a marketing strategy that puts the company name in the customers' minds in the right place at the right time. Finally, there is simply no substitute for excellent customer service, resulting in a high percentage of repeat and referred sales. Widgee World will serve individual customers with common needs.

V. ADVERTISING AND PROMOTIONAL STRATEGIES

Due to its localized target market, Widgee World will implement an advertising and promotional strategy that addresses the greater metropolitan area. Our initial annual budget will be $50,000.

A. *Message Conveyed*

Widgee World recognizes the profitable opportunity in the products we presently offer in the kiosk. Creating a positive brand image for the store and its products are most important. Pricing will not be an issue, as it is competitive, but customer service must be superior.

B. *Product Rollout Strategy*

Widgee World has every intention of implementing advertising and promotional strategies prevalent among the national retail outlets, but at a local level. These strategies are encouraged to accomplish:

- Offsetting the employee compensation and benefits costs expected to represent a significant portion of the total operating overhead
- Gaining access to a growing market of targeted customers who can now be found through less-traditional media
- Maximizing exposure in less-expensive media venues

2008 MARKETING TECHNIQUES: WIDGET OUTLETS

Media Outlet	% Participating
Sponsorship of Community Event	82%
Limited-Time Menu Offering	80%
Direct Mail	79%
Radio	78%
Newspaper	74%
Website	74%
Handouts or Flyers	72%
Sponsor a Sports Team or Event	72%

The table above reflects responses of retail-widget outlets nationwide, surveyed by the National Widget Association. Widgee World has every intention of implementing part or all of these strategies as the budget allows and competitor activity in the geographic locale suggests is successful.

C. *Specific Advertising and Promotional Strategies*

Our target customers tend to be from middle- and upper-class neighborhoods. They also tend to reflect traditional family household environments with more degrees of education. To that end, we will contract an advertising agency to assist in implementing the following strategies:

1. Affiliations and Memberships—We will consider memberships in the New York Widget Association, local chambers of commerce, and the National Widget Association.
2. Sponsorship of Community Events—Primarily through the chambers' activities, we will sponsor events that attract our target market and draw attention to Widgee World.
3. Website—Given the sociodemographic nature of our customers, we know a presence on the Internet will be beneficial.

4. Traditional Media Outlets—We will rely on our contracted ad agency to identify the most opportune traditional media outlets for targeting our customers in our geographic markets, and within budget.

5. Press Releases—All proceeds donated to local charities and events will be promoted through the distribution of press releases to the traditional media outlets and on the Internet.

These activities are commonplace strategies among our successful competitors, with the exception of charitable contributions, websites, and Internet promotions.

VI. OPERATIONS

Our experience operating six kiosks in Stone Mountain Park has provided extensive experience and insight that will improve our likelihood of success, including customer service, ideal employee profiles, product knowledge, competition, and ideal decorum. In addition, we have key individuals who will be the driving force.

A. Key Corporate Management

There are two individuals who will be the driving force in the start-up and operation of Widgee World's transition from mall kiosks to retail outlets.

1. John Doe—John is President and founder. His background includes:

   - Graduate of Central High School, 1996
   - Ownership, management, and operational experience (9 years) in the retail industry
   - Senior Sales Manager for a telecommunications firm; quarterly regional sales awards

- Store Manager for three years at ABA Retail
- Developed growth strategy and retail concept, which include an experienced management team to implement expansion
- Active volunteer in local charitable organizations

2. Joe Doe is Chief Financial Officer and Accountant. His background includes:

   - BBA from Central State University
   - Passed the CPA Exam in 1995
   - Staff Accountant for an international accounting firm, 1990–1995
   - Started a CPA practice in 2005 with 600 percent and 150 percent growth in 2006 and 2007 respectively
   - Volunteer, local hospital relief program

B. Personnel

Each location will be staffed with a store manager and 6–10 employees at any one time. The financial assumptions in Section VII (Financial Analysis) detail the compensation and benefits expenses associated with management and staffing.

C. Staffing—Job Descriptions

Well-trained and friendly employees flourishing in an environment of teamwork will be critical to our success. The job descriptions for each position are as follows:

1. Store Manager—Responsible for the management of operations, which includes:
   - Managing staff and creating a positive work environment
   - Opening and closing of store

- Responsible for cash on hand and safe procedures
- Responsible for store maintenance
- Responsible for creating positive company exposure and PR
- Weekly store inventory and payroll
- Ensure store and merchandise layouts are consistent with optimum traffic flow

2. Assistant Store Manager—Responsible for the management of operations, which includes:
   - Managing staff and creating a positive work environment
   - Opening and closing of store
   - Responsible for training of staff
   - Responsible for cash on hand and safe procedures
   - Responsible for creating positive company exposure and PR
   - Responsible for all salesperson activities in absence of the store manager
   - Ensure that all merchandise is replenished and fronted

3. Salesperson—Responsible for the following:
   - Consistently excellent customer service and follow up
   - Knowledge of use of all merchandise
   - Accountable for cash control and register drawers
   - Stock merchandise shelves, counters, and displays as needed

D. Office Facilities

At the outset, ownership foresees no reason to establish a corporate headquarters outside of a home office setting. Until such time as that need arises, all activities associated with a headquarters will be conducted at the residence of Mr. John Doe.

E. Store Facilities

1. Interiors

All merchandise will be stocked on shelves in predetermined locations. Shelving units will run in a pattern that optimizes exposure of all merchandise to the customer. Product display units will be implemented for end caps at the end of each aisle. The checkout register will be strategically located near the entrance of the store to adequately serve traffic flow and allow sales staff to observe any potential shoplifting. The floor will be a dark hardwood laminate, consistent with the nature of the merchandise sold. The store's office will be situated at the rear, away from the entrance, enhancing security of the store safe and cash on hand.

2. Exteriors

We intend for the exterior to be very attractive, yet consistent with the nature of the surrounding commercial outlets. Exterior décor will be limited by the policies and codes of the real-estate management firm and local building codes. Exterior signage will be positioned so as to stand out from surrounding retail outlets.

3. Hours of Operation

We will maintain hours of operation that are considered ideal to promote our merchandise. As a contingency, hours of operations will be adjusted according to local foot traffic, observations of surrounding retail outlets, and seasonal events, including Thanksgiving, Christmas, and New Year.

WIDGEE WORLD HOURS OF OPERATION	
Day	**Hours**
Monday through Thursday	9 A.M. TO 5 P.M.
Friday	9 A.M. to 7 P.M.
Saturday	8 A.M. TO 7 P.M.
Sunday	10 A.M. to 5 P.M.

Hours of operation on Friday night and the weekends are established due to the sales trends noted by the National Widget Association.

4. Locations

Widgee World projects the opening of three storefront operations in each of the first three years of operation. All will be located in the greater metropolitan area, and in locations near middle- and upper-income communities and high retail foot traffic. We rely on economic census data to help target the three storefront locations.

VII. FINANCIAL ANALYSIS

A. Key Financial Assumptions

The financial projections have been developed from information gathered during the Company's analysis of the industry and key assumptions developed by management using their experience. Provided below are the key assumptions used to develop the Company's financial projections.

The financial projections that follow are based on the operations of one store. It is assumed that the first store will begin operations in January 2009. The second store will begin operations in April 2010. The third store will begin operations in April 2011.

1. Owners' Investment

To date, $50,700 has been invested from the following equity owners:

SOURCE OF FUNDS	
Source	Amount
John Doe	$19,000
Jane Doe	$23,700
Janie Doe	$8,000

The funds were used for fixed-asset start-up expenses in the kiosk.

BREAKDOWN OF USE OF FUNDS— OWNER'S INVESTMENT	
Activity	Amount
Shelving	$37,775
Custom Display Racks	$8,700
Storage Bins	$300
Registers	$750
Miscellaneous	$950
Licensing Permits	$450
Legal fees	$2,500

2. Capital Requirements

The Company is seeking financing in the amount of $305,000. The Company intends to use the proceeds as follows:

BREAKDOWN OF USE OF FUNDS		
Item	Cost	Total Cost
Store Build-out	$80 per s/f @ 1000 s/f	$80,000
Shelving	$20,250	$20,250
Displays	$7,200	$7,200
Interior signage	$8,500	$8,500
Legal fees	$3,500	$3,500
Store set-up	$29,900	$29,900
Insurance	$3,700	$3,700
Additional store equipment	$3,800	$3,800
Additional leasehold improvement expenses	$8,900	$8,900
Professional fees	$7,200	$7,200
POS system	$22,000	$22,000
Exterior signage	$10,200	$10,200
Initial inventory	$15,000	$15,000
Initial payroll	$25,000	$25,000

BREAKDOWN OF USE OF FUNDS—*continued*

Item	Cost	Total Cost
Additional working capital	$25,000	$25,000
Subtotal		$270,150
Other start-up costs		
Marketing—campaign development	$10,000	$10,000
Initial marketing expense	$10,000	$10,000
Brand—identity activities	$12,000	$12,000
Subtotal		$32,000
Licenses and Permits		
Business license	$850	$850
Permits	$2,000	$2,000
Subtotal		$2,850
Grand total		$305,000

WIDGETS

Size	Retail Price (Unit)	Cost
Small	2.95	0.48
Medium	3.95	0.72
Large	4.95	0.96
Extra Large	7.75	1.94
Commercial	25.95	7.79

WIDGET ACCESSORIES CATEGORY 1

Size	Retail Price (Unit)	Cost
Small	1.20	0.09
Medium	1.95	0.15
Large	2.45	0.22
Extra Large	3.05	0.31
Commercial— Regular	5.75	0.59
Commercial— Large	10.95	1.17

WIDGET ACCESSORIES CATEGORY 2

Size	Retail Price (Unit)	Cost
Medium	4.25	0.85
Large	4.95	0.87
Commercial	21.95	4.84

3. Payback Strategy

In return for the financing, the owners are offering an equity position in Widgee World with an option for a buyback. The equity position and buyback amounts will be negotiated at the time of financing.

4. Sales Projections

The storefront will generate a weighted revenue average from the sale of the following products at the retail level:

- Widgets (50%–60%)
- Accessories Category #1 (10%–15%)
- Accessories Category #2 (20%–25%)
- Other (5%–10%)

Note: Figures in parenthesis indicate the percentage of total sales that a particular group of products will account for.

5. Marketing and Advertising

Marketing and advertising will include the following activities:

- Public Relations Firm/Consulting—$35,000
- Printing—$5,000
- In-House Promotions—$10,000

6. Salaries

PERSONNEL COMPENSATION	
Position	**Salary**
John Doe, CEO	$0
Jane Doe, COO	$0
Janie Doe, Human Resources Manager	$0
Store Manager (1)	$40,000
Assistant Store Manager (1)	$8–$10 per hour
Salespersons (4–10)	$7.25–$8 per hour

Note: Payroll taxes and benefits estimated at 20 percent. Management will defer compensation until such time as the cash flow reaches and consistently maintains positive monthly results.

7. Fixed and Variable Administrative Expenses

FIXED AND VARIABLE ADMINISTRATIVE EXPENSES—MONTHLY		
Line Item	**Fixed**	**Variable**
Contributions		2%
Insurance	$333	
Legal and Accounting	$1,000	
Office Supplies	$150	
Lease	$3,333	
Repairs and Maintenance	$250	
Shipping	$125	
Telephone	$415	
Travel/Lodging	$417	
Utilities	$250	

Notes: Fixed and Variable Administrative Expenses:

- Contributions—Included in the contributions are 2 percent of sales in support of charitable organizations and activities.
- Legal and accounting—Estimated at $1,000 per month for year 1. That figure is expected to drop to $750 per month in year 2 and year 3.
- Telephone—Includes landline ($65), cell phone ($250), and broadband connection ($100).
- Travel and lodging—Reflects trade shows and local-event sponsorships.

B. Profit and Loss Statement—Annual

	YEAR 1	YEAR 2	YEAR 3
REVENUE			
Total Sales	426,000	821,000	1,215,000
GROSS REVENUE	426,000	821,000	1,215,000
COST OF GOODS SOLD			
Cost of Goods Sold	85,200	164,200	243,000
Total Cost of Goods Sold	85,200	164,200	243,000
GROSS MARGIN	340,800	656,800	972,000
% of Net Revenue	80%	80%	80%
SALES, GENERAL & ADMIN EXPENSES			
MARKETING			
Sales and Marketing	50,000	50,000	50,000
Total Sales & Marketing	50,000	50,000	50,000
% of Net Sales	12%	6%	4%
OTHER S.G&A EXPENSE			
Administration	225,180	407,585	639,760
Total Other Expenses	225,180	407,585	639,760
TOTAL S,G&A EXPENSES	275,180	457,585	689,760
% of Net Revenue	64.60%	55.74%	56.77%
EBITDA	65,620	199,215	282,240
	15.4%	24.3%	23.2%
Depreciation	33,000	66,000	99,000
Interest	5,000	10,000	15,000
Total Depreciation & Interest	38,000	76,000	114,000
NET PROFIT (LOSS)	27,620	123,215	168,240
	6.5%	15.0%	13.8%

C. Balance Sheet—Annual

	YEAR 1	YEAR 2	YEAR 3
ASSETS			
Current Assets			
Cash and Cash Equivalents	190,199	205,436	261,949
Accounts Receivable, net	5,175	8,377	16,001
Inventories	10,282	19,540	38,078
Other Current Assets	50,000	50,000	50,000
Total Current Assets	255,656	283,352	366,028
Intangible Assets	0	0	0
Less Amortization	0	0	0
Net Intangible Assets	0	0	0
Fixed Assets			
Property & Equipment	165,000	330,000	495,000
Less Accumulated Depreciation	(33,000)	(66,000)	(99,000)
Net Fixed Assets	132,000	264,000	396,000
TOTAL ASSETS	387,656	547,352	762,028
LIABILITIES & SHARHOLDER EQUITY			
LIABILITIES			
CURRENT LIABILITIES			
Accounts Payable	45,036	81,517	127,952
Accrued Liabilities	10,000	10,000	10,000
Other Current Liabilities	0	0	0
Total Current Liabilities	55,036	91,517	137,952
Line of Credit	0	0	0
Long Term Debt	0	0	0
Long Term Liabilities	0	0	0
TOTAL LIABILITIES	55,036	91,517	137,952
SHAREHOLDER EQUITY			
Equity	305,000	305,000	305,000
Paid In Capital	0	0	0
Distributions	0	0	0
Current Earnings/(Loss)	27,620	123,215	168,240
Retained Earnings	0	27,620	150,835
TOTAL SHAREHOLDER EQUITY	332,620	455,835	624,076
TOTAL LIABILITIES & SHAREHOLDER EQUITY	387,656	547,352	762,028

D. Cash-Flow Statement—Annual

	YEAR 1	YEAR 2	YEAR 3
Cash Flow from Operating Activities			
Net Income/(Loss)	27,820	123,215	168,240
Adjustments to Reconcile Net Inc/(Loss)	50,449	226,312	376,855
Add Back Depreciation Expense	33,000	66,000	99,000
(Decrease) Increase in Accounts Payable	3,753	6,793	10,663
(Decrease) Increase Other Current Liabilities	833	833	833
(Increase) Decrease Accounts Receivable	(5,175)	(8,377)	(16,001)
(Increase) Decrease in Inventories	(10,282)	(19,540)	(38,078)
(Increase) Decrease in Other Current Assets	(50,000)	(50,000)	(50,000)
Cash Provided By Operating Activities	**50,199**	**345,237**	**551,513**
Cash Flow from Investing Activities			
Purchase of Fixed Assets and Start Up Expenses	(165,000)	(330,000)	(495,000)
Cash Provided By Investing Activities	**(165,000)**	**(330,000)**	**(495,000)**
Cash Flow from Financing Activities			
(Decrease) Increase Long Term Payable	0	0	0
(Decrease) IncreaseEquity Investment	305,000	0	0
Cash Provided By Financing Activities	**305,000**	**0**	**0**
Net Change in cash Decrease/Increase	190,199	15,237	56,513
Cash at the Beginning of the Period	0	190,199	205,436
Cash at the End of the Period	**190,199**	**205,436**	**261,949**

E. Break-Even Analysis

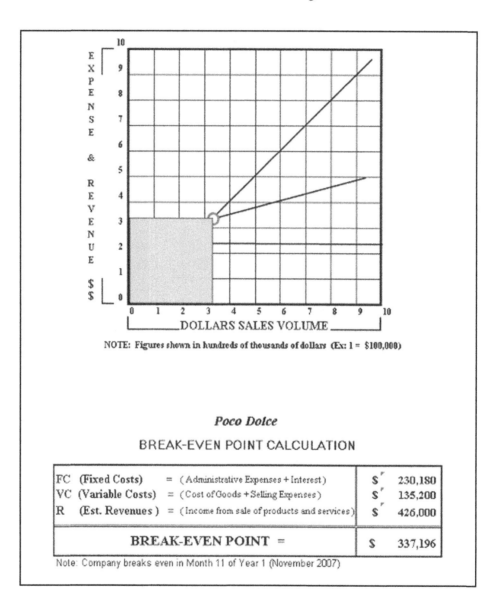

NOTE: Figures shown in hundreds of thousands of dollars (Ex: 1 = $100,000)

Poco Dolce

BREAK-EVEN POINT CALCULATION

FC (Fixed Costs) = (Administrative Expenses + Interest)	$	230,180
VC (Variable Costs) = (Cost of Goods + Selling Expenses)	$	135,200
R (Est. Revenues) = (Income from sale of products and services)	$	426,000
BREAK-EVEN POINT =	$	337,196

Note: Company breaks even in Month 11 of Year 1 (November 2007)

Note: Widgee World breaks even in month 11 of year 1.

F. Profit and Loss Statement—Year 1

	1	2	3	4	5	6	7	8	9	10	11	12	TOTAL
REVENUE													
Total Sales	26,122	27,398	28,706	30,018	31,335	32,656	33,981	36,541	39,106	41,676	46,711	51,752	426,000
Gross Revenue	**26,122**	**27,398**	**28,706**	**30,018**	**31,335**	**32,656**	**33,981**	**36,541**	**39,106**	**41,676**	**46,711**	**51,752**	**426,000**
COST OF GOODS SOLD													
Cost of Goods Sold	5,214	5,480	5,752	6,016	6,283	6,550	6,820	7,323	7,828	8,335	9,307	10,282	85,200
Total Cost of Goods Sold	**5,214**	**5,480**	**5,752**	**6,016**	**6,283**	**6,550**	**6,820**	**7,323**	**7,828**	**8,335**	**9,307**	**10,282**	**85,200**
GROSS MARGIN	**20,908**	**21,909**	**22,954**	**24,002**	**25,052**	**26,105**	**27,161**	**29,218**	**31,278**	**33,341**	**37,403**	**41,470**	**340,800**
% of Net Revenue	80%	80%	80%	80%	80%	80%	80%	80%	80%	80%	80%	80%	80%
SALES, GENERAL & ADMIN EXPENSES													
MARKETING													
Sales and Marketing	50,000	0	0	0	0	0	0	0	0	0	0	0	50,000
Total Sales & Marketing	**50,000**	**0**	**0**	**0**	**0**	**0**	**0**	**0**	**0**	**0**	**0**	**0**	**50,000**
% of Net Sales	191%	0%	0%	0%	0%	0%	0%	0%	0%	0%	0%	0%	12%
OTHER S.G&A EXPENSE													
Administration	18,765	18,765	18,765	18,765	18,765	18,765	18,765	18,765	18,765	18,765	18,765	18,765	225,180
Total Administrative Expenses	**18,765**	**18,765**	**18,765**	**18,765**	**18,765**	**18,765**	**18,765**	**18,765**	**18,765**	**18,765**	**18,765**	**18,765**	**225,180**
TOTAL S,G&A EXPENSES	**68,765**	**18,765**	**18,765**	**18,765**	**18,765**	**18,765**	**18,765**	**18,765**	**18,765**	**18,765**	**18,765**	**18,765**	**275,180**
EBITDA	**-47,857**	**3,144**	**4,189**	**5,237**	**6,287**	**7,340**	**8,396**	**10,453**	**12,513**	**14,576**	**18,638**	**22,705**	**65,620**
Depreciation	2,750	2,750	2,750	2,750	2,750	2,750	2,750	2,750	2,750	2,750	2,750	2,750	33,000
Interest	417	417	417	417	417	417	417	417	417	417	417	417	5,000
Total Depr., Amort, Interest	**3,167**	**3,167**	**3,167**	**3,167**	**3,167**	**3,167**	**3,167**	**3,167**	**3,167**	**3,167**	**3,167**	**3,167**	**38,000**
NET PROFIT (LOSS)	**(51,023)**	**(23)**	**1,022**	**2,070**	**3,121**	**4,174**	**5,229**	**7,286**	**9,346**	**11,409**	**15,472**	**19,538**	**27,620**
% of Net Revenue	-195%	0%	4%	7%	10%	13%	15%	20%	24%	27%	33%	38%	6%

Acme Time Management Consultants, Inc. Business Plan

123 Main Street | Main, NY 12345
123-456-5555 | 123-456-7890
www.AcmeTimeManagement.biz

CONTENTS

I. EXECUTIVE SUMMARY

According to the *Time Management Journal*:

- The average American businessperson loses six weeks a year searching for lost or misplaced articles from messy desks and files.
- That translates into a loss of $3,125 for each $25,000 employee, when an hour a day is spent unproductively. Multiply that toward your hourly rate, or by the number of employees in your office. This unproductive time amounts to a significant financial loss for a business.

Company Overview

Acme Time Management Consultants, Inc. (ATMC), incorporated under the laws of the State of New York, is a start-up company seeking to establish itself in the professional organizing service industry. The mission of ATMC is to help the business professional balance his/her career and family by professionally organizing time, office, and home environments.

ATMC will be strategically located at 123 Main Street in downtown Main, NY. We will be taking our business to the clients, thus our location has easy access to major highways within ATMC's geographic target market. Our hours of operation will be Monday through Saturday from 8:00 A.M. to 9:00 P.M. and Sunday from 11:00 A.M. to 5:00 P.M. eastern standard time.

Services Offered

People always read and hear how to increase their productivity, take control of time, and create an organized environment in the office and home. However, studies have proven that people learn to change their behavior more effectively when they have hands-on experience to physically adapt to a new strategy.

A professional organizer is someone who provides information, products, and or services to help people get organized. This professional should have a good understanding of the tasks to perform, a thorough knowledge of organizing products and services, and, of course, excellent organizational skills.

Professional organizers assist with many tasks of organization in business, corporate, and home environments. The services we will provide include:

- Time and paper management
- Clutter control
- Behavior modification
- Space planning
- Filing
- Training and coaching
- Wardrobe and closet systems
- Event planning
- Financial and records management
- Computer usage/software/systems
- Public speaking and seminars

The Professional Organizer

Many such consultants come from varied backgrounds, including corporate management, counseling, social work, teaching, and many other professions in which organizational skills are essential to success.

The ATMC professional organizer will have the objective to establish a definite relationship with clients, helping them lead a simpler, more organized life. To accomplish this goal, ATMC will lead them through a specific, four-step strategy, ultimately developing a sense of tranquility and greater success in their professional and or personal lives.

1. Assess the current living and working conditions to help the clients define where they are now and where they want to be. This step gives

ATMC an understanding of clients' needs and desires, allows them to witness their level of commitment, and develop a strategy specifically designed to help those clients accomplish their goals.

2. Develop a time-management plan to define priorities, identify time-wasting activities, set realistic goals, schedule and delegate activities. The plan highlights clients' responsibilities and magnifies time allocation.

3. Implement the plan. This is the most critical stage of the partnership with the client. There is no improvement if the client is not willing to change. Our clients will demonstrate their commitment to reaching a higher pursuit of productivity. We will have the opportunity to assist them in attaining the desired goals.

4. Conduct ongoing analysis to determine effectiveness of the current strategy and implement any adjustments necessary to improve time management. We will record progress, reinforce positive activities, highlight and reinforce strengths and opportunities, and make adjustments to address continued weaknesses and threats to the plan.

The process allows clients to experience significant progress. Time will no longer control the client; rather, the client will control time.

Company Founder

Ms. Jane Doe, founder and President of Time Management Organizers, has twelve years of organizational activities working with prominent individuals in the public and private sectors throughout the United States. She has retained levels of authority, in assistance to these individuals, as a corporate secretary, executive assistant to a corporate vice president in the electrical industry, eventually rising to the position of Assistant Vice President for a highly successful local public-relations firm, charged with overseeing account executives for the South Florida region.

Ms. Doe is a Certified Professional Organizer (CPO), a certification issued by the National Association of Professional Organizers (NAPO) and the Board of Certification for Professional Organizers (BCPO).

Funding Requirements

A sum of $40,000 is anticipated, for which ATMC is seeking outside capital investment of $25,000 for the start-up and initial operation of office facilities, leasehold improvements, office equipment, staffing, and operating overhead. The funding allows the company to start, promote, and generate sales in a time frame necessary to generate consistent, positive cash flow and accumulate pretax earnings by the second year of operation.

Sales projections (see Figure 1 below), elaborated in detail later in this plan, are expected to increase in excess of 140 percent and 53 percent in years two and three respectively.

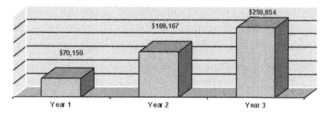

Figure 1: Annual Gross Sales Projections.

Ms. Doe will inject an initial cash investment of $15,000. The remaining $25,000 will be conventionally financed at the rate of 12 percent over a period of thirty-six months. Collateral is offered in a combination of homeowner equity and or the deposit and freezing of cash funds to an interest-bearing account of the commercial lender's choice. Gross-sales projections accommodate and dictate the level of financing over a period of three years.

II. MARKET RESEARCH

Changing Work Conditions

The age of technology and the ever-expanding global economy, for many, have eroded the standard 9-to-5 job. Downsizing, outsourcing, layoffs, the growth of small and home-based businesses are additional factors forcing executives and entrepreneurs to spend upward of ten to sixteen hours daily racing against the clock to meet obligations. They feel overwhelmed, resulting in higher levels of stress that often reduce productivity.

The home environment, especially for a woman wanting to raise children, is not immune to these changes in professional lifestyles. It requires juggling a career and family, especially for the working mother. It is compounded if she is a single working mother. Many of them often feel guilty for not devoting more time to their families.

Industry Trends

Most people are not familiar with time-management consultants and professional organizers and what they do, as the profession is relatively new compared to many traditional consulting professions. In recent years, the time-management and organizing industry has become lucrative, as more people seek simplicity and serenity to manage their lives.

Being organized is not an option; it is a necessity. Professional time-management consultants are now capitalizing on that need. Though ATMC prefers to define itself as a time-management consulting firm, the industry most relevant to this terminology and profession is that of the professional organizer. And it is from

that industry our market research data is culled. Some industry trends and conditions include:

- There are approximately 2,000+ professional organizers specializing in different areas throughout the U.S.
- The cost for a professional organizer is based on the tasks to be performed, skill, experience, and self-worth of the individual organizer, and can range $55–$145 per hour, and in some cases up to $1,000 daily.
- Corporate and residential planning and organizing represent the specific high-growth markets. The majority of these professionals in the United States are obtaining the largest share of this personal-service industry in New York and California.
- The National Association of Personal Organizers (NAPO), founded in 1985, has a roster that grew from 1,000 members in 1999 to nearly 4,000 in 2008.

Over the next few years, the number of professional organizers entering this industry is expected to increase, as more people become aware of the ability to take control of their professional and personal lives with coaching and hands-on assistance of a professional organizer.

In general, professional organizing is a relatively new sector within the consulting industry. However, it is the opinion of ATMC and its consultants that due to continued technology changes, a robust economy, and the pace at which society operates, there is a growing need for organizing professionals. The biggest growth in the organizing industry is taking place in the area of corporate and residential planning and organizing. The number of professional organizers entering this industry is expected to continue to increase, as more people become aware that they can take control of their professional and personal lives with the coaching and hands-on assistance of a professional organizer.

Industry Associations

There are two distinct associations related to the personal-organizing industry:

- **National Association of Professional Organizers (NAPO)**, *www.napo.net*: NAPO is an organization of, by, and for professional organizers. Founded in 1985, NAPO is a not-for-profit organization with a mission to encourage the development of professional organizers; promote recognition of, and advance the profession of the organizing industry. NAPO currently has eleven chapters. Chapter membership is voluntary, while active national membership, $150 annually, is required for chapter membership. Some chapter meetings and programs are available to nonmembers.
- **ARMA International**, *www.arma.org*: ARMA International is a not-for-profit association serving more than 10,000 information-management professionals in the United States, Canada, and over thirty other nations. ARMA International members include records and information managers, MIS and ADP professionals, imaging specialists, archivists, hospital administrators, legal administrators, librarians, and educators.
- **The Professional Organizers Web Ring (POWR)**, *www.organizerswebring.com*: POWR is an online resource for information, products, services, and links to the websites of professional organizers. Our observations suggest POWR may eventually become a major competitor to NAPO as the preferred PO industry association.

POWR allows Internet users to locate many professional organizers in one step without having to do numerous searches or needing to know individual website addresses. POWR is multinational and has no affiliation with NAPO; however, many of its members are NAPO members and are from the USA.

Obviously, NAPO and POWR are directly devoted to promoting the personal organizers' profession. ATMC will maintain membership in each of these two organizations. Membership in ARMA will be determined after further investigation to determine relevance to networking opportunities, substance of services offered, and prestige associated with the agency's image.

ATMC Services Offered

ATMC's full spectrum of organizing services provides short-term and long-term benefits to enhance the quality of personal and professional life. Organizing services are categorized in three major areas:

- **Time Management** is designed to highlight responsibilities and identify where the majority of time is being allocated—specifically focusing on time wasters and the process of elimination; Define Priorities, Develop Action Plans, Short-/Long-Term Goal Setting, Delegate Task and Activities, and Appointment Scheduling.
- **Office Organizing** implements the principles of time management to organize, declutter, simplify, and clean the office in order for our clients to pursue a higher level of productivity and provide more time for business at hand; Office Setup/Maintenance, Computer Consulting, Paper and Records Management, Filing System and Space Planning/Setup.

- **Residential Organizing** implements the same principles at the office to be used at home to help our residential customers turn their house into a home by getting everyone in the family involved in the process; Family Management, Space/Closet Planning, Packing/Relocating/ Moving, and Financial Management.

Personal-organizing services to the business environment will include individual and group offerings. Residential offerings will be limited to the individual.

In the office, our hands-on approach will allow ATMC to take positive steps to help executives and entrepreneurs alleviate the mental and physical pressures of stress at the office. ATMC will specialize in teaching these harried individuals the secrets of how to rearrange schedules, focus on important priorities, create quiet time to avoid interruptions, declutter and streamline paper flow, and organize desktops to make office equipment user friendly.

In the home, no one appreciates the essentials of time management better than the working mother. We specialize in teaching her how to avoid being pushed and pulled in too many directions. The techniques used in office organization will be used in the home environment. The working mother will act as manager and the family will represent the team. The manager (mother) will plan, delegate, motivate, train, and supervise each team (family) member to ensure the household responsibilities are executed fairly amongst the members. This technique eliminates the working mother having to carry the entire load alone and gives her a sense of control to manage her family and career.

ATMC intends to provide services that will help the individual in the office and in the home to overcome the overwhelming demands and stress in each of these environments.

Target Clients

It is likely that our clients have a clear understanding regarding the benefits of being in full control of their time and having an organized environment at the office and or home.

- **Corporate Business Executives:** Our typical business clients are corporate executives and others within their organization, plus small to medium-sized and home-based business owners who need to get organized at the office. These clients are limited in time, skill, and space. ATMC will target the 200 largest public and private companies as listed in our geographic market. Typical clients will include bankers, investment firms, cruise lines, and computer-technology firms.
- **Small and Home-Based Businesses:** Feature articles in recent editions of popular magazines have featured the need to organize home-based businesses. Besides, substantial data from the public and private sectors continuously indicate continued growth of this type of entrepreneur.
- **Residential:** Our typical residential client is the person who influences the decision making for the household: the housewife or mother. She understands the household necessities and knows what it will take to get and keep it in working order. Our typical residential clients will have household earnings in the range of $50,000–$100,000 per year, if not more, and retired persons living in middle- to upper-class residential areas.

Research indicates that these groups of clients are not as sensitive to pricing differences among competitors as they would be to other types of consulting services. In fact, research indicates these people are willing to spend their money on ways that improve their way of life, giving them freedom to live it to the fullest. It is our task to educate the client(s) on the superior quality of our services and the long-term affects it will have in their lives.

Geographic Target Market

Key points in defining the market segment for our business and residential services are our geographical location, the lifestyle of our targeted customers, and economic and demographic census data from the Bureau of the Census. ATMC will occupy a local market base targeting the populous counties in and around Main, NY, the ATMC offices being centrally located in that area. Furthermore, census data indicates continued population growth relatively above the national average for household income.

Pricing

The cost for professional organizing services is based on several key factors including skill, experience, and the self-worth of the individual organizer. The fees charged in this industry are diverse. Hourly rates typically vary between $60 and $150 per hour, with several in the profession earning as much as $1,000 per day.

Though personal organizing is a relatively new industry sector, demand for the service is growing. ATMC will offer introductory, discount pricing for the first six months of operation. Anticipating positive results, the price structure will then be increased to a more customary rate.

PRICING STRUCTURE		
Type	**Discount**	**Customary**
Business—Single	$30	$60
Business—Group	$165	$200
Residential	$25	$50

Group rates are noted in the pricing table to represent an approximate median of the range from $150 to $175 an hour for 3–10 individuals. The exact price charged within the group rate depends on the number of participants and materials used to provide the service. For ease of calculations, the group medians listed in the pricing table are implemented in the financial projections.

Competitive Analysis

Identifying competitors in this market was challenging. Four of the eleven professional organizers have no website but are listed in the yellow pages. The remaining seven higher-profile competitors are:

- **A Personal Organizers** offers a broad range of services, including space planning, clutter control, filing systems, archiving, and photography.
- **B Personal Organizers** targets businesses and individuals, organizing their desks, filing systems, offices, and homes. It specializes in a one-hour, on-site seminar for businesses, with individual follow-up for each employee.
- **C Personal Organizers** targets residential and business organizing, on-site workshops, and a booklet on eliminating clutter.
- **D Personal Organizers** targets organizational-systems analysis, ergonomics, checkbook reconciliation, accounts payable/accounts receivable, scheduling, income tax summary, medical-claim submission, and wardrobe coordination.
- **E Personal Organizers** promotes consulting, training, and hands-on organizing for your office, home, and life. They specialize in home offices, clutter control, closet organizing, and residential space management, paper, and time management for individuals and small business.

- **F Personal Organizers** offers services that include training and consulting, product sales, business computer set-up, merchandising, seminars, and other services.
- **G Personal Organizers** focuses on setting up paper-flow and clutter-control systems, paper and desk management, setting up a finding system, seminars and guest-speaking engagements.

For lack of industry data, having a majority of local competitors on the Internet with websites affords the valuable opportunity to itemize general observations, leading ATMC to develop a strategy of advertising and promotion. Some of the following observations are unqualified, but we are confident they present a relatively accurate image of the competition:

- The overwhelming majority appear directed to home-based businesses.
- Most appear to be one-person operations.
- Most websites are affiliated as subsites, not wholly owned sites, of web-hosting services.
- Several use before-and-after photos to demonstrate their space-organization work.
- POWR and NAPO are the dominant affiliations.
- No pricing is listed at any of the sites.
- Space organization and employee organization are the most prevalent service offerings.
- Those offering seminars primarily address employee organizational issues, but the sites offer no details of seminar content.
- The majority appear to have been in business for one year or less. Only two note personal organizing experience of several years.
- The longer-standing, older companies extend their services to well-known corporate clients.

The website observations support the assumption personal organizing is a new industry sector in our geographic market. None of them boasts certification or educational experience. There is also a strong tendency to draw on alliances with associations, chambers of commerce, and apparently reputable online sources for professional legitimacy.

Sales Projections

The lack of industry data requires establishing in-house sales goals based on projected billable hours. The level of billable hours are balanced by the need to meet obligations of operating overhead, cost of sales, minimally acceptable net profit, and the note payable to finance this venture. The pricing structure is adjusted to meet those needs. Business group pricing at introductory and regular rates are at the middle and top of the customary pricing scale respectively. Business and residential individual rates at introductory levels are discount, and at the middle to high end of the customary pricing scale after the introductory pricing period. Assumptions leading to projected sales are:

- Residential, Business Individual, and Business Group sales are 40 percent, 50 percent, and 10 percent respectively of total sales.
- Monthly increases will be 10 percent, 15 percent, and 15 percent for Residential, Business Individual, and Business Group sales respectively, reflecting a shifting reliance on business-category sales. This is based on the assumption business clients will be more difficult to establish at the outset but will result in more sales from networking references.
- Introductory pricing is in effect only for the first six months of operation.
- There will be no sales generated in the first month of operations.

- ATMC will recruit one new personal organizer every three months after the first six months of operation.
- Personal organizers will be offered a commission rate of 28 percent on total sales.

The three-year sales summary is:

THREE-YEAR SALES SUMMARY

Service	Year 1	Year 2	Year 3
Residential	$25,934	$57,146	$81,477
Business—Individual	$38,933	$101,212	$162,043
Business—Group	$5,284	$10,810	$16,334
Total	$70,150	$169,167	$259,854

The billing hours are listed as follows:

THREE-YEAR PROJECTION OF BILLABLE HOURS

Year	Residential	Business— Individual	Business— Group	Total
1 mn. 1	0.0	0.0	0.0	0.0
1 mn. 2	48.0	50.0	1.8	99.8
1 mn. 3	50.4	54.0	1.9	106.3
1 mn. 4	52.9	58.3	2.1	113.3
1 mn. 5	55.6	63.0	2.2	120.8
1 mn. 6	58.3	68.0	2.4	128.7
1 mn. 7	61.3	73.5	2.5	137.3
1 mn. 8	64.3	79.3	2.7	146.3
1 mn. 9	67.5	85.7	2.9	156.1
1 mn. 10	70.9	92.5	3.1	166.5
1 mn. 11	74.5	100.0	3.3	177.8
1 mn. 12	78.2	107.9	3.6	189.7
Total Yr. 1	681.9	832.2	28.5	1,542.6

THREE-YEAR PROJECTION OF BILLABLE HOURS —*continued*

Year	Residential	Business— Individual	Business— Group	Total
2 Qtr. 1	248.9	350.4	11.5	610.8
2 Qtr. 2	272.0	394.2	12.7	678.9
2 Qtr. 3	297.2	443.4	14.1	754.7
2 Qtr. 4	324.8	498.8	15.7	839.3
Total Yr. 2	1,142.9	1,686.8	54	2,883.7
3 Qtr. 1	354.9	561.1	17.4	933.4
3 Qtr. 2	387.8	631.1	19.3	1,038.2
3 Qtr. 3	423.8	709.9	21.4	1,155.1
3 Qtr. 4	463.1	798.6	23.7	1,285.4
Total Yr. 3	1,629.6	2,700.7	81.8	4,412.1

Again, due to the lack of industry data, the intent is to set a series of goals, via billable hours, at a level that can be supported by the company's initial resources and conservative growth that will not burden the anticipated growth of those resources. The strategies, assumptions, and formulas for the billing hours and sales are as follows:

- The greatest burden for growth is placed on business/individual sales and the least burden is on business/group sales.
- Residential sales are anticipated to be the more likely source of sales opportunities at the outset, allowing time to develop business source opportunities, testimonials, and referrals.
- Anticipating leveling off of growth over time, with a conservative approach, monthly sales growth is 5 percent, 8 percent, and 7.5 percent for Residential, Business/Individual, and Business/Group sales respectively.
- Those growth levels for years two and three are 3 percent, 4 percent, and 3.5 percent respectively for each category.

- Projected resources in years 2 and 3 cannot justify the same level of growth as in year one.
- ATMC has the option to expand PO force based on a balance between market demand and individuals' level of productivity.

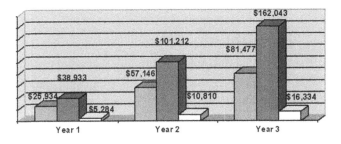

Figure 3: Annual Sales Projections by Category of Service

This format establishes profitability goals via billable hours, controls demand on resources, and allows flexibility in the future contracting of POs. Finally, categorical sales goals can be measured on a monthly basis in year one, the critical period for reaching continuous, sustainable positive cash flow.

III. Marketing Strategies

SWOT Analysis

The development of a marketing strategy must begin with a SWOT analysis (Strengths, Weaknesses, Opportunities, and Threats).

1. Strengths:
- Owner's varied organizational experience in corporate and residential environments
- Owner's acquaintance with many individuals in the local corporate world
- ATMC office strategically located in the geographic market
- Low operating overhead
- Competitive pricing structure

2. Weaknesses:
- Start-up company with no track record
- No individuals, as yet, identified to fill Office PO positions requiring specific organizational skills

3. Opportunities:
- Professional organizers are a relatively new professional in the targeted geographic market
- The Internet is increasingly becoming a primary source for seeking goods and services
- Population and economic census data indicate existence and continued growth of the specific types of office and residential clients ATMC will target

4. Threats:
- Some competition may react with lower price ranges
- Competitors will promote existing client base and experience
- Continued recession in the region may cut into total potential client base for all competitors

SWOT ANALYSIS STRATEGIES	
Strengths *Opportunities*	**Weaknesses**
1. Promote experience.	1. Focus on service offerings that reflect strengths of owner and contractors.
2. Use website.	2. Expedite brand awareness through inexpensive novelty advertising and yellow pages.
3. Nurture existing professional network.	

Strengths	Weaknesses
Threats	
1. Briefly offer. discounts	1. Recruit staff that reflects shortcomings of experience and strengths of competitors.
2. Offer competitive pricing.	

Balancing resources, conservatively projected revenues, and the strategies resulting from the SWOT analysis result in a clearly defined advertising and promotional program.

Strategies

The strategies and their influencing factors are:

1. Immediate development and promotion of the company website; seven of the eleven local competitors have websites and apparently rely heavily on those websites for promotion.
2. Immediate membership application to national and local organizations that are specific to personal-organizing and business-development networks; the more competent competitors rely on memberships and affiliations for networking and image building.
3. Prioritize promotion of residential services to County A; growth of and existing median household income in County A is much stronger than in County B, and more consistent with national trends.
4. Prioritize promotion of business services to County B; older companies and their sheer number are much greater in County B.
5. Shift promotional activities in one or both of the counties if categorical sales trends are justified.

6. Advertise in traditional media as is customary in the management-consulting industry and within company budget.

The mix of advertising media and their related costs are based on the six market-research factors above.

Website

ATMC has developed a primary website at *www. acmetimemanagement.biz*. There is significant data to support using the website as a primary vehicle to promote our services:

- Seven local competitors have websites, of which three demonstrate track records and significant hyperlinks to affiliations, networking relationships, and support vendors.
- The reputable Internet research firm IDC reports management-consulting e-business will grow from $25.46 million to $50 million from 1999 to 2004.
- An Amercia Online/Roper Starch Worldwide study indicated online purchases grew from 31 percent to 42 percent and will increase to 56 percent by the end of 2000 among survey respondents.
- *American Demographics* indicates the percent of the U.S. work force working from home or maintaining a satellite office at home will grow from 5 percent to 20 percent by 2005.
- The reputable Internet research group Jupiter Communications indicates women are now more active using the Internet, representing 50.4 percent of users.

This last item is of particular interest in that residential organizing services will more likely be promoted to a female audience. Website development, maintenance, and hosting costs are projected at $5,700 in the first year.

Affiliations and Networking

ATMC will actively seek memberships in organizations directly related to the personal-organizing industry and local business organizations that maintain membership rosters reflecting the targeted clients for business-organizing services.

Organizational memberships and annual dues will include:

- NAPO, one of two national associations of personal organizers ($150)
- POWR, the other national association for personal organizers ($150)
- County A Economic Development Council ($1,000)
- County B Alliance business network group ($175)
- County B Chamber of Commerce ($250)
- Greater Main Chamber of Commerce ($190)

Expansion on the roster and types of memberships will expand as the budget allows and marketing opportunities arise.

Conventional Advertising

It cannot be ignored that four of ATMC's competitors, though not on the Internet, are listed in the yellow pages. Furthermore, absent industry-sector research data to the contrary, there is reason to believe some income referrals will derive from a yellow pages listing. In addition, the listing in this publication also affords ATMC a listing in the online yellow pages. Anticipated first-year cost is $2,200.

Additionally, ATMC will develop brochure and seminar materials. Depending on these costs, there may or may not be allowance for novelty advertising items like pens, miniature day organizers, and personal pocket phone books to be distributed at networking events. The budget for year one is $4,000.

Promotional Offerings

Additional means of promotion include:

- Gift Certificates can be purchased by anyone who would like to bring relief to a friend or client needing help getting organized at the office or home. These can be used toward any of our professional organizing services: time management, office, and/or residential organizing. Each certificate will be equal to the cost of our services offered. How can you give a quote on this item without first having assessed the client needs?
- A 15 percent discount will be granted to any client who uses $500 of our services (including purchases). Each time a client reaches this amount, this discount will be automatically subtracted from the total cost of their next purchase/request for our services.
- Souvenir Specialty Items will be distributed as an extra incentive for clients and prospects to remember ATMC's name and the services provided. ATMC plans to distribute coffee mugs, mouse pads, desk and pocket calendars, hats, T-shirts, and other advertising specialties with the company logo and slogan.

These promotional activities are contingent on better-than-expected positive cash flow. They are not implemented in the financial projections at this time.

IV. OPERATIONS

Ownership and Management

Ms. Jane Doe, President

Responsibilities: develops and maintains the vision of the company. Oversees marketing, finance, administrative, and customer service. Approves all financial obligations. Seeks business opportunities. Directs and coordinates financial programs to provide funding for new or continuing operations in order to maximize return on investments and increase productivity. Recruit, hire, and train professional organizers on corporate culture and job functions.

Ms. Doe's education includes a BS and MBA in Business Management. Past experience includes:

- Marketing and selling training services to over 2,000 white-collar professionals
- Evaluating and conducting need assessments for in-house training
- Developing and updating training modules
- Corporate training on office computers and software
- Financial analysis and evaluation
- Set-up and implementation of bookkeeping and accounting systems
- Extensive exposure to larger corporate management environments

Her personal and professional experiences allow communication in the diverse environments and types of individual personalities that can be expected in this type of business enterprise.

Outside Management Support

Budgeting, financial oversight, and website development represent the two outside sources of contracted management support.

- Ms. Jane Black, of Black & Associates, will provide bookkeeping and accounting services.
- Mr. John White, a computer consultant and programmer, will provide webmaster services for the websites.

Each will also be contracted on an individual, as-needed basis for clients having organizational needs related to their professions. This allows ATMC to maintain lower operating overhead associated with compensation and benefits.

Staffing

ATMC will recruit and hire one staff member for the position of Recruiter. This person will perform multiple tasks, including reception, secretarial duties, and promoting the company services to all potential clients via incoming telephone calls and website inquiries. The position requires excellent written and verbal communication skills.

Potential applicants for the contracted position of PO must demonstrate one of two types of background:

- The Office POs need approximately seven to ten years experience working in senior and corporate management environments, and must be strongly familiar with the essentials of time management and organization in an office environment.

- The Home PO is one whose background demonstrates organizational skills, but must be able to develop sales opportunities and communicate in a residential environment. The ability to relate to the experiences of the typical residential client, the housewife, will be critical to this PO's success.

The number of POs contracted will be based on demand. However, we have presently projected the first PO will be contracted and begin producing sales at the beginning of the seventh month of operations. The Recruiter will be hired to begin work the first week of operations.

Compensation and Benefits

The Recruiter will be hired at the rate of $25,000 annually, with annual increases of 5 percent in each of years two and three. Benefits will be limited to Social Security until such time as cash flow actually allows contracting medical and other benefits programs.

PO compensation will be based exclusively on a commission basis at the rate of 28 percent on total contract sales generated.

Ms. Doe's compensation will be determined as a percentage of her own sales. Dividend deductions against net earnings are not projected at this time. At any point in time should cash flow not be sufficient, Ms. Doe will defer her compensation to insure all indebtedness and other obligations are met.

A weighted average of 20 percent has been incorporated into the financial projections to account for Social Security, Medicare, workman's compensation, unemployment compensation, and any added benefits that can be accommodated within that budget.

Office Site and Facilities

ATMC will lease an office space at the rate of $1,000 monthly with a deposit of $2,500 to cover the space and any utility deposits. Leasehold improvements are projected to $2,000 for accommodating one reception area, five separate cubicle offices, and installation of office equipment.

Start-Up Expenses

Based on the information above, the start-up expenses prior to day one of operations are:

Item	Amount
Office Lease and Utility Deposits	$2,500
Leasehold Improvements	$2,000
Licenses	$300
Professional Services	$2,400
Unanticipated Expenses	$800
Total Start-Up Expense	$8,000

V. FINANCIAL ANALYSIS

The financial projections in this business plan are developed on the cash basis of accounting.

Source and Uses of Funds

Sources	Loan Proceeds	$25,000	
	Equity Investment (25%)	$15,000	$40,000
Uses	Start-Up	$ 8,000	
	Operating Overhead	$32,000	$40,000
Total Initial Investment		$40,000	
Start-Up Expenses		- $8,000	
Balance Forward to Operations			$32,000

Income Statements

Year One monthly income projections are:

Item	Jan	Feb	Mar	Apr	May	Jun	Jul	Aug	Sept	Oct	Nov	Dec	Total
Income													
Residential		1,200	1,260	1,323	1,389	1,459	1,532	3,216	3,377	3,546	3,723	3,909	25,934
Business/Individual		1,500	1,620	1,750	1,890	2,041	2,204	4,761	5,141	5,553	5,997	6,477	38,933
Business/Group		300	321	343	367	393	421	546	584	625	668	715	5,284
Total Income		3,000	3,201	3,416	3,646	3,893	4,156	8,523	9,102	9,723	10,389	11,101	70,150
Expenses													
Prof. Organizer Commissions								2,386	2,549	2,723	2,909	3,108	13,675
Recruiter	2,083	2,083	2,083	2,083	2,083	2,083	2,083	2,083	2,083	2,083	2,083	2,083	25,000
Taxes & Benefits	417	417	417	417	417	417	417	417	417	417	417	417	5,000
Mileage		319	340	363	386	412	439	468	500	533	569	607	4,937
Utilities	120	120	120	120	120	120	120	120	120	120	120	120	1,440
Advertising	1,100	1,100	1,100	1,100	1,100	1,100	1,100	1,100	1,100	1,100	1,100	1,100	13,200
Memberships	1,915												1,915
Office Supplies	30	30	30	30	30	30	30	30	30	30	30	30	360
Insurance	100	100	100	100	100	100	100	100	100	100	100	100	1,200
Maintenance	75	75	75	75	75	75	75	75	75	75	75	75	900
Legal and Accounting	100	100	100	100	100	100	100	100	100	100	100	100	1,200
Licenses	150								150				300
Telephone Service	200	200	200	200	200	200	200	200	200	200	200	200	2,400
Office Equipment Lease	175	175	175	175	175	175	175	175	175	175	175	175	2,100
Miscellaneous	30	30	30	30	30	30	30	30	30	30	30	30	360
Office Lease	1,000	1,000	1,000	1,000	1,000	1,000	1,000	1,000	1,000	1,000	1,000	1,000	12,000
Bank Loan / Line of Credit	136	136	136	136	136	136	136	136	136	136	136	136	1,636
Total Operating Expenses	7,631	5,886	5,907	5,929	5,953	5,978	6,006	8,421	8,765	8,822	9,044	9,282	87,623
Net Profit (Loss) Pretax	-7,631	-2,886	-2,706	-2,513	-2,307	-2,086	-1,849	101	338	901	1,345	1,820	-17,473

Year Two quarterly projections are:

Item	Qtr 1	Qtr 2	Qtr 3	Qtr 4	Total
Income					
Residential	12,446	13,600	14,861	16,239	57,146
Business/Individual	21,027	23,652	26,605	29,927	101,212
Business/Group	2,300	2,550	2,827	3,134	10,810
Total Income	35,772	39,802	44,293	49,301	169,167
Expenses					
Professional Organizers	10,016	11,144	12,402	13,804	47,367
Recruiter	6,563	6,563	6,563	6,563	26,250
Taxes & Benefits	1,313	1,313	1,313	1,313	5,250
Mileage	1,955	2,173	2,415	2,686	9,228
Utilities	396	396	396	396	1,584
Advertising	3,630	3,630	3,630	3,630	14,520
Memberships	1,953				1,953
Office Supplies	100	100	100	100	400
Insurance	330	330	330	330	1,320
Maintenance	248	248	248	248	990
Legal and Accounting	330	330	330	330	1,320
Licenses	0	0	0	0	0
Telephone Service	660	660	660	660	2,640
Computer Lease	578	578	578	578	2,310
Miscellaneous	99	99	99	99	396
Office Lease	3,150	3,150	3,150	3,150	12,600
Bank Loan / Line of Credit	409	409	409	409	1,636
Total Operating Expenses	31,728	31,121	32,621	34,294	129,765
Net Profit (Loss) Pretax	4,044	8,680	11,672	15,007	39,403

Year Three quarterly income projections are:

Item	Qtr 1	Qtr 2	Qtr 3	Qtr 4	Total
Income					
Residential	17,745	19,390	21,188	23,153	81,477
Business/Individual	33,664	37,868	42,596	47,915	162,043
Business/Group	3,475	3,852	4,271	4,736	16,334
Total Income	54,884	61,111	68,056	75,804	259,854
Expenses					
Professional Organizers	15,367	17,111	19,056	21,225	72,759
Recruiter	6,891	6,891	6,891	6,891	27,563
Taxes & Benefits	1,378	1,378	1,378	1,378	5,513

Year Three quarterly income projections—*continued*

Item	Qtr 1	Qtr 2	Qtr 3	Qtr 4	Total
Expenses					
Mileage	2,987	3,322	3,696	4,113	14,118
Utilities	436	436	436	436	1,742
Advertising	3,993	3,993	3,993	3,993	15,972
Memberships	1,992				1,992
Office Supplies	110	110	110	110	440
Insurance	363	363	363	363	1,452
Maintenance	272	272	272	272	1,089
Legal and Accounting	363	363	363	363	1,452
Licenses	0	0	0	0	0
Telephone Service	726	726	726	726	2,904
Computer Lease	635	635	635	635	2,541
Miscellaneous	109	109	109	109	436
Office Lease	3,465	3,465	3,465	3,465	13,860
Bank Loan / Line of Credit	409	409	409	409	1,636
Total Operating Expenses	39,496	39,583	41,902	44,488	165,469
Net Profit (Loss) Pretax	15,388	21,528	26,154	31,316	94,385

Cash-Flow Statements

Year One cash-flow projections are:

Item	Jan	Feb	Mar	Apr	May	Jun	Jul	Aug	Sept	Oct	Nov	Dec	Total
Opening Balance	$32,000	23,675	20,414	17,355	14,511	11,896	9,529	7,424	6,832	6,476	6,683	7,334	32,000
Sources of Funds:													
Total Sales	0	3,000	3,201	3,416	3,646	3,893	4,156	8,523	9,102	9,723	10,389	11,101	70,150
Total Sources	0	3,000	3,201	3,416	3,646	3,893	4,156	8,523	9,102	9,723	10,389	11,101	70,150
Uses of Funds:													
Personnel Expenses	2,500	2,500	2,500	2,500	2,500	2,500	2,500	4,886	5,049	5,223	5,409	5,608	43,675
Other Operating Expenses	4,995	3,249	3,270	3,293	3,316	3,342	3,369	3,398	3,580	3,463	3,499	3,537	42,312
Mileage Payment Delayed	-319	-340	-363	-386	-412	-439					2,260	0	

Year One cash-flow projections—*continued*

Item	Jan	Feb	Mar	Apr	May	Jun	Jul	Aug	Sept	Oct	Nov	Dec	Total
Loan Payments	830	830	830	830	830	830	830	830	830	830	830	830	9,964
Total Uses	8,325	6,260	6,260	6,260	6,260	6,260	6,260	9,115	9,459	9,516	9,738	12,236	95,951
Net Cash Flow	-8,325	-3,260	-3,059	-2,844	-2,614	-2,368	-2,104	-593	-356	207	651	-1,135	-25,801
Ending Cash Balance	23,675	20,414	17,355	14,511	11,896	9,529	7,424	6,832	6,476	6,683	7,334	6,199	6,199

Year Two quarterly cash-flow projections are:

Item	Qtr 1	Qtr 2	Qtr 3	Qtr 4	Total
Opening Balance	6,199	8,161	14,759	24,349	6,199

Sources of Funds:

	Qtr 1	Qtr 2	Qtr 3	Qtr 4	Total
Total Sales	35,772	39,802	44,293	49,301	169,167
Total Sources	35,772	39,802	44,293	49,301	169,167

Uses of Funds:

	Qtr 1	Qtr 2	Qtr 3	Qtr 4	Total
Personnel Expenses	17,891	19,019	20,277	21,679	78,867
Other Operating Expenses	13,428	11,693	11,935	12,206	49,262
Loan Payments	2,491	2,491	2,491	2,491	9,964
Total Uses	33,810	33,203	34,703	36,376	138,093
Net Cash Flow	1,962	6,598	9,590	12,925	31,075
Ending Cash Balance	8,161	14,759	24,349	37,274	37,274

Year Three quarterly cash flow projections are:

Item	Qtr 1	Qtr 2	Qtr 3	Qtr 4	Total
Opening Balance	37,274	50,579	70,025	94,097	37,274

Sources of Funds:

	Qtr 1	Qtr 2	Qtr 3	Qtr 4	Total
Total Sales	54,884	61,111	68,056	75,804	259,854
Total Sources	54,884	61,111	68,056	75,804	259,854

Uses of Funds:

	Qtr 1	Qtr 2	Qtr 3	Qtr 4	Total
Personnel Expenses	23,636	25,380	27,324	29,494	105,834
Other Operating Expenses	15,451	13,794	14,168	14,585	57,998
Loan Payments	2,491	2,491	2,491	2,507	9,980
Total Uses	41,578	41,665	43,984	46,586	173,813
Net Cash Flow	13,306	19,446	24,072	29,218	86,041
Ending Cash Balance	50,579	70,025	94,097	123,314	123,314

Balance Sheets

Balance-sheet projections for the end of each of the first three years of operation are:

Item	End of Yr. 1	End of Yr. 2	End of Yr. 3
Assets			
Cash	$6,199	$37,274	$123,314
Fixtures and Equipment	$2,000	$2,000	$2,000
Prepaid Expenses	$2,500	$2,500	$2,500
Total Assets	$10,699	$41,774	$127,814
Liabilities			
Initial Funding Loan	$16,672	$8,344	$0
Shareholder's Equity			
Common Stock	$15,000	$15,000	$15,000
Retained Earnings	-$20,973	$18,430	$112,814
Total Equities	$10,699	$41,774	$127,814

Additional Assumptions and Notes

- Please review sections on Pricing and Sales Projections for assumptions used to develop income and related expenses.
- Mileage payments to Ms. Doe are deferred until cash on hand and positive cash flow are sufficient to meet the expense.
- Cash flows, as with income projections, are developed with a conservative approach. Cash on hand is more than sufficient to cover negative cash flow through the first nine months of operation. At the beginning of the tenth month cash funds increase, allowing for any planned growth that would tax existing resources.
- Organizational costs of $3,500, incurred at start-up, are not amortized. They are incorporated as expenses against income. That represents the differential between retained earnings (-$20,973) and the net pretax loss (-$17,473) on the income projection at the end of year one.
- Mileage is billed at the rate of thirty-two cents per mile.

- Taxes and benefits are determined at the rate of 20 percent of compensation to personal organizers and recruiters.
- As a contingency, Ms. Doe will defer personal compensation, when necessary, to meet all expenses and maintain sufficient cash on hand.
- Ms. Doe's compensation is consolidated into the line-item expense labeled "Personal Organizer."
- If Ms. Doe opts for a smaller operational start-up, she will assume the roles of ownership, management, personal organizer, and recruiter. Under such circumstances, she is allowed a lower capital demand at start-up and operating expenses until such time as income and demand for services allow recruitment of additional organizers on a contractual basis.

Copyright © Acme Time Management Consultants, Inc. Business Plan Copyright © Windhaus Associates (*www .windhaus.com*)

Sample Business Plans

The CD included with this book contains the following seventy free sample business plans:

Aircraft Rental—Instruction: Lansing Aviation

Airline—Regional: Puddle Jumpers Airline

Animal—Horse Reseller—Livestock: GFX: Gravestat Farm eXchange

Automotive—Car Wash: Soapy Rides Car Wash

Automotive—Parts Retailer: Southeast Racing

Automotive—Repair: Quick and Dirty Auto Repair

Bakery—Specialty: Morningstar Bakery

Bar—Historic Irish Pub: McKnight's Pub

Bar—Sports: Take Five Sports Bar

Bed & Breakfast: Coach House Bed and Breakfast

Beverage—Machine Rental: Margarita Momma

Beverage—Shave Ice: Ice Dreams

Cafe—Coffee Kiosks: Daily Perc, The

Cafe—Internet Café: JavaNet Internet Cafe

Computer Consulting—Technical: Calico Computer Consulting

Computer Hardware—Reseller: AMT Computers

Construction—Formwork: Concrete Fabricators

Consulting—High-Tech Marketing: Acme Consulting

Consulting—High-Tech Mktg—UK: Acme Consulting--UK

Drapery Fabricator: Cutting Edge Drapery

Engineering—Consulting: StructureAll Ltd.

Event Planning—Personal: Occasions

Export—Coffee: Silvera and Sons

Export—Watch Mfr: Grutzen Watches

Food—Salsa Manufacturer: Salvador's Sauces

Food—Vending Services: Chef Vending

Furniture Mfr—Office: Willamette Furniture

Furniture Mfr—Office—UK: Fulham Furniture Manufacturer--UK

Hair and Beauty Salon: Trend Setters Hair Studio

Health Fitness Program: Corporate Fitness

Heavy Equipment Manufacturer: Tricky Widgets Manufacturing

Import—Artificial Flowers: Fantastic Florals

Insurance—Brokerage: Acme Insurance

Internet—ISP—Ongoing: Web Solutions, Inc.

Machine Tooling—Construction: Machine Tooling

Magazine Publisher—Editorial: Group Publishing, Inc.

Mail Order—Returns: QuickReturns

Marketing—Global: West Pacific Marketing

Medical Billing Service: Physicians 1st Billing and Claims

Medical Equipment Developer: Medquip, Inc.

Medical Equipment Mfr—Aircraft: Stretch 'r Wings

Nightclub: Nightclub Sample Plan

Nonprofit—Trade Association: CMBA— Connecticut Motorsports Business Association

Online Education—Children: InteliChild.com

Online Print Shop—Start Up: PrintingSolutions .com

Organizer—Start Up: Acme Time Management Consultants, Inc.

Painting Contractors: Barnum Painters

Photography—Pets: Adorable Pet Photography

Plan Administration—Benefits: Employee Benefits Administration

Plan Administration—Health: Southeast Health Plans

Printing Job Brokerage: R and R Printing

Promotional Products Mfr.: Elsewares Promotional Products & Packaging

Property Management—Development: MSN Real Estate

Real Estate—Brokerage: RJ Wagner and Assoc. Realty

Restaurant—Organic: Studio67

Restaurant—Steak Buffet: Sagebrush Sam's

Retail: Widgee World Retailers, Inc.

Self-Storage: Westbury Storage, Inc.

Software—Business Planning: Corporate Software Sales

Software Publishing: Sample Software Company

Sports—Inline Skating Products: Pegasus Sports

Sports—Retail Tennis Shop: Tennis Master Pro Shops, Inc.

Sports Equipment—Cafe: Boulder Stop

Sports Programs—Indoor Courts: Supreme Courts, The

Sports Protective Equipment Mfr: Professional Athletic Equipment

Theatrical Producers—Music: Edgar Risk Ventures, Ltd.

Travel Agency—Adventure: Adventure Travel International

Truck Stop: Interstate Travel Center

Trucking—General Freight: Mike's Trucking Service

Wedding Consultants: TLC Wedding Consultants

You can find 442 additional example business plans available with the purchase of the Standard or Premier Editions of Business Plan Pro (*www.bplans.com*).

Business Plan Glossary

Business has a unique language. This glossary of business terms can help you understand and be understood in the world of business planning.

Accounts payable
Money that you or your business owes to others.

Accounts receivable
Money owed to you or your business.

Accrual
An accounting term for the increase over time of expenses incurred by your business. They are accrued up until the time they are paid.

Acid-test ratio
A measurement of how well a business can meet its short-term financial obligations without selling any inventory.

Acquisition
The takeover of a business by another company.

Added value
The process of going the extra mile with a customer. Added value is also used to describe when products and services include additional features beyond what is generally desired by the customer, at no additional cost.

AIDA
Attention, Interest, Desire, Action.

Anchor store
A major retailer chosen for its ability to drive traffic to the mall or shopping center in which it's located.

Asset
Things of value. Tangible assets include cash, receivables, inventory, and buildings. Intangible assets include goodwill.

Automatic reordering system
Program that reorders merchandise when in-store supplies fall below a pre-determined level.

Average inventory cost
Average inventory cost is found by adding the beginning cost inventory for each month plus the ending cost inventory for the last month in the period. If calculating for a season, divide by 7. If calculating for a year, divide by 13.

B2B
A sales organization whose primary effort is selling to and doing business with other businesses.

B2C
A sales organization whose primary effort is selling to and doing business with consumers or with individual users.

Base salary
The guaranteed portion of a salesperson's monetary compensation. Base salaries reward salespeople for their accumulated experience and overall selling efforts.

Benefit
The value experienced by the customer as a result of the purchase of a product or service. Salespeople who focus on communicating benefits and aligning those benefits to a customer's business objectives increase the likelihood of gaining a sale.

Big-box store
Large standalone store specializing in one category of merchandise (e.g., Home Depot).

Bill of lading
A contract between a freight company and a shipper regarding transportation, which includes the exact contents of the delivery.

Body language
The gestures, body movements, and mannerisms by which a person communicates his outlook or frame of mind.

Bonus
In sales compensation, this refers to a type of incentive payment, typically awarded when the salesperson or sales team achieves predetermined financial objectives.

Brand
A name, term, or symbol used to identify the products and services of the selling organization and to differentiate them from those of competitors.

Brand awareness
A gauge of marketing effectiveness measured by the ability of a customer to recognize and or recall a name, image, or other mark associated with a particular brand.

Break-even point
The point in business where the sales equal the expenses. There is no profit and no loss.

Brick and mortar
Brick-and-mortar store refers to retail shops that are located in a building as opposed to an online shopping destination, door-to-door sales, kiosk, or other similar site not housed within a structure.

Business cycle
A sequence of economic activities typically characterized by recessions, recovery, growth, and at times, decline.

Business plan
A detailed document describing the past, present, and future financial and operational objectives of a company.

Buyer
The person who purchases or procures the product or service you are selling. This person may also be the decision maker, but not necessarily.

Buying process
The steps a customer organization or a buyer actually takes in making a purchase for a product or service.

Buying signal
A statement or indication from a prospect or customer that suggests he is considering making a purchase.

Capital assets
Long-term assets used to produce income, such as buildings and equipment.

Cash discount
A percentage reduction in price for payment within a specified period of time.

Cash flow
The movement of money in and out of a business and the resulting availability of cash.

Chain store
One of a number of retail stores under the same ownership and dealing in the same merchandise.

Channel
The means by which an organization sells their products. A company who uses their own sales force is said to have a direct channel. Other channels include distributors, wholesalers, retailers, and agencies.

C-level executive
An executive in the organization whose title is often preceded by the word Chief, such as CEO, COO, CIO, CFO.

Close
The point at which the salesperson asks for a commitment to purchase the product or service being evaluated.

Commission
In sales compensation, this refers to a type of payment or revenue sharing resulting from achieving a sale or attaining a given sales level. Commissions are typically expressed as a percentage of the selling price for the product sold.

Commodity
Competing products or services that bear the same or similar characteristics.

Competitive advantage
Those areas deemed to have preferential value to a customer versus a similar competitive product.

Confidentiality agreements
Agreements between two parties affirming that the information exchanged during a relationship is maintained within the confines of the agreement and not shared beyond the agreement.

Contribution margin
The difference between total sales revenue and total variable costs. The term is applied to a product line and is generally expressed as a percentage.

Convenience products
Merchandise that is purchased frequently, without advance planning,

including staples, impulse items, and emergency items.

Conversion
The methodology used to convert a customer's use of one product or supplier to another.

Cooperative
A group in which several retailers pool their resources to buy products at a discount from manufacturers; also called group buying.

Corporation
A legal entity that can buy, sell, and enter into contracts as if it were a person.

Cost-benefit analysis
The method a customer (or sales organization) follows to assess the viability of a recommendation, by examining the total amount of money, time, and resources used relative to the value being received.

Cost of goods sold (COGS)
The price paid for the product, plus any additional costs necessary to get the merchandise into inventory and ready for sale, including shipping and handling.

Customer profile
A document that outlines the critical information about a particular customer.

Customer relationship management (CRM)
The process used internally to manage customer relationships.

Demographics
Characteristics of a specific group of people, such as potential customers.

Desire
A longing, a wish. Strong desire drives ambition and performance.

Destination retailer
Retailer to which customers will make a special trip, even if it entails going out of their way.

Differentiation
The process of distinguishing services or products through design.

Direct marketing
The process of marketing directly to an end user. The most known form of direct marketing is direct mail.

Discount
A reduced amount (typically from list price) that is offered by the seller or the selling organization to encourage purchase of a product being offered.

Discount store
A self-service retail store with low markups. Example: Wal-Mart, Kmart.

Distributor
An indirect sales channel that markets or sells a product or service. Distributors are used by selling organizations to capitalize on the distributor's local presence and capacity to support the manufacturer.

Double entry
An accounting system that requires two balancing entries, a debit and a credit, to be made for each transaction.

Draw
In sales compensation, this refers to a cash advance, in anticipation of future sales performance.

Durable goods
Products that can be used frequently and have a long life expectancy, such as furniture, jewelry, and major appliances.

E-business
The term used to refer to conducting business via the Internet.

Economic benefit
The financial value of your product or service. This is tied closely to the term ROI, or return on investment.

Electronic shopping
Shopping over the Internet or through a TV cable channel.

Elevator speech
Sales slang for a short, thirty-second overview of who your company is, what it does, and what you do, with the intent of gaining an individual's interest to learn more and seek further discussion.

Empathy
The ability to communicate and understand someone else's situation and feelings.

Employer identification number (EIN)
Also known as a Federal Tax Identification Number, is used to identify a business entity. Most businesses need an EIN. You may apply for an EIN in various ways, including online.

Executive summary

Often considered the first page or first several pages in a business plan, summarizing the key issues, solution, and value a customer will receive by implementing the recommendation.

Feature

A characteristic of your product or service. The distinct parts of your product or service that can be described.

First in, first out (FIFO)

A method of stock rotation where goods that are received first are sold first. Newly received product is stocked behind the older merchandise.

Forecast

A salesperson or a sales manager's prediction of sales results as a result of analyzing where opportunities are in the sales cycle.

Free on board (FOB)

Shipping term used to indicate who is responsible for paying transportation charges. FOB factory means the buyer must pay shipping from the factory.

Free-standing store

Store that's not part of a shopping center or a mall.

Full line

Describes department stores that carry a full line of merchandise, from appliances and hardware to clothing and jewelry.

Goods

Tangible products for sale that can be held or touched.

Gross income

Total income derived from a business.

Gross margin

The difference between what an item costs and for what it sells.

Gross profit

Profit calculated after deducting all costs of merchandise, labor, and overhead.

Hard lines

A store department or product line primarily consisting of merchandise such as hardware, housewares, automotive, electronics, sporting goods, health and beauty aids, or toys.

Image

The impression customers have of a company or service.

Impulse items

Products that people purchase without planning for it, such as magazines or candy bars.

Inventory turnover

The number of times during a given period that the average inventory on hand is sold and replaced.

Just-in-time (JIT)

A term often used to denote the availability of goods and services when needed.

Keystone pricing

A method of marking merchandise for resell to an amount that is double the wholesale price.

Liabilities

Amounts that a business owes to suppliers and other creditors.

Loss leader

Merchandise sold below cost by a retailer in an effort to attract new customers or stimulate other profitable sales.

Loss prevention

The act of reducing the amount of theft and shrinkage within a business.

Manufacturer's representative (rep)

An independent salesperson that represents your organization and non-competing products.

Margin

The difference between the cost of a product and its selling price, expressed as a percentage or dollars-per-unit.

Markdown

Planned reduction in the selling price of an item, usually to take effect either within a certain number of days after seasonal merchandise is received or at a specific date.

Market area

Geographic area from which a store draws its customers.

Market penetration

Your ability to enter and gain share in a specified market, generally measured in percentage terms.

Market share

An organization's portion of the total market, typically expressed as a percentage.

Marketing

The process followed by organizations to satisfy the needs, wants, and demands of their customers through the application and promotion of products and services that satisfy those customer requirements.

Marketing calendar

A tool used by retailers to show what marketing events, media campaigns, and merchandising efforts are happening when and where, as well as the results.

Markup

A percentage added to the cost to get the retail selling price.

Merchandise mix

The breadth and depth of the products carried by retailers. Also known as product assortment.

Mission statement

An organization's purpose for being. Mission statements typically communicate what an organization values.

Needs

That which is required or wanted by a customer. The ability of a sales professional to surface viable "must-address" needs (versus wants) leads to greater sales success.

Needs analysis

The process of formally evaluating a customer's needs and requirements.

Net lease

Lease in which the tenant pays the base rent plus property taxes. Also known as a single-net lease.

Net-net lease

Lease in which the tenant pays the base rent plus property taxes and building insurance. Also known as a double-net lease.

Net-net-net lease

Lease in which the tenant pays the base rent plus property taxes, building insurance, and maintenance. Also known as a triple-net lease.

Niche market

A unique segment of the market a selling organization is targeted toward. This unique segment, if served well, can provide areas of distinctive competitive value.

Nondurable goods

Products that are purchased frequently and used in a short period of time, such as beauty supplies and cosmetics.

OEM

Original equipment manufacturer.

Operating expenses

The sum of all expenses associated with the normal course of running a business.

Partnership

An entity where two or more people own a business.

Point-of-purchase display (POP display)

Marketing materials or advertising placed next to the merchandise it is promoting. These items are generally located at the checkout area or other location where the purchase decision is made. For example, the checkout counters of many convenience stores have numerous cigarette and candy POP displays.

Point-of-sale (POS) system

Combination of hardware and software that records customers' purchases, accepts payments, and adjusts inventory levels.

Point-of-sale terminal

An electronic machine at a checkout station that feeds information from product tags directly into a computer.

Price

The monetary value placed on a product or service.

Private label

Products that are generally manufactured or provided by one company under another company's brand.

Process

A series of steps bringing about a desired result.

Product breadth

The variety of product lines offered by a retailer.

Product depth

The number of each item or particular style of a product on the shelves. Also known as product assortment or merchandise depth.

Profit margin

A ratio of profitability calculated as earnings divided by revenues. It measures how much out of every dollar of sales a retail business actually keeps in earnings.

Pro forma

Refers to the process of preparing a hypothetical income statement for a customer, based on a given set of assumptions.

Purchase order (PO)
A written sales contract between buyer and seller detailing the exact merchandise or services to be rendered from a single vendor.

Quantity discount
A reduction in price based on the amount purchased. May be offered in addition to any trade discount.

Request for proposal (RFP)
Used by customers to assess who will respond and evaluate solutions being posed.

Retail
The sale of small quantities of goods directly to the user.

Retailers
Businesses that buy goods from wholesalers or manufacturers and resell them to customers.

Return on investment (ROI)
The amount, expressed as a percentage, earned by an investment.

Sales floor
The location of a retail store where goods are displayed and sales transactions take place. For example, the receiving of merchandise takes place in the stock room, but all direct sales and customer interactions are done on the sales floor.

Service
A product/service mix that offers only a service, with no accompanying product needed or wanted, such as an insurance policy.

Shrinkage
Retail shrinkage is a reduction or loss in inventory due to shoplifting, employee theft, paperwork errors, and supplier fraud.

Softlines
A store department or product line primarily consisting of merchandise such as clothing, footwear, jewelry, linens, and towels.

Sole proprietor
One person (or a married couple) who owns a business.

Specialty products
Products that solve a specific want or need for specific customers, often expensive products with special characteristics or brand identity.

Standard industrial classification code (SIC Code)
A coding system using four digits to identify specific industrial sectors within the federal government. The first two digits identify the broad industrial sector and the last two digits represent a facility's specialty within this broad sector.

Stock-keeping unit (SKU)
A number assigned to a product by a retail store to identify the price, product options, and manufacturer.

Supportive services
Free services offered to customers to increase convenience, make shopping easier, and entice customers to buy more.

Target market
The set of customers or organizations that you deem most viable for your product or service.

Trade credit
An open account with suppliers of goods and services.

Trade discount
A discount on the list price given by a manufacturer or wholesaler to a retailer.

Turnover
The number of times during a given period that the average inventory on hand is sold and replaced.

Universal product code (UPC)
Bar code used for electronic entry.

Value
The relative worth, utility, importance, or financial benefit that is assigned by a buyer to the product or service an organization sells.

Wholesale
The resale of large quantities of goods to a retailer.

Wholesaler
Sales channel typically engaged in the sale of goods in large quantities for resale.

Widget
An unnamed article or gadget used as a hypothetical example.

Word of mouth
Verbal recommendation and positive approval by a satisfied customer.

INDEX